Going God's Way

BY

REUBEN K. YOUNGDAHL

AUGUSTANA BOOK CONCERN
ROCK ISLAND, ILLINOIS

GOING GOD'S WAY

Copyright, 1951, by
AUGUSTANA BOOK CONCERN

⟦ PRINTED IN U·S·A· ⟧

AUGUSTANA BOOK CONCERN
Printers and Binders
ROCK ISLAND, ILLINOIS
1951

Dedication

To my beloved parents who, during
their earthly sojourn, traveled
God's way, and who found
at the end of the journey
"the house of many
mansions"

Foreword

IN a very vital sense the problems which face the church and the nation have their origin in the home. Anything written, spoken, or produced, which is designed to strengthen the home and deepen the faith and courage of its members, is of major importance.

It is to that purpose that the author of this book, in a convincing and inspiring manner, has dedicated his ministry, and now in a specific manner, this book entitled, GOING GOD'S WAY.

The Christian Church today needs a revival of the family altar. When father, mother, and children pray with one accord, and with singleness of heart break bread together, the home will become and remain the source of strength it should be.

Wise in practical suggestions, and abundantly illustrated with concrete examples, this book comes from the heart of this parish pastor, who so effectively and increasingly gives himself to his gospel ministry.

The author of this book starts out the daily devotional series with a thought-provoking and soul-searching question, "Are you going God's way?" Every day of the year the family is faced with that question as they use this book, and each day its members are guided and encouraged along God's way.

Dr. Youngdahl is pastor of a large city church. Under his leadership the Mount Olivet Lutheran Church of Minneapolis has grown and prospered. To accomplish this result there have been years of consecrated prayer, effort, and organization. The congregation has followed its pastor as he led the way in using every new method of communication developed. He insisted that these effective means of proclaiming the gospel should be used by the church. So Dr. Youngdahl has made special use of the radio to increase the outreach and effectiveness of his ministry.

"Going God's Way," a radio devotional program, has become a daily source of strength and guidance for thousands of listeners. Beamed to the family circle, calling upon the listening family to participate and to use the radio devotional and music as part of their family altar service, this program has done much to re-establish the home as the center of faith and hope and courage.

These devotional messages are surcharged with confident faith in Jesus Christ as the answer to the confusion of the world today and call upon every church member to be a living witness for the Lord and His Church, starting at the family altar, through school and business, through work and worship.

As a personal friend of the author, an appreciative member of his congregation, and as a co-worker in the gospel ministry, I know that this book has been written with the earnest prayer that through its use a great host of people will be helped along "God's way."

S. E. ENGSTROM

Minneapolis, Minnesota, October 1951.

Author's Preface

FOR several years it has been my privilege to enter the homes of our community by means of the radio. As many as fourteen broadcasts originate each week from our church. The primary purpose has been to help build the family altar. I have always been convinced that if people set aside time each day to talk with God and to read His Word, they will soon discover what a living partnership with Him can mean.

Each morning at these broadcasts this has been our opening salutation: "Up and away, for this is God's day! Are you going God's way?" We attempted in the meditations that followed to speak some word that would encourage the listener to take the high road that God intended we should travel, that means glorious living today and eternity with Him tomorrow.

Many of our listeners have encouraged the writer to put into devotional form the many illustrations that have been used. They have suggested the illustrations be in language children can understand. This book is the answer to that request.

Some of the stories you have heard before, others have been currently chosen from our daily newspapers, but most of them are actual experiences of people in my own congregation.

I would like to suggest that the Bible verse for the day be memorized by the members of the family. The Table Talk at the end of the meditation gives opportunity to discuss the practical application of the message to everyday living. It is important that the children be allowed to give their viewpoint.

It would be well if the devotional period closed by having each member of the family participate in prayer, with all joining in the Lord's Prayer and the Benediction.

God is present in this world today. He is still the all-powerful, loving God, seeking His children to give them more abundant life. It is my hope that these meditations will help lead you into the secret of His presence that you may discover the partnership that makes you unconquerable.

I am deeply indebted to a congregation that has willingly heard God's Word and has experienced a miracle because of faith. Then, I am grateful to my staff who have been most helpful and consecrated in the Kingdom's work and in preparing this manuscript. I would speak a special word of thanks to Mahala Kemp, who has carried the total load of the stenographic work; Marian Lack Ehlers, and Reynold and Sylvia Anderson, who have corrected and revised these devotions; Aldys Holmes, who selected many of the Bible verses and gave suggestions for Table Talk; Lorraine Telander, Ruth Peterson, and Paul Beckstrand for suggestions used in many of these daily meditations; and Richard Burg, who designed the cover.

It is my hope and prayer that you may discover the power of God in your living and that each day you may have ever expanding horizons to keep beckoning you on!

This is God's day. Are you going God's way?

REUBEN K. YOUNGDAHL
Mount Olivet Lutheran Church
Minneapolis, Minnesota

GOING GOD'S WAY

*Up and away, for this is God's
day! Are you going God's way?*

JANUARY 1

Are You Going God's Way?

Cause me to hear thy lovingkindness in the morning: for in thee do I trust: cause me to know the way wherein I should walk; for I lift up my soul unto thee. Psalm 143:8.

You are writing a record—a chapter each day. The pages before you are blank. But every thought, word, and deed will be recorded upon them. This is the day of beginning again. By the grace and mercy of God the past can be forgotten. We do not have to carry into today the cares and worries and mistakes that have burdened us in the past. It is a new year, and it is God's day. Are you going God's way?

Pick up a seed in your hand and get into conversation with it. "Little seed, what do you plan to become? You are so small and insignificant." The little seed would reply, "Some day when the warm weather comes I am going to bury myself in the ground, but that will not mean death for me, for, nurtured by the rains that fall from the heavens and the sun that will shine so brightly, I will grow into a beautiful flower that might some day even be chosen for a bouquet that will adorn the table of a king." You look at the seemingly insignificant seed and say, "How can you ever become anything like that? And the seed replies, "Not I—but God and I."

God and you are unconquerable. You do not have to be afraid to face the future, no matter what it might bring. There is always hope and assurance of victory if you walk hand in hand with Him, going His way. You will continue to make mistakes. There will be some ugly blotches on the record, but there will also be His redeeming grace to grant you forgiveness.

Each one of us has tremendous value in the sight of God. There is something for us to be doing in His great work. Our course has not been charted for us, for none of our lives have been predestined. We choose the pathways we will take. But if we follow the Master, we will know that some day we shall reach our desired goal, for He is well acquainted with the pathway.

It is beginning time again. This is God's day. Are you going God's way?

TABLE TALK: *Discuss what resolutions you can make which will help keep you going on God's way.*

1

JANUARY 2

Stop, Look, Listen

The heavens declare the glory of God; and the firmament showeth his handiwork. Psalm 19:1.

Many times as you have traveled about, you have come to a sign which reads "Stop, Look, and Listen." It is a warning that soon you will be crossing a railroad track and if you want to be sure to cross it safely you must heed the advice which is given. If you do not, tragedy may result.

As you travel along spiritually, it would be well from time to time to observe like signposts. It is well for us to stop in the busyness of life as it is lived today to take a look at ourselves and to see the direction in which we are traveling. So often we are anxious to get places in a hurry and when we arrive we have not the least idea where we have been. If ever there was an age that needed to stop to let its soul catch up with its body it is ours. Great scientific advancements have added luxuries and comfort for all of us which were unheard of in previous generations, yet there are heartaches in millions of lives and a vacuum that cannot be filled with the things of the world.

We need to stop and look. Too many of us have our eyes focused upon the things of earth to the extent that we cannot appreciate the glory of God that surrounds us. Go out into the wide open spaces and look up into the sky some night and see the stars and let the song of your heart become, "The heavens declare the glory of God." Living will then take on new meaning for you. You will discover your worth in the sight of God as you say, "What is man, God, that Thou art mindful of him?"

We need to stop and look and listen. We have been so busy working in the marketplace, hearing the shouting, the sounding brass and tinkling cymbals, that we have been unable to discern the still small voice of God so anxious to speak to us and tell us the way that we should go.

Decide to go God's way!

TABLE TALK: *Have you ever started a task without first planning your procedure? Imagine what would happen.*

Let Your Light Shine

That ye may become blameless and harmless, children of God, without blemish, in the midst of a crooked and perverse generation among whom ye are seen as lights in the world.

Philippians 2:15.

Several hundreds of years ago in a country village in England a young lad began to learn the shoemaking trade. Though he worked hard and long at his cobbler's job, he spent a great deal of time studying and reading. He especially liked geography and the languages of various foreign countries. One day, one of his fellow workers told him about God—and how Jesus died upon the cross that we might have eternal life. This boy became a devoted Christian. He was later destined to leave his shoemaking trade to become one of the greatest missionaries the world has ever known.

His name was William Carey, who for more than forty years battled the pagan ideas in India. Though trouble, heartache, and disappointment met him at every turn, William Carey began a Christian church in India and translated the Bible into thirty-five languages, for the thousands of people who had never before heard the word of Christ. William Carey's life as a devoted Christian could be traced to that small cobbler's shop and to a fellow workman who loved God enough to tell others about Him. It seems like such an insignificant witness, but just think of the tremendous results!

What joy there can be in your heart if others find Christ because of your influence. You are privileged to be a lamplighter. God's light can shine through you. You are an example to the world about you, by indicating that you are for God or against God. You lead others to the Saviour or you drive them away down the rough and crooked paths. God is counting on each one of us to spread the good news of salvation not only to the whole world and the people in faraway lands, but to our neighbor who may be living very close by. God will give you the power and the strength to be a soul winner.

TABLE TALK: *Whose example did you follow in becoming a member of the church? Are you a good example for others?*

Reach for the Stars

Beware of false prophets, who come to you in sheep's clothing, but inwardly are ravening wolves. Matthew 7:15.

Not long ago a man made a very interesting experiment. He wondered whether people would truly appreciate good music if they heard it unexpectedly. He was one of the foremost violinists in one of our metropolitan orchestras. He went out into the street dressed as a shabby beggar, and began to play his beautiful music. He appeared to be as any other person. But his music was more wonderful than people could imagine. In a week's time he actually earned hundreds of dollars and was convinced that people, as indicated by their generous gifts, were truly appreciative.

The worth-while things of life cannot be hidden by cheap clothes. A wonderful opportunity of rendering spiritual music comes to each one of us regardless of rank or station. Our lives should reflect the goodness and kindness which filled the heart of the Master as He walked upon the earth, healing the sick, giving bread to the hungry, and bringing happiness to those who were sad. If in our lives we play beautiful music, it matters little whether we are dressed as a lowly pauper or as a wealthy prince.

Bobby Jones, one of the world's greatest golfers, once said that the secret of his success was that he was never as much interested in beating his opponent as he was in reaching the goal which he had set for himself. He always worked for the ideal score no matter how good or how poor his opponent might be. He never played the game just to get by. He always tried to produce to the very best of his abilities.

The standards we set for our lives determine the qualities of character which shine in our everyday living. How we live, what we think, our whole state of mind, can be reflected in the fruits of our efforts. No matter how lowly our earthly rank, we reach for the stars as our souls soar to the heavenly music.

TABLE TALK: *Some people think clothes make a difference. Discuss.*

JANUARY 5

Set Your Light on a Hill

But ye shall receive power, when the Holy Spirit is come upon you: and ye shall be my witness both in Jerusalem, and in all Judaea and Samaria, and unto the uttermost part of the earth.
Acts 1:8.

There are not enough ministers in this world to save it by the preaching of the gospel but let it not be forgotten that there are Christians who, each in his daily occupation, can perhaps preach more effectively than many of those who are ordained.

During the days of war when hotel accommodations were difficult to secure, a certain Christian layman was told that he could find lodging for the night only if he would be willing to share a room. This he readily agreed to do. When it came time to retire he turned to his new-found friend with whom he was sharing the accommodations of this hotel and said to him, "I don't know what kind of faith you have or what church you go to, but I never retire at night without first reading the Bible and having a word of prayer. I would be happy if you would like to join me in my evening devotions." The man accepted the invitation. Later, he indicated to some friends that the reason he had found a new life of peace and happiness was that a traveling salesman had one night led him into the presence of the Lord by asking him to join in his evening devotions.

All of us can be witnesses. In a certain community there lives one whose executive ability is known throughout the land. But his first concern is the church. He travels a lot by private plane. But wherever he is, when the Lord's day comes, he is found at a worship service. When he is at home he not only gives unselfishly of his time but also generously of his means, and he gives not to be seen of men. When there is a special need he will present his gift, with the request that his name is not mentioned. Many souls will find their way into the eternal kingdom because of him and the sermon that he preaches as he goes about doing good. In this life he may never know what a real inspiration he has been, but God knows, and great will be his reward.

TABLE TALK: *Discuss how each of you can be a daily witness.*

5

JANUARY 6

Come into My Heart

Jesus said unto him, If thou wouldest be perfect, go, sell that which thou hast, and give to the poor, and thou shalt have treasure in heaven: and come follow me. Matthew 19:21.

One day a little lad and his sister decided that they wanted to do something for somebody else. They agreed that they would find some boys and girls who were poor and who did not have any toys or dolls and that they would give them some of their playthings. So they took out all their toys and games, and put everything they were going to give away in a large box. Then they brought all these things to the poor boys and girls.

The little sister was especially proud of what had happened, but the little brother looked very unhappy. When his sister asked him what was the matter, he said, "I have done something very wrong, because I gave those other boys and girls all the toys that I didn't want any more. I kept my best ball and glove and the red fire truck and all the things that are best." Then the sister began to remember that she had done the same thing. She asked her brother, "Jimmy, do you think God always wants the best?" Jimmy replied with one word: "Always."

When we give God the best, He is merely keeping it for our future use, because we are going to live some day in the house that we are constructing now. What are you searching for in life? A way to make more money, a plan to get out of doing much work? Material gain, even if it means acquiring it at the expense of others? If you look far enough, you may find all of these things. But suddenly some day you will discover that they have all been taken from you—you stand empty handed and silent as you are being asked a few simple questions. "Whom have you made happy? God has done so much for you. What have you done for Him?"

Are you aware that Christ is watching your living today? Every time you show love to a friend or a stranger, or when you do an act of kindness, or give help to someone in need, you are receiving Him into your heart.

TABLE TALK: *Have you ever had the same experience as the little boy or girl? Discuss what they should have done.*

6

Tomorrow, a Beautiful Day

For with thee is the fountain of life: in thy light shall we see light. Psalm 36:9.

A son was called home because his mother was very seriously ill. She lived in a little cottage on the shore of the great Pacific Ocean. Throughout their lives there had been a warm bond of love and understanding which had held them closely together. It was not easy for the boy now to see his mother at the end of the journey and to think of the loneliness which would be his until some day they would meet again.

The day was far spent and the evening shadows were beginning to fall. The sun was setting in majestic glory over the great body of water which only God would have the power to create. It streamed through the window and reflected in the radiant face of this saint of God who was on her way home. The boy got up to pull down the shade whereupon the mother turned to him and feebly whispered, "Ernest, don't pull down the shade." They both silently looked for a moment into the faraway horizon. The great Artist had splashed the colors of gold and amber and red upon the tapestry of the evening sky and, evidently thinking of the old adage, "Red sunset at night, sailors' delight," this Christian woman of great faith turned to her boy and said, "Ernest, tomorrow is going to be a glorious day!"

Her words were most prophetic. By the time morning came her soul had been carried by angel wings into the eternal paradise of God. She had claimed the promises of Christ her Saviour and now she knew the reality of all that she had ever hoped for.

When we have faith to believe we, too, live in the promise of tomorrow being more glorious than today. Life can be lived on the ascendency. Every step goes higher, higher. Each day is more glorious than the one that has preceded it. And life's final day is the most glorious of all for it means the life of God without earthly separations and sorrows and sin.

TABLE TALK: *Discuss the possibilities of improvement in your way of life which will make tomorrow more wonderful. Recall the mistakes you made today. Resolve to correct them that tomorrow may find you reaching higher.*

JANUARY 8

You Are Your Brother's Keeper

No longer as a servant, but more than a servant, a brother beloved, specially to me, but how much rather to thee, both in the flesh, and in the Lord? Philemon 1:16.

There is an organization which is known as "Big Brothers." Being a member is an act of true unselfishness. It consists of members who are willing to be counselors and friends to boys who need help and companionship.

This is a story of a "big brother" whose job has been more difficult than all. The befriended youngster comes from a broken family and has been placed by the state in a boarding home. At the age of fifteen he has a crushing personal problem. He suffers from muscular atrophy, a disease from which his brother died. He must be carried everywhere, and someone must feed him. He attends a special school where his spirit shines. But there are long stretches of loneliness. Here is where "big brother" stepped in.

A real estate man was assigned to the boy and for a period of over a year he has called for him each Saturday afternoon. He has carried George to the car for a trip to the country, to a baseball or football game, or to a movie. Together, George and his "big brother" have explored the countryside, have listened to the songs of birds, and looked at the color of the flowers. They have followed the stars together as they have watched them on clear nights. Because of this businessman, a new world of glory has opened up for George. Before, he was a lonely, helpless lad, but now, because of the help of somebody else who cared, he has been able to know something about abundant living.

Not only has George been helped, but the "big brother" has been blessed as well. He has learned that only as you invest yourself in others will you receive dividends in life. As he 's followed the Master in going about doing good, he has rece. d the thrill that comes to those who plant flowers in the barren places and who cause songs to be sung in the night.

TABLE TALK: *Discuss the influence some older person has had upon you. What could each member of the family do as "big brother" or "big sister" to someone you know?*

JANUARY 9

Your Best Friend

Greater love hath no man than this, that a man lay down his life for his friends. John 15:13.

Maybe you can remember the first time you went away from home. A strange feeling came over you when you realized Mother was not there to answer when you called. You had to make all your decisions yourself. No doubt you got lonesome and it seemed mighty good to run up those front steps and open the door to home again.

There is nothing quite so discouraging as being lonely and downhearted. Life seems so empty when we do not have friends to whom we can talk. Once there was a young man far away from home who in desperation sent this telegram to his father: "I am in the big city without friends or money. What shall I do?" It was not long before his father wired back a reply, "Make some good friends at once."

One of the things everyone admired about Jesus when He walked here on earth was His friendliness. He had a kind word for the little children who were playing in the street. He would stop and talk to the merchants along the highways and He had a smile of encouragement for the sick and downhearted. The Master was a friend of all men, willing to share happiness and love wherever He went. He is the same today.

There is a story of a boy who helped change a whole day for everyone in his family. It was one of those mornings that happen so often in every house. Daddy was late for work. The children were in a hurry to get off to school, and Mother had a busy day ahead of her. Quickly everybody sat down to the breakfast table and started to eat—that is, everybody but little Tommy. He just silently sat there for a moment. Then with a rather worried expression on his face he turned and said, "Why, Mother, we forgot Jesus!" The family had always said grace, but in the hurry they had forgotten.

Never forget your best friend. He is the one who can cheer you up and give your life new meaning.

TABLE TALK: *Discuss the importance of family prayer and table grace. Do you daily remember your friend in prayer?*

9

JANUARY 10

Walking in Others' Shoes

The Lord is gracious, and merciful; slow to anger, and of great lovingkindness. Psalm 145:8.

A few years ago an unusual thing took place on the streets of one of our metropolitan cities. A man stepped off the curb into the path of an approaching streetcar. The motorman sounded the bell, but the man kept on walking. Suddenly the streetcar struck him, knocking him to the ground. The motorman jumped out to help him, but when he saw he was not hurt, he let loose a tirade on the carelessness of pedestrians. But the hurt man was very apologetic and said, "I am sorry that I crossed in front of you. It wasn't your fault." Then he continued, "I hope you will forgive me, but you see, I am deaf and I didn't hear you coming."

Sometimes we are quick to criticize and then afterwards we are sorry that we have been so harsh. Biting words are quickly spoken before we realize the circumstances. Certainly one of the virtues which a real Christian possesses is to be slow to anger, thinking clearly and wisely before saying anything that might hurt somebody. How often an unkind remark has caused someone else a hurt that has taken away his joy in living!

One of the most pointed verses in the Bible is this: "If a man say, I love God, and hateth his brother, he is a liar: for he that loveth not his brother whom he hath seen, cannot love God whom he hath not seen." There can be no doubt about the meaning of that sentence. It says frankly that if you do not have understanding, consideration, and love for your fellow men, you cannot love God.

When the land of our country still belonged to the Indian tribes there was a custom among the Indians of appointing judges who went from village to village trying those who had done wrong. One young brave used as his simple prayer: "Forbid that I should judge any man until I have walked in his moccasins."

TABLE TALK: *Stop and think! Have you judged someone unjustly in the last few days? Discuss what you should remind yourself of every time you pass judgement on someone.*

10

It Is Worth the Price

One God and Father of all, who is over all, and through all, and in all. Ephesians 4:6.

Many years ago there was a courageous preacher who defied his lawless and heathen government. He kept on telling his people about the love of God. The emperor threatened to destroy him and throw him into exile on a deserted island. The faithful preacher gave this answer: "There is not such a thing as exile. The whole world is my Father's house and you can never get rid of Him." Then the emperor said he would have him killed, but he only replied, "I cannot die, for my life is hid in Christ." The next threat was to take away his treasure but the answer came, "My treasure is in heaven and you can never take that from me." Then they threatened to destroy all his friends and leave him alone in the world. "You cannot banish all my friends for I have one who will never leave me. In truth, there is really nothing that you can do to hurt me, for I have Christ."

The Christian way of life demands sacrifices and hardships. But nothing can really hurt you when Christ is your king. His power is greater than all the tribulations of the world. His strength is mightier than all the armies and His promises are surer than all earthly threats. The road that you must walk may not always be an easy one to travel, but the will of God is always there willing to help you across the pitfalls and to ease the pain of bruised steps. The Master wants you to know happiness and peace and He constantly seeks to guide you away from the discouragements and tribulations of the world. But when they come, He offers grace sufficient for them.

Look at the Christian facing a troubled world after a long day's work. Stop and ask him if he is sorry that he has walked the way of Christ. Listen to him as he smiles and answers, "Sorry? How could I be sorry when my heart is full of happiness and love." No price is too great to pay for such a reward. It may mean that you will have to stand alone in the riotous crowd that ignores God. It means to put yourself last, but it is worth it!

TABLE TALK: *What makes your religion worth fighting for, and worth the ridicule of a crowd? Discuss.*

JANUARY 12

Onward, Christian Soldiers

Fight the good fight of the faith, lay hold on the life eternal, whereunto thou wast called, and didst confess the good confession in the sight of many witnesses. 1 Timothy 6:12.

As you go through the city or travel through the countryside you will see spires pointing heavenward indicating that there are people in these communities who have faith in the power of God and who gather in these places to sing their praises unto Him. Wherever your church may be, it stands up boldly to the world as a fortress against the storms of unrest and war. And the forces of evil can never destroy it as long as you, the soldiers of Christ, hold fast to all of its eternal values. When Christians come together in the house of God they witness as a mighty army stronger than the sword of hatred, and with God's help this army shall never be conquered.

The town of Newbury, across the sea, was virtually bombed out during the last war and only the skeletons of a few buildings were left standing. In one block, the church had been bombed and on one side of the ruins was the wreckage of a schoolhouse, on the other side the rubble of a hospital. It appears as if the enemy had blotted out the town's religion, its education, and its institution of mercy, and still the village had hope. One wall of the church was still standing and on the very top of that wall was a golden cross still shining in all its glory. Though the bricks and mortar had been leveled to the ground, the symbol of the things eternal still remained unchanged.

There is no enemy great enough to destroy the faith that lives in the hearts of devoted Christians. That is our reason for hope today. The church has the power to stand against tyranny and dishonesty because it is built upon the solid foundation of God. And we have the promise that His Word will endure forever.

Each day that you live you are preaching a sermon. You are indicating to people that life holds no future, or you are an apostle of hope with the faith built upon the Rock of Ages.

TABLE TALK: *Sing together "Onward, Christian Soldiers" and then discuss how each of you can be a soldier of Christ in victory over sin.*

JANUARY 13

Each One an Author

And having been made perfect, he became unto all them that obey him the author of eternal salvation. Hebrew 5:9.

Each one of us is an author. Perhaps you have never recognized any literary gifts among your talents. Maybe you think you have nothing about which to write. It might be that you object to such a thought since you have never had training in literary expression. Even in the face of such denials from many of you, I would repeat that everyone of us is an author.

When God gave us life, He put a pen in our hands, and with the things we do and the things we say, we are writing a book. Every day is a clean new sheet that God gives us on which we write our record. No one else can write that book for us. We must select and phrase what will go into it, and people about us readily see the story which our life is weaving.

When God first put that pen into our hands they were tiny ones and we handled it quite clumsily. We were new in this world and inexperienced. For such a time God gave us parents and other loved ones who took our hands in theirs and helped us shape the first lines which we wrote in this book of life. They taught us how to spell love and thoughtfulness and happiness. They traced pictures of God for us with which to better understand the purposes to which we were dedicated.

But the day comes when every one of us must direct the writing with his own hand. We would do well to spend time as we select our words and phrases. If we wish to build toward a story with a happy ending we must put into our living, actions that will lead in such a direction. It takes time to write a book that is going to be worth reading. It takes quiet times of concentration and meditation to build a life that is worth living. We must often pause to dip pens into the wells of God's grace if we are going to leave an imprint that will not fade. Only God can give us the inspiration we need to go on writing this book of life so that it will have real meaning.

TABLE TALK: *What kind of reading would your book make? Discuss what changes you would make in your daily actions if your life were an "open book"?*

13

God's Unchanging Love

The Lord appeared of old unto me, saying, Yea, I have loved thee with an everlasting love: therefore with lovingkindness have I drawn thee. Jeremiah 31:3.

A country pastor was visiting his members who lived on farms surrounding the village. As he approached one of them he saw a new weather vane upon the top of the large barn. Painted on each side of it were the words, "God Is Love." When the pastor met the farmer he asked him about the new addition, suggesting that people might get the wrong idea from it. The minister said that every time the wind changes the sign turns and people might get the notion that God's love is unsteady and changing. The farmer understood all right but had a prompt reply. "It is just the other way around. The weather changes and the weather vane turns, but it still says, 'God Is Love.' It really means that whatever way the wind may blow God is still love."

We can be sure of God. His love is stable and abiding for it does not depend upon the changes in times or circumstance. He loves the rich just as He loves the poor. All people are His children, regardless of the color of their skin, regardless of the country in which they live. There is only one distinction that He makes: Do you serve Him or do you deny Him? If you are following His way, He shares goodness and mercy without asking what kind of a house you live in or what your social standing may be. If you serve him, your life is full of light; if you deny him, you walk in darkness.

Only as our world turns away from the sun in the sky does its brightness not come upon us. God's love can brighten every corner and make every heart burn with joy and happiness if only we do not turn away. Does it not give you confidence to know that never need you be separated from this great love?

God is Love. His love is everlasting and unchanging.

TABLE TALK: *Why not stop and think of all the ways in which God's love is evident—in nature all about you, in the very fact that day dawns anew, in the laughter of little children, in the love of a friend—and then remember, that God's love is far greater than you can ever imagine.*

JANUARY 15

Your Soul Is Your Fortune

For what doth it profit a man, to gain the whole world, and forfeit his life? Mark 8:36.

Very frequently, we should take inventory of what we have. It would make us much more grateful. Everything that we possess has been given to us! We came into this world with nothing, except a body, mind, and soul which were created by Almighty God and which therefore belonged to Him. Everything we have created since is the result of the original capacities given us by the hand of our benevolent Father.

Not often enough do we think of these original gifts of God. You possess a wonderful body. Just take, as an example, your ability to see. If you have never thanked God for your eyesight, you ought to visit an institution for the blind to observe these handicapped people, and then to compare your more favorable lot with theirs. Or think of your mind, the capacity you have to think clearly. If you have not been grateful for this gift, you ought to visit a hospital and observe the mentally ill.

And what about your soul? It is a sky parlor that looks up to heaven. Nothing can close off that view for you. Perhaps you may be encircled with trouble and difficulty, but no one can stop you from looking up to Him who has promised to be your helper in every time of need. And upon that soul is the stamp of the divine. He made you in His very own image, and He has meant that you should belong to Him, not only because He has made you but also because He has redeemed you, and because He has promised to go with you along the entire journey of this life, and then through the valley into the life that is to come.

One day Jesus said that if you piled up all of the material possessions of the world and placed them on one side of a scale, and then put the soul on the other side, the one soul would outweigh all these other things, and would be of more value in the sight of God. "For what doth it profit a man, to gain the whole world, and forfeit his life?"

TABLE TALK: *Take inventory of what you have. Discuss the ultimate source of each possession and then decide how you can show your gratitude.*

15

JANUARY 16

Take the High Road

Lord, make me to know mine end, and the measure of my days, what it is; let me know how frail I am. Psalm 39:4.

The next time you take your watch to be fixed, stop and watch the jeweler as he goes to work. Somewhere in those intricate wheels something has gone wrong. But even the watchmaker's expert eye cannot discover it. So he uses a little magnifying glass and in just a few moments he usually has found the trouble.

Something is wrong with this world! But so many people cannot seem to discover what it is. They need a vision more powerful than their own. If they would only look at mankind through the eyes of God they would quickly find the reasons for the despair which seems to abide in the hearts of men everywhere.

The hope for peace and contentment has been buried under selfish desires and misguided values. There are so many people who seem to be willing to risk losing their eternal soul in order to win a few years of worldly power. What we need today is a vision which goes far beyond the ends of the earth, and that reaches deeper than the pride of wealth and power. The only road that travels farther than the eye can see is that straight and narrow way which Christ traveled Himself many years ago. That highway is still open to the trusting traveler today. If you believe in God then you must live in Him. You will then hold high the banner of His love and stand up boldly for His name. If you are to help save the world, He must first save you. And then you will be given a vision of how you can help others.

As we observe the sin in life all about us, it is so much easier to look at someone else and find his faults than it is to discover our own. We act like Jimmy who said his prayers one night. His mother asked him if he had asked God to make him a good boy. "Yes," replied Jimmy, "I asked God to help me, but I spent most of my time putting in a good word for Bill next door."

Face your own fears first. Be honest with God and confess your weakness. Ask Him to show you the way.

TABLE TALK: *Examine your life closely. Are you able to correct your faults with the help of God, and then be of greater service to your fellow men?*

16

JANUARY 17

Like a Little Child

Except ye turn, and become as little children, ye shall in no wise enter into the kingdom of heaven. Matthew 18:3.

One day the Master was lecturing to the Pharisees about some divorce matters. Near him were some mothers with their children, clamoring for attention. The disciples, thinking the Master would be disturbed by the confusion, went to them and said, "Our Master is a busy man. He has a full calendar. Can't you see you're disturbing Him?"

Jesus heard them speak these words and said, "You are very mistaken. I am happy to bless these children. Allow them to come to me. Do not forbid them, for of such is the kingdom of heaven; and if one does not become as a little child, he cannot enter into the kingdom of heaven."

If we think it through carefully, it is not difficult to understand why Jesus indicated that we enter the Kingdom by being like a little child. As yet unspoiled by the world, they retain the endearing qualities that Christ wants for all His children. You have often seen how humble they are.

Then note how dependent they are. They have absolute faith in their parents, and the words that they speak to them are truth. They are willing to rely on their decisions, and if ever they get into trouble, they turn to them for help, confident that they will receive it.

And what imitators they are! The little girl wants a dress like her mother's and the boy wants to do just as the father does. So God would have us be imitators of Him. He has revealed Himself to us through Christ His Son, and each day we should try to live as He did when He walked the streets of men.

Anyone may enter the kingdom of heaven. You do not need long merit lists, nor do you have to possess a college education or great material riches. But you need to be childlike, humbly confessing your need of God's forgiveness.

TABLE TALK: *"A little child shall lead them." You have often heard that. Do you know of any instances where a child has been an example for its parents?*

Build Spiritual Foundations

But we received, not the spirit of the world, but the spirit which is from God; that we might know the things that were freely given to us of God. 1 Corinthians 2:12.

The story is told concerning a certain young couple who were looking into the crib at their first-born child. They seemed to be dreaming. The mother was thinking that her young son would grow up some day to become, perhaps, a great statesman. Suddenly she turned to her husband and said, "And dear, what were you dreaming about?" He replied, "I was just wondering how they could build a cradle like that for $3.98."

We are living in a materialistic age. Most values seem to be measured in dollars and cents. We seem to have lost sight of the fact that ideals, hopes, and dreams are important, too. The most important things in life cannot be purchased across the tables of trade. They are gained by sacrifices made in the realm of the spirit.

Consider, for example, salvation. You cannot buy it, no matter how many stocks or bonds you possess, and no matter how large your bank account might be. It was purchased for you on Calvary by the Son of God, who willingly died that your sins might be forgiven. The only condition imposed upon you is that you accept the gracious gift which is given to you. When you do, you seek out of gratitude to love and serve Him.

There are always tragic results when a person builds on material things to the exclusion of the spiritual. How often we dream of great ambitions we would like to attain, and how seldom we dream of a life that would be more Godlike.

It is important to make a living. We need a house in which to live, and food to eat, and clothes to wear. But more important than any of these is to build within our souls a spiritual fortress that will enable us to face any situation confidently and victoriously. The Master has promised to give us that strength. Let us speak with Him in prayer and read His Word.

TABLE TALK: *You cannot buy love, or faith, or health, or friendship with dollars and cents. Discuss how each of these are obtained, that is, what spiritual sacrifices are made for each.*

JANUARY 19

Leave the Light Burning

God is light, and in him is no darkness at all. If we say that we have fellowship with him and walk in the darkness, we lie, and do not the truth. 1 John 1:5-6.

Sometimes when you are unhappy and sorrowful, and the hours of the day seem long and almost endless, remind yourself of this promise which will give you hope, "I can do all things through Christ who gives me strength." In spite of what the hours may bring, there is so much to make you happy and so much to keep you smiling. Always remember that the power of Almighty God is behind you. You can be sure that the Master will show you the way, step by step, that He will take you over the highest mountain and through the deepest valleys.

Then, find some task that will challenge you. It will take your mind off your troubles as you invest your life in some great cause. There is something for each one of us to do. And the results of that doing will live far beyond the span of our own life.

There is a story about a little girl who visited the old home of Abraham Lincoln in Springfield. She had heard so often about this great man who did so much for so many people. And she was very anxious to see the house where he had lived. When she came up to the old homestead she noticed that the lamps inside were burning just as they were many years ago when Lincoln lived there as a young man. Then the little girl stopped, looked up at her mother, and said, "Mr. Lincoln left the lights on when he went away."

There are many lights still burning because of great souls who will always remain as an inspiration to every generation. Christ spoke of John as a burning and shining light. What a wonderful benediction it would be if the Master could say the same of our lives today! God has sent us into this world to be the bright lights which can destroy the darkness of sin so that others need not stumble along the way.

TABLE TALK: *There is always some task that needs to be done. Name some leaders in the religious, political, and spiritual fields who "left a light burning." What qualities made them admirable?*

JANUARY 20

God's Love Is Constant

They that know thy name will put their trust in thee.

Psalm 9:10

No matter how far away you may go, you cannot escape the troubles of this world. No matter where you may choose to hide, you cannot avoid its sorrow and grief. Even though there will be some darkness in life, a Christian always has faith that a new day will follow closely behind.

The assurance that you have in your heart that sunshine will come after rain, and that God can work out all things for good, we call "faith." It is not "believing things you know ain't so," as the little boy defined it, and it is not a logical formula for letting someone else do your work. Faith is the soul's discovery that enables you to stand up against anything that happens and still know that because of a power beyond yourself you will be victorious.

One night some years ago, a strange sight appeared in the sky. It seemed as if a great number of stars were falling out of the heavens, and they left trails of flame as they fell toward the earth. Some people thought that it meant that the end of the world was near. They ran to an old man known for his faith who lived near by to ask him what they should do. There they found the wise old man sitting in the door of his cabin looking up at the stars with a smile on his face. They told him they were afraid and that they needed his help. He slowly pointed up at the sky and said, "That is a mighty beautiful sight. See those little stars shooting across the heaven? But look at those big ones, they haven't moved an inch."

What if the little things of life are continually being shaken, with many of them falling to the ground broken and destroyed. The important things live on unchanged. God in His love still shines brilliantly in all of His beauty. That is the kind of a star to which you can hitch your life, one that points to eternal salvation and lights the way before you.

TABLE TALK: *Have you ever been frightened by a storm, or a loud noise, or the dark? What would help you to overcome these fears?*

JANUARY 21

In Need of Grace

For all have sinned, and fall short of the glory of God; being justified freely by his grace through the redemption that is in Christ Jesus. Romans 3:23-24.

Some years ago, a giant waterway was built in southern California in order to keep a treacherous river from spilling its destruction into the near-by countryside. Huge walls were constructed which engineers carefully calculated to withstand the tremendous pressure of the water. But not long after this project was completed, the giant concrete walls collapsed and the rampant river swept down the valley destroying the rich land and causing the loss of many lives.

An investigation was made and witnesses were brought in to give their explanations of the great disaster. Among them was the chief engineer of the waterway project. Standing before the investigating committee he made this statement. "Don't blame anyone else. I planned this structure and I am responsible for it. If there was an error in judgment or calculation the error was mine."

In this age of "blame shifting," it takes an added bit of courage to admit boldly that we are wrong, even though our mistakes are many more than we can count. And that is the reason why so many of us hold ourselves apart from God. There is one condition that He makes that we must abide by, if we are to receive His forgiveness! We must come to Him with penitent hearts, admit our mistakes and say, "I am sorry. Forgive me." This is not an easy world in which to live. There is not anybody who is perfect. Even though we try desperately to make the right choices and follow the good rules of living each day we fall short and are in need of God's forgiving love.

Never forget that you are a sinner standing in the need of grace, but remember also the wonderful assurance which can be yours, that your mistakes will be forgiven and forgotten when you take them to the Master with an honest, open, and sincere confession.

TABLE TALK: *Perhaps you have made a mistake recently. Was it hard for you to admit it? Discuss.*

JANUARY 22

How Big Are You?

And Jesus advanced in wisdom and stature, and in favor with God and men. Luke 2:52.

Mary and Joseph no doubt took all the delight in their children that parents do today. The mother certainly must often have bent over the little cradle of Baby Jesus and slowly and distinctly pronounced the Hebrew words for father and mother. She must have been happy to hear Him say these words for the first time. We can also imagine her watching Him stand on His own feet for the first time and then helping Him to take those first faltering steps.

Very little information is given us about the boyhood of the Master. We, therefore, ponder much over the few single statements we find, a significant one being, "And Jesus advanced in wisdom and stature, and in favor with God and man." In almost every home where there are growing children one can discover somewhere in the house a place where there are notches or pencil marks drawn horizontally in varying heights. Jimmy will be proud to step up and tell you that this line shows how tall he was on his last birthday and now look how much he has grown since then. Ask little Susan how big she is. She will delightfully stretch her little arms as high above her as she can reach and say, "I am so big."

It is right for children to be happy about their growing up. However, there is a normal time for physical growth to cease. But in our spiritual lives we are dwarfed and retarded if we do not continue to grow. Paul says that we can never be satisfied until we have attained the measure of the stature of Christ. We must move on. We are called to build and to rise and to dream dreams and to put them into action.

Have you measured your spiritual growth? Are you growing each day in favor with God and man? You can grow each day in wisdom and stature only as you feed your soul on the spiritual food He has prepared for you. How big are you?

TABLE TALK: *Spiritual growth is gained through worship and study and service. Discuss how the family can grow spiritually together.*

22

Living in Confidence

Behold, I stand at the door, and knock: if any man hear my voice and open the door, I will come in. Revelation 3:20.

One of the gifts of God is the beautiful scenery He has given His children in His creation. Have you ever had the experience of standing on the shore of a beautiful lake on a crisp, clear night, looking into the sky at the millions of stars shining as lights in the window? Then perhaps the northern lights would appear and the longer you stood watching, the more breathtaking the picture became. The Lord seemed to be everywhere.

When you enter into partnership with the Master you are attracted by His magnificent love and tenderness. And the longer you live side by side with Him the more this partnership comes to mean to you. Just as you get to know your friends and acquaintances better as you share their company day by day, so you will get to know the Master as you walk and talk with Him each hour. You will gradually get to know the strength which can be yours. You will begin to realize the tremendous depth of His love. You will understand better the meaning of His Word and promises.

Not only has Jesus promised to receive the penitent sinner and to change his direction of living in one act of forgiveness, He has also given us the assurance that He will continue to help His children grow and mature in their Christian life.

When a friend asked a neighbor if she had found salvation, the woman replied, "No, but I am working hard at it." The thoughtful friend sincerely answered, "I am afraid you won't discover it that way. Christ did all the work and all you need to do is to accept it as a wonderful gift."

God reaches out His hand to save you from the temptations which crowd in on you on every side wherever you go. With tender care He offers to help you grow strong and more beautiful every day. Why not open your heart to Him and really live in confidence as hand in hand He leads you down life's way?

TABLE TALK: *How would you explain God's forgiveness to a sinner? Discuss.*

JANUARY 24

Pray Without Ceasing

Pray without ceasing. 1 Thessalonians 5:17.

When I was a little boy I heard a Bible verse that really puzzled me. I just could not understand how anyone could truly follow the admonition to "pray without ceasing." To me the command seemed quite foolish. Who spent all of his time praying? Did not a person have to earn a living? Did he not have to take time to eat, talk to his friends, and have a good time, and to sleep?

I went to an older minister who was a very understanding man and asked him this question: "What does it mean to pray without ceasing?" He sat down with me and asked, "You love your father and your mother very much, don't you?" "Yes," I replied, "better than anyone in the whole world." Then this good old preacher friend of mine reminded me that even though I loved my parents I was not thinking of them every minute of the day. I ate my meals, I went to school, I played ball with the fellows, I talked to my friends, and I slept at night. But whenever I stopped to think of my parents I felt warm and good inside because I knew that they were loving me even as I loved them.

And so it is with God. There are many activities in the day which keep us busy and to which we must give our full attention, but any time we want to we can stop and think of God and speak to Him in prayer. It makes us feel good inside to know that He is always with us. In fact, our heart should always be in an attitude of prayer so that God is constantly directing us in the way that we should go, in the thoughts that we think, and in the words that we speak. One's whole life should be lived in the spirit of prayer; then whenever there is a decision to be made, the divine Partner will always be taken into consultation so that His will might be done.

The happy souls I know are those who never for one moment walk alone. They have learned the secret of His presence.

TABLE TALK: *Do you ever stop during the day to think of God? Make "prayer without ceasing" a part of your everyday living.*

JANUARY 25

Daily We Are Building

He is like a man building a house, who digged and went deep, and laid a foundation upon the rock: and when the flood arose, the stream brake against that house, and could not shake it: because it had been well builded. Luke 6:48.

Maybe you remember the song sung in Sunday school—some of the lines run something like this: "Building, daily building, while the moments fly; we are ever building, for our home on high."

It is often well to consider the things that are necessary if we shall build well this house of life. We certainly want to be sure of our foundation. What can be more discouraging than to build a fine home, constructed with the finest materials, only to find after a time that the foundation begins to crumble? It is a sad and costly experience in building our house of life. We shall want to be sure that we are building on the Rock of Ages.

Of what shall we build the walls in our house of life? The one toward the north should be of love—warm and strong against the cold, sharp winds of hate. On the opposite side, let us build a wall of understanding that may include all people regardless of color, or faith, or social station. To the east, let us erect a wall of faith which looks toward the sunrise and believes that the new day holds possibilities the like of which were never known before. On the west, we shall want a wall of hope that will spring eternal even though facing the setting sun.

We want windows to give us vision of the needs about us so that we may be of service to our fellow men. We would do well to have a window toward the sea to remind us of friends and children of God throughout the whole world. We would want a window in which we might set a lamp to show the way to some-one who may be groping in darkness.

"We are building, daily building." Let us never forget that in the house we build today we shall live tomorrow.

TABLE TALK. *Discuss instances of people who are forgetting the most important things in living and whose lives are therefore not built on firm foundations, and others who are taking time to put the right kind of materials into life.*

25

He Has Gone Before You

If any man would come after me, let him deny himself, and take up his cross, and follow me. For whosoever would save his life shall lose it; and whosoever shall lose his life for my sake and the gospel's shall save it. Mark 8:34-35.

A brother and a sister lived with their parents in a little country home close to a valley. The little girl had been told in her early childhood that there were goblins down there of which she should be afraid. There was a beautiful hill on the other side but never had she had an opportunity to see its glory at close range because she was afraid that there might be those in the valley that would harm and destroy her. Her brother tried to convince her that it was not true, that the person who told her about those goblins did not know what he was talking about. For many months he tried every kind of an argument with little success.

One day he said to her, "Now, Sister, if I go down into the valley and come up on the other side and you see me there, will you promise me that you will come over there to meet me? Just to prove to yourself that there is really nothing down there that will harm you." After hesitating a moment, the sister agreed to the plan.

One morning the boy started out. He descended to the valley and climbed up the hill on the other side. When he reached his destination he waved back to his sister proving to her that he had arrived safely. She had to keep the promise she made, so she started out, still a little fearful of what she might encounter. What did she find? A quiet little stream running there, and some beautiful flowers that she plucked. Then she ran up the hill on the other side, threw her arms around her brother and said, "Thank you for going before me. Now I will never be afraid of any valley again."

Is it not a wonderful hope to be able to live each day knowing that there is not a single undirected mile in life?

TABLE TALK: *Think of some problem you have in business, at home, or in school. Could Christ show you by His example what you could do to solve it? Discuss this.*

JANUARY 27

The Everlasting Arms

The Lord upholdeth all that fall, and raiseth up all those that are bowed down. Psalm 145:14.

Often when play gets too rough, when feelings get hurt or a knee gets skinned, the child goes running to his mother for consolation and solace. And then, in her arms, all problems are soothed away and happiness returns to his little world. All of us at times have felt the need of the encircling arm and the lullaby of a soft voice saying, "Everything is going to be all right."

Many of us have now grown into men and women, and some of us no longer have a mother to whom we can turn. It is God our heavenly Father who speaks to us now as He says, "You can trust your mother's God. I care for you. I know that you are engaged in the rough game of living. There are so many opportunities for you to get knocked around and bruised. But you can come to me, and I will help you and will bind up your wounds in love."

To really be victorious in our lives we must get into our consciousness the fact that God *does* care, that He is concerned about even the little hurts which life inflicts upon us. He knows the problems we face in life today. He knows, because He is present with us in our living. But likewise He knows He has the strength and the power to help us overcome, no matter what the difficulty might be.

God is not detached from this world, nor from us. His presence is as real as anything can be. Any time we choose we can talk to Him and know that He will answer us. Today, remind yourself of the presence of one who is stronger than any foe that you will have to face, and then stay close to Him, and you will discover how thrilling it is to have Him conquer for you. When life gets too rough, when your feelings are hurt, you have Him for consolation and solace. You can rest in His everlasting arms!

TABLE TALK: *Have you ever felt homesick for your mother or someone you hold dear? Were you able to find solace and companionship with God instead?*

JANUARY 28

A Loser or a Winner

And every man that striveth in the games exerciseth self-control in all things. Now they do it to obtain a corruptible crown, but we an incorruptible. 1 Corinthians 9:25.

A teacher told the story of a young girl who had finished a stenographic course in school, graduating with the highest honors in her class. A call came from a large and prosperous business concern that was looking for a capable secretary. The school highly recommended this particular girl. An appointment was made for an interview with the office manager and her chances for getting the job seemed good. But as the manager waited for her at the appointed hour, she failed to arrive on time. She did not get the job!

You miss a train just by a few moments. The track star is just a few steps behind the winner. Either way, you are the loser. Paul suggested that in life we are running a race. Some will win and others will lose. But unlike other races, you can determine the outcome. You can be a winner or a loser just by choosing God or by rejecting Him. If you are on His side, you may be confident that some day you will wear the victor's crown.

If someone came to you today and offered to give you a priceless gift, something you have always wanted but could never get yourself, and if it were offered to you without cost, I am sure you would receive it gratefully. Right now, God stands at the door of your heart offering you the most precious gift of all life, a peaceful mind and a victorious soul. Certainly you would not turn away from Him without accepting it. Not only will He be disappointed if you refuse Him, but you will lose life's supreme opportunity.

No one wants to be a loser, but no one wants to win unless there is a worthwhile prize. Nothing could be more disheartening than working for a useless thing. It is wonderful to know that God offers us a priceless gift.

You choose either a perishable wreath, or a lasting crown!

TABLE TALK: *Do you know anyone who has only earthly goods? Discuss what they are missing in life.*

JANUARY 29

Keep Watching the Signals

Turn ye from your evil ways, and keep my commandments and my statutes, according to all the law which I commanded your fathers, and which I sent to you by my servants the prophets. 2 Kings 17:13.

One day I was really frightened. We were driving down a busy metropolitan avenue which was designated as a one-way street. When one travels on such a street he usually goes with more speed and assurance because he knows that he need not cope with oncoming traffic. Suddenly the lights of a car coming the wrong way from a side street turned against us. We swerved fast and miraculously avoided a head-on collision. The lights of many automobiles began blinking at the driver and many horns tooted to let him know that he was a wrong-direction driver. Due to the heavy traffic, the car was unable to back up and had to make its way as best it could the length of the block. It must have seemed like a very long block to that driver.

As we drove on into the night, I thought of how easy it is for any driver to miss the one-way-traffic sign and get into trouble. But is it not just as easy for us on the highway of life to miss our signals and to get into more serious danger? For example, God tells us that we should not take His name in vain. But there are people who become careless and forget that warning signal and before they know it, they are not even aware that they are taking His name in vain. God tells us that we should speak to Him in prayer. When we start missing the signal and forget to talk to Him as we should we get into trouble, for then we have no one to guide us in the way that we should go. Life becomes unbearably long for those who are thus separated from Him.

It is always wise when driving an automobile to obey the signs. It is even wiser in the living of a life to obey the Commandments God has given us. Only so can we reach our goal.

TABLE TALK: *Discuss together instances of people who have violated the laws of God and suffered severe consequences because of it.*

JANUARY 30

Strong in His Strength

Speaking one to another in psalms and hymns and spiritual songs, singing and making melody with your heart to the Lord.
Ephesians 5:19.

Not long ago the world witnessed the departure of a dear Christian mother. She had been a woman of great spirit and much enthusiasm for living, and her family of four had grown to fine womanhood and manhood. Alive to all that was fine, she was the sort of a woman who was staunch and genuine, with no trace of what we might term a "Pollyanna" attitude toward events. Yet she was the kind about whom it was easy to say, "She surely had a heart of gold." More rightly, it should be said that what made her life so radiant was that she had laid hold on the heart of God and it was He who lived so freely through her loving deeds, kind words, and noble thoughts.

Even though a person was not actually related to her, it was the natural thing to call her "Aunt Ruth." Some months past her health had begun to fail and finally she was utterly confined to her home. There she busied herself with writing letters to her friends who needed cheering, to her son and daughter-in-law who had recently lost their only child, to a daughter who had been a polio victim, and to a grandchild who had been ill nigh unto death.

This valiant soul never complained, even at the last. And when she was called to take the final journey through the valley, there was a song in her heart and upon her lips. "Praise God from whom all blessings flow." She had learned the great secret of being able to give thanks for all things.

St. Paul, in writing to the Ephesians, gives us this advice: "Be filled with the Spirit; speaking one to another in psalms and hymns and spiritual songs, singing and making melody with your heart to the Lord; giving thanks always for all things in the name of our Lord Jesus Christ to God, even the Father."

TABLE TALK: *Too often we become absorbed in our own affairs and do not follow the admonition of St. Paul. Think of someone you know who would appreciate a card, a note, or a friendly call, and then do something special for this friend.*

JANUARY 31

Thank You, God

And all things, whatsoever ye shall ask in prayer, believing, ye shall receive. Matthew 21:22.

A minister was instructing a class of young boys about their attitude in worship, especially upon entering the church. He told them that when they had seated themselves, they should always bow their heads in prayer. He then gave them some suggestions about what they might pray. After the instruction session, he brought the class upstairs to the sanctuary, and the boys took their places in the pews, each one silently saying a prayer. Then the minister questioned each one about what he had said when he bowed his head. Each boy told the pastor about what he had prayed. Finally he came to little Jimmy, and said, "And what did you pray about?" Jimmy replied, "Sir, I didn't say nothing. I was just loving Him a while."

Often we have been told that we should take a look at ourselves. It is good to take inventory from time to time. Another appropriate suggestion is that we take a look at our prayers.

Do we talk to God only when we want to ask Him for something? Do we just talk to Him when we are in trouble or when something serious has come into our home? As parents we would be very disappointed if our children spoke to us only when they wanted some selfish desire satisfied. Sometimes God must become quite disturbed "as daily He provides us with all the necessities of life" and we in return fail to come to Him to just thank Him for all that He has given us.

It would be a good discipline during the course of each day to set aside one prayer session when you would do nothing but thank God for all the things He daily provides for you. Perhaps at night, just before you go to sleep, it would be well to take a look at the day which you have lived and to think in terms of all the good things that have come to you during that time at the hand of Almighty God. Some time each day turn to God in prayer to tell Him what a wonderful, loving Father He is.

TABLE TALK: *Discuss specific instances in your lives when God has answered prayer.*

FEBRUARY 1

We Live with Courage

The thief cometh not, but that he may steal, and kill, and destroy: I came that they may have life, and may have it abundantly. John 10:10.

Many people today are painters of pessimism. They portray the day in which we are living as a black and raging storm that ultimately is destined to sweep goodness and righteousness out of the picture.

Undoubtedly there are stormy clouds that float overhead, but above and beyond is the greatest artist of all, who has painted a brilliant sunrise, flaming with hope and courage. The eye of the faithful Christian can see through the black mist into the time when truth and purity will forever shine brightly.

Jesus Himself has given us the promise of something greater that is to be. He says, "I came that you might have life, and might have it abundantly." If Christ is the king of your heart, you do not have to wait until tomorrow for the wonderful day of victory. You have already found it today. When troubles or problems face you, do not give up hope. With the Master as your partner, you are always marching steadily onward and upward. And you are never afraid, for this is the song of your heart: "All the way my Saviour leads me. What have I to ask beside?"

No matter what kind of future may be ahead, if we have faith, we live with courage. Christ is a guide who never loses His way, never forgets His direction, nor ever leads us astray. The pathway which He travels is not always the easiest way. Sometimes there are mountains to climb and valleys to cross. The road is not always smooth and wide, but the more difficult the traveling becomes, the greater the help you receive from your God.

Live each day with Christ as your partner. Ask yourself, "What would He have me do and how would He have me live?"

TABLE TALK: *Discuss ways in which you can overcome a pessimistic view of life. Show how Christ was an optimist.*

FEBRUARY 2

Room to Fly

And ye said, Behold, the Lord our God hath showed us his glory and his greatness, and we have heard his voice out of the midst of the fire; we have seen this day that God doth talk with man, and he liveth. Deuteronomy 5:24.

Lao-tze, father of Taoism, says: "Clay is molded into a vessel; the utility of the vessel depends upon its hollow interior. Doors and windows are cut out in order to make a house; the utility of the house depends on the empty spaces."

Few of us realize that the importance of empty space is not a modern idea, but was even a part of the thinking of a Chinese philosopher more than 2,500 years ago.

At an exhibition of Chinese paintings, a visitor was overheard saying to the artist that she would buy the picture of a bird on a bare branch but that she considered the painting too empty and asked him if he could not add a few more branches and leaves. "If I added that," the Chinese artist answered, "there would be no room for the bird to fly." In his conception, the main feature of the picture was a suggestion of infinite space.

Not only the birds need room to fly. Too many lives are daily hemmed in by the pressures of so many appointments, and, duties, and cares. Frequently we should consider the planning of our days so that we might have the opportunity to eliminate as many nonessential activities as possible.

Very rarely does any great person ever complain about the fact that he does not have a free moment of time. In his planning he usually leaves some time available for any emergency which may develop; for opportunities to help those with special needs whose paths he might cross that day.

To get the proper direction in living we need moments set aside for frequent talking with God. It is possible to become so busy that one loses his effectiveness. We must be on guard against filling our days so full of activity that making a living becomes more important than making a life.

TABLE TALK: *Let each analyze the activities of the past few days, looking for wasted energies and nonessential activities. Was enough time given to talking with God?*

Guard the Treasure

But lay up for yourselves treasures in heaven, where neither moth nor rust doth consume, and where thieves do not break through nor steal. Matthew 6:20.

A story is told about a traveler who was making his way across the desolate plain of Africa. He was searching for a fortune in diamonds but so far his journey had been in vain. One day he came to a small native village and asked if he might stay there to get some rest and a few supplies. The natives agreed and they gave him a hut in which to sleep.

As he awakened the next day, he walked about the village and came upon a group of youngsters playing in a small clearing nearby. He walked over to watch them. He noticed that they drew a circle in the ground and then threw some rough stones in the center. Suddenly he realized that these stones were not just ordinary bits of rock but were uncut diamonds. Quickly he rushed over and gathered them up and ran to the native chief with them. "I would like to take these stones with me as a souvenir," he told the chief. "I will pay you for them." Then he dug out a rusty pocket knife, a few coins, and a colored handkerchief. "I will give you these in exchange." The chief looked for a moment and then replied, "Take the stones if you want them. I will trade." And the traveler hurried off with his pockets bulging with valuable diamonds.

There are too many people in the world today who are willing to trade eternity for this world. And because of it they are living in the darkness of sorrow and despair. They have lost the only real treasure. Within their hearts the sun never seems to shine. They never face life with a smile. Only the deep lines of regret and countless complaints can be seen and heard.

Do not sell, for any price, your great treasure. God is the only power that can conquer sorrow and sin. He not only gives salvation—He *is* salvation. Without Him, all hope is gone—with Him, we have eternal life!

TABLE TALK: *Some people, like the chief, possess treasures they do not even realize they have. Enumerate your material and spiritual possessions.*

FEBRUARY 4

Is There Music in Your Soul?

Set your mind on the things that are above, not on things that are upon the earth. Colossians 3:2.

"Slivers" was one of the highest paid clowns in the country. He made a fortune because he had the capacity to make other people laugh. He had a beautiful home, a big bank account, and apparently was in perfect health. But one night he took his own life because he had a heart that could not laugh!

Nothing is more important than music in the soul. It is not something that can be purchased with material means. Rather it is a free gift of God and the condition is the total commitment of self to Him. Some people seem to be happy living apart from their heavenly Father as they build their lives on the things of the world. Then, suddenly, comes the rude awakening. They discover that they have nothing which is of eternal significance.

One noon hour a couple of men were about to eat their lunch. As the one opened his sandwiches he discovered that the first was made with peanut butter. He pushed it aside and said, "I don't like peanut butter." He opened the second and found that it was made of ham, which he liked, so he ate it. The third he again discovered to be peanut butter so in disgust he refused to eat it.

The man sitting beside him said, "Sam, are you married?" His answer was "Yes." "How long?" inquired the friend. "Fifteen years," came the answer. "You mean you have been married for fifteen years and your wife doesn't even know that you don't like peanut butter?" "Say listen, Buddy," replied Sam, "don't bring her into this. I made this lunch myself!"

What you create today you will either suffer for or enjoy tomorrow. Therefore, create wisely! And believe in your creations. To make others laugh, you must have a heart that laughs. To enjoy the fruits of your labor, you must plan wisely the kind of work you want to do.

TABLE TALK: *The clown did not believe in his own laughter! Discuss what he should have done to solve his problem.*

FEBRUARY 5

Keep Dreaming

God, my rock; in him will I take refuge:
My shield, and the horn of my salvation, my high tower, and
  my refuge;
My saviour, thou savest me from violence. 2 Samuel 22:3.

Some people face tremendous battles in living as conquerors—
they never give up. Others are easy quitters who quickly get
discouraged. They forget that sometimes it is that last bit of
hope that wins a battle even after everything seems lost.

If you stand on picturesque a hill near the spot where New
York and Vermont come together you can look out over beautiful Lake Champlain. Nearly 350 years ago, the famous explorer
after whom this lake was named, started a voyage at its very
source. His small boats traveled many miles into the very heart
of the lake, and he was hoping to find a passageway into the
Canadian wilderness. But when Champlain found what seemed
to be the last large bay his party was weary and a bit discouraged. As they came to the most distant shore line they gave up
their search and turned back.

Now we know that this famous explorer made a great mistake
because just a few miles down the shore line from where he
stopped there was a tiny outlet that led into another vast ex-
pansion of uncharted waters. Just a little more searching and
he would have discovered his ultimate goal.

Sometimes in our hopes and dreams we seem to come to an
insurmountable barrier that stands in our way. The wise choice
might be to turn back and start all over again. But the chances
are that there is a way to overcome the barrier so that we can
travel on. It may take a lot of time to discover the tiny outlet
which leads to the greater victories beyond. It will mean many
talks with God and an untiring allegiance to His commands.
But somewhere for the Christian there is always at last a narrow
road which leads to his ultimate goal.

When problems and doubts confront you, do not give up. The
answer to your question may be just around the corner!

TABLE TALK: *Can you recall a time when a problem seemed
almost too difficult and then a solution was found?*

36

FEBRUARY 6

A Lamp Unto My Feet

In the beginning was the Word, and the Word was with God, and the Word was God. John 1:1.

In God's Word we find courage to keep us living victoriously in spite of everything. There we find happiness for each day and strength for every moment. God has meant that His Word should be the key to victorious living throughout the ages.

If you should visit the great museum in Boston, you would see there a collection of many interesting objects. One of the oldest is the collection of mirrors. Among them is one, hundreds of years old, dating back into the early centuries. But when you look into that old mirror today you do not see the ancient characters in weird costumes who once peered into it. Rather you see only the reflection of yourself.

So it is with the Bible. It has been read by people of all times. But when you read it today you discover there the way of life for the present and not an outmoded and ancient philosophy. God's Word is the only way that can make your life worth while.

As you continue to read it and live by it, faith and encouragement will be added to your every day. You will become stronger because of it. You will find answers to many questions which come to you. The Bible is universal and yet it is extremely personal. In it are words of advice, words of comfort, and words of encouragement just for you. But you must read it to find those things for which you are seeking. You must recognize that it is The Book of all books.

You recall the name of Sir Walter Scott, as one of the great authors of the centuries. As he lay on his deathbed, he said to a friend who stood close by, "Read to me from the book." "Which one?" asked the friend. "There is only one—the Bible," came the reply.

God's Word is our great heritage today. Take time to search for the answers and discover the strength which is found in these wonderful words of eternal life.

TABLE TALK: *What is your favorite Bible story? Retell it.*

37

FEBRUARY 7

Where Are You Going?

Now may our God and our Father himself, and our Lord Jesus Christ, direct our way unto you. 1 Thessalonians 3:11.

A little boy and his mother were about to enter a large department store. The sign at the entrance said, "Please use revolving door." The prospect intrigued young Jimmy. He wanted to do it alone, so his mother gave him a start to send him into the circling maze. She stayed outside, however, waiting until she was sure that he had stepped out on the other side. But as she watched, she noticed that Jimmy was having a confusing time. The doors had spun around to the place where he should have stepped out and into the store. But the little boy seemed uncertain of himself. He just kept shuffling his little feet between the two doors that formed a little cell for him. And presently he had made the complete circle and was right back at the starting point. There Mother took his hand and drew him out again. Jimmy began a half whimpering recital of what had transpired. "Mother, I just went round and round and didn't know where I was going. I just didn't get any place."

There are a lot of Jimmys in this world. We get caught in a whirl of "busyness." We find ourselves just going round and round, running here and there in behalf of inconsequential things. Many times we do not even know where we are going. We are wise when we see that such living gets us nowhere.

God has given us many things in this life to help us enjoy it. He has given us family and friends, food and clothing, travel and books, and all of nature's glory. The list of His blessings is really endless. To the consecrated life, all of these things are as doors to be used in this great business of living to the great glory of God. These blessings inspire us to seek opportunities to live with the love of Christ in our hearts.

Where are you going? Are you caught in the whirl of the things of earth, or do you see the lights of the Heavenly City?

TABLE TALK: *Analyze your activities. Are you spending a lot of time on inconsequentials? Which comes first, club or church; a show or choir practice; an all-day picnic or Sunday school? Discuss.*

FEBRUARY 8

Live Close to God

Being therefore always of good courage, and knowing that, whilst we are at home in the body, we are absent from the Lord (for we walk by faith, not by sight); we are of great courage, I say, and willing rather to be absent from the body, and to be at home with the Lord. 2 Corinthians 5:6-8.

Two friends once met in busy Grand Central Station in New York City. As one of them was hurrying to catch a train the other asked where he was going. "I'm going to a country cottage in Vermont," he answered. "It is much too lonely in New York."

There are many people who are surrounded by friends and relatives and yet share this feeling. They have not learned that life must be filled from within. There must be a joyful heart and an understanding mind if you are to have real contentment and happiness. Only God can give you these. The big city is a lonesome place to the person who has no friends, and the open spaces are a whole world to a man who loves the sky.

The story is told of a family who lived in the mountains of Kentucky. For fifty years they had scraped the ground trying to make crops grow so that they could buy the things that they wanted. Seldom, if ever, in that time had they left their own little community. One day they decided to pack their few belongings and to start out for new land. They headed for the rich bluegrass country, which everyone said was the place to make money and to have a decent home in which to live. As the family trudged across the country, hour after hour they walked slower and slower until finally they stopped altogether. It was the father who spoke. "I don't like being so far from the things I know about. I feel like a stranger already." And so the family turned back again to the old home they had learned to love.

There is a sense of security and belonging when you live close to God. When you wander away from His presence you feel like a stranger in a far-off country. You are afraid of losing your way. But when you walk with God you know the way leads home.

TABLE TALK: *Sometimes you feel lonely until you count your friends. See how many earthly friends you can name to whom you could turn. Are you ready to help them?*

FEBRUARY 9

The Virtue of Patience

Be still, and know that I am God: I will be exalted among the nations, I will be exalted in the earth. Psalm 46:10.

Some people think that patience is an old-fashioned, outdated sort of virtue. In these times when life is geared to such a tremendous speed, patience seems to be a characteristic left over from a day gone by. Our modern philosophy has adopted the attitude that the faster something is accomplished the greater it is. Sometimes we even base our chance of existence on the speed of an airplane or the production of an assembly line.

In the midst of all our speed and hurry, let us stop to remember that it takes fifty years or more to make a forest of beautiful trees. It takes many months to build a cathedral, and it takes countless hours of sunshine to make one small flower burst into bloom. In fact, God does not count time by hours or days or years. His is the calendar of one page and that is marked eternity.

Too often we expect God to do things on the spur of the moment. If our prayers are not answered within the next hour, we give up hope and lose our trust. God's will is not always accomplished in a day, or a year, or even in a lifetime. The road of the Christian life goes on forever. Eternity beckons us to keep traveling on. During our journey we are commanded to go and win others for Christianity. Jesus did not say, "Go out and teach other men about God, but if at the end of two months no one believes it, just forget about it all." The command was to go and keep going until the whole world should know about the Father in heaven and the victorious living that is found in His way.

As you go about His work, you need not look for overnight miracles. But slowly, steadily working, you can win others to His way.

You have a task to do. Patiently seek the will of God and you will know the victory.

TABLE TALK: *Stop and consider how many things you hurried to do in the last few days. In the light of the Great Commission, were they important?*

FEBRUARY 10

In Our Time of Need

I will instruct thee and teach thee in the way which thou shalt go: I will guide thee with mine eye upon thee. Psalm 32:8.

Over the bed of a little boy there hung a beautiful silhouette. It was delicately cut and pictured a guardian angel walking beside a little lad as he was crossing a footbridge over a ravine. The angel had his hand extended to give the boy special care, for at this moment a slat was missing at the foot of the bridge just ahead of where the little lad was to step next.

What a fine reminder for life that picture was, to be imprinted indelibly on that little mind and heart. He had something to take with Him all his life! God does take care of His children in all circumstances. He sees and knows the pitfalls ahead, the places where the slats are missing. He knows how deep the precipice is below. God does not just sit by as an idle spectator. His loving heart impels Him to do something to help His children avoid misfortune and harm. To fall into evil is disastrous to the soul and often leaves an awful imprint on the body, too. God tries to guide us by sending us whispers of conscience to help us know which way to go. For this is His promise: "I will guide thee with mine eye upon thee." What strength to know that He who keeps us neither slumbers nor sleeps. He is always near.

Just as there is a peaceful watchfulness on the part of God, so there can be a peaceful acceptance of the counseling of God on our part. God sees what can befall us and He does something about it. He warns us through conscience and through the wise counsel found in the Word of God. Then it is up to us to choose whether to step over that place in the bridge where the slat is out or to step into it. If we choose the latter course, then we cannot blame God for the consequences. But if we accept the guidance and the strength that God gives us to surmount the stumbling point of sin, it is victory for the soul.

Our sin is just as real as that barbed word we spoke to some friend today. It is just as real as the breaking of a promise. May each of us be willing to accept the power to rise above our sins.

TABLE TALK: *Have you ever violated the voice of conscience? Discuss the consequences of your actions.*

FEBRUARY 11

Heaven Begins Today

Today shalt thou be with me in Paradise. Luke 23:43.

When we think of the wonderful eternity called heaven, a sense of gratitude and peace fills our hearts. Some people insist that it will be a great city with gold-paved streets and pearly gates. When they are plagued with troubles, they think of it as a place where troubles will disappear like magic. When they are tired and weary of long hard work, they think of it as eternal rest where all labor is ended. When clouds fill their sky, they think of sunshine that will last forever.

Perhaps heaven will mean all these wonderful things but it is something much more. It is being with God. The Bible seldom speaks about what the life after death will be like. It does talk to us frequently, however, about what this hour, right now, can become.

Oftentimes we wish that we could have lived in those wonderful days when Jesus walked here on earth. It would have been a rich experience to walk and talk with Him as He traveled from place to place. But what attracted the people most was not the miracles He performed when He used His unusual powers. They were most amazed at the everyday reality of His religion. That is the message that Christ brought to those people of long ago and it is the same message that He brings to us today. Our Christian faith is not some mystical power that comes to us only in the quiet of a beautiful cathedral or in a mysterious dream. It is the strength and abundance of living that fills the hours we spend on the job, at home, in the market-place, or on the street.

That is what our Christianity is, and in truth, that is what our heaven is. If we have found our Saviour in everyday living, then we have found today the peace and contentment which others reserve for the life which is to come. We can have faith to believe that our God will lead us into victory each day and that our faith will ultimately be crowned with eternal light.

TABLE TALK: *Have you ever been restless for better days to come when you will be financially secure, and have abundant leisure time? Discuss enjoying each day fully.*

FEBRUARY 12

Christ Liveth in Me

I have been crucified with Christ; and it is no longer I that live, but Christ liveth in me: and that life which I now live in the flesh I live in faith, the faith which is in the Son of God, who loved me, and gave himself for me. Galatians 2:20.

A young student at Harvard University read intently one of the great biographies of Abraham Lincoln. After he finished the book, he said, it was not long until he found himself trying to live like Lincoln. He tried to meet circumstances and people in the same way that this famous statesman would have done.

This same young lad had never been very much interested in church, though he had a great admiration for the Christian faith. He began to wonder if perhaps he could not find the same sort of experience in reading about Christ as he had with Abraham Lincoln. So he began to read the Bible and especially the Gospels, which tell about the life of Jesus and His experiences. Some time later he was talking with one of his friends and said, "You know, I have been reading about Jesus and all the things that He did, and now He has become an entirely new person to me. I seem to be living with Him and I think I have found out what it really means to be a Christian."

No doubt this young man had truly discovered the meaning of Christianity. He had come to the conclusion that it was not only a set of rules in a book but that it was a devoted life through the hours of every day. The Apostle Paul caught the true spirit of a soul dedicated to the things which are lasting and eternal when he said, "It is no longer I that live, but Christ liveth in me."

Have you caught the vision of what it means to live with God as the architect of everything you do and the author of everything you say? He is willing to share with you His wisdom and strength and He offers you the possibility of meeting the problems of every day with His understanding, and to enjoy each bit of happiness with His love.

TABLE TALK: *Name personalities whom you know or have read about whom you admire. What qualities would you like to attain?*

FEBRUARY 13

Our Help Comes from the Lord

I will lift up mine eyes unto the mountains: From whence shall my help come? Psalm 121:1.

Mountains suggest towering strength. They breathe serenity and stability. They look with quiet eyes upon the world about them. Their height gives them vantage point so that they can see things in perspective. Trivialities are lost in the haze below. The mountain has its feet placed firmly on the earth but its snow-covered head is close to the starlight of eternity. The soft white clouds of God's presence drift silently but visibly about it.

There is much to learn from the mountains. Perhaps the Psalmist had these things in mind when he said, "I will lift up mine eyes unto the mountains: From whence shall my help come? My help cometh from Jehovah, who made heaven and earth."

Sometimes life throws deep shadows on our way. Perhaps there is a great misunderstanding between you and someone whom you have respected and loved. Tension and mistrust have crept in to mar the relationship or perhaps death has taken from you one whom you have depended upon for love and understanding. Or it may be that you have suffered loss of employment, or serious illness, or an accident. There are many things that bring shadows in our lives. Life is not without its disappointments, anxieties, and hardships.

But let us remember that the sun is always shining somewhere. God is, and always will be. While the shadows seem to linger over us let us look to the crimson peaks reminding us that dawn will come to us again. The problems somehow are solved and life takes on new color.

We who have tested God's peace of mind and heart know that He will never leave us nor forsake us. The shadows are only temporary. Morning is breaking and will come again in all its glory to give us hope.

TABLE TALK: *Describe any mountains you have seen. Did you have any vivid impressions at your first sight of them?*

A Chart and a Compass

And the peace of God, which passeth all understanding, shall guard your hearts and your thoughts in Christ Jesus.

Philippians 4: 7.

None of us can be positive of what is going to happen in the course of a day. Most of us make some kind of plans and we can imagine what is likely to occur, but we cannot be certain. Every day can be a real adventure!

There is always the opportunity of doing something that will help change the world for the better. With complete faith in God, you can live the day persuaded that you are going to have count. And there are always opportunities to tell others of the the courage to stand up boldly for the things in life that really wonderful friend you have in your Christ.

But if you are going to make this day a real adventure you need a chart to follow, a compass to point you to the right road, and a star to light your way. Your map will be God's Word which shows you the straight and narrow highway. Your compass will be the cross which forever points upward. Your star will be the light of God's love. If you follow the course and obey the signs along the way you will find that your adventure will become a rich experience. But if you stray from side to side taking the roads which seem attractive for the moment, you will be off the main highway and are likely to be in danger.

Why not begin today by resolving to go on an adventure for God, working and living to bring some dark corner the light of salvation and the hope of victory? As you travel along God's road, lend a hand to those who stand near by crying for help. Point them to the great Physician, who can heal their wounded hearts and soothe their troubled minds. Invite them to join God's army of soldiers who march with the sword of the Spirit and with the banner of the peace that passeth all human understanding flying high.

Follow the chart, the compass, and the star!

TABLE TALK: *Plan what you can do today that will help change the world for the better. It may be only a small deed, but it will have real significance.*

FEBRUARY 15

There Is Power in Prayer

In nothing be anxious; but in everything by prayer and supplication with thanksgiving let your requests be made known unto God. Philippians 4:6.

Loneliness is often associated with the stillness and solitude of a quiet night when one is all alone. But a soldier out on the Korean battlefield with the noise of battle in the distance and his buddies lying close beside him was very lonely. He thought of home and the feeling of loneliness so engulfed him that he felt he could not bear it much longer. "I wonder what Mom's doing?" he thought and then the answer came to him, "At home, it is time for morning devotions. I think I'll join Mom in prayer." His loneliness melted away and he felt that power of prayer.

Prayer does do something! Something always happens when we turn our hearts to God. Prayer opens the gates to the understanding and love of our heavenly Father. It gives the spirit of the Master the chance to fill our hearts with the things that are good in life and cleanses our minds of cheap and worthless thoughts. Prayers are meant to be sincere and loving. Even the desire to ask God for help gives a person a different spirit and added hope. When we pray, we link ourselves with the power that has made the universe. It is the power that can meet and conquer any situation that the world constructs. It is the power that is open to anyone who will tap its great source. This power has breathed His very life into every soul. Each day He calls upon us to abide with Him so that His power might be ours.

When the Master walked on earth He oftentimes went to the quietness of the hilltop and talked in prayer to His Father in heaven. He gained strength for the ordeals of His journey. He received power to walk steadfastly toward Jerusalem, and the courage to die upon the cross praying for the forgiveness of His enemies. His life was constantly in tune with God through prayer.

TABLE TALK: *Name instances when you have turned in prayer to God and He has given you power.*

46

FEBRUARY 16

The Penitent Is Forgiven

Create in me a clean heart, O God; and renew a right spirit within me. Cast me not away from thy presence; and take not thy holy Spirit from me. Psalm 51:10-11.

Each Sunday as we go to church, and certainly many times during the course of the week, we come as humble children of God to confess our many sins before Him. We are sorry not only for the acts that we have committed that are contrary to His will but also for those things we have failed to do in behalf of His kingdom work. But we come in absolute assurance that God is faithful and righteous to forgive us our sins and to cleanse us from all unrighteousness. Only when we fail to acknowledge our mistakes and our shortcomings need we be afraid. Excuse-making and pride are not acceptable in the sight of God.

Some years ago, it is said, a royal nobleman visited the city of Barcelona, Spain. In the harbor was a prison ship on which were many criminals, chained in dark dungeons. The duke went aboard and visited each one of them, asking what crimes they had committed to bring them there. One after another they offered excuses, all in turn trying to assure the duke that actually they had done nothing wrong. One said that the judge had been unfair. Another spoke of how the witnesses had lied. Still another mentioned that his friends had deserted and betrayed him. Finally the duke came to one of the prisoners who had a different story to tell. "Sir, I deserve to be here. I stole a purse of money and I was justly convicted." The nobleman was so amazed at the honest man's conviction that he turned to the young prisoner and said, "You are much too bad to be left among these 'innocent' men. You, my friend, have your pardon."

God knows better than we do the many wrongs we have committed. He knows perfectly well our guilt. Excuses will gain for us nothing but suffering and untold agony in the end. But a simple, humble confession from the heart will win for ourselves grace and pardon.

TABLE TALK: *Does society always pardon those who have admitted their guilt and served their term? Discuss our system of punishment, etc. What changes would you make?*

FEBRUARY 17

Above All, Be Genuine

But there arose false prophets also among the people, as among you also there shall be false teachers, who shall privily bring in destructive heresies, denying even the Master that bought them, bringing upon themselves swift destruction. 2 Peter 2:1.

A little girl—her name was Margie—had a doll. But this doll had seen her best days, as far as her appearance was concerned. Margie had forgotten her out in the yard one night when it happened to rain. The next morning the sun had beaten down on the doll's face and the combination of dampness and heat had dealt cruelly with it. The finish of the doll's face had begun to crack and peel. She was a sorry sight!

But the little girl picked her up with no less devotion than she had always tendered her. She carried her fondly in her arms as she went over to visit the neighbor. When Margie came into the house, this young mother was holding her own real baby. The little girl walked over to the chair where they were sitting. She looked first at the baby and then at her own little doll, and then she looked at the baby again. The contrast was so evident— the cheap and peeling finish on her doll, and the clear skin of the baby's face. With a trace of envy in her expression, she made this comment: "My, you have kept your baby nice."

Of course Margie was right in this, the mother had taken good care of the child. But there is more to the story than that. The face on Margie's doll was just a veneer. It was only an imitation, a shallow surface disguising a lifeless form. But the baby was genuine. His every feature spoke of life.

We have two choices. There are lives like Margie's doll. For a time they may look lovely but when the stress of hard circumstance comes, the veneer cannot stand it. It chips and crumbles. There are those whose every action is prompted by the love of Christ. They are able to meet the storms and trials of life.

TABLE TALK: *Discuss some of the "veneers" an impressionable child is likely to admire: for example, glamor, adventure, fame, and fortune. What can be done to counteract the undesirable influence? Name some of the ideal examples a child could admire.*

FEBRUARY 18

God Goes with Us

Forsake me not, O Lord: O my God, be not far from me.
                                                    Psalm 38:21.

A chaplain of the last war was one day counselling with a young soldier, who made this request of him: "I've got to go into a bad battle. Will you stay here and pray that I might come back safely?"

The chaplain was very wise when he gave the young man this answer: "There are boys out there that are going to be killed in battle. War is bad, very bad. You might be one of those whose life is taken. No, I can't pray that your life will be spared, but I will tell you what I will do. I'll go with you."

God is trying to tell us each day that sin creates a lot of suffering and sickness and death. "I cannot promise you that you will not have to suffer," He says. "I cannot promise you that you will not have heavy burdens to carry or temptations to face. I cannot promise you that the way will not be rough and steep, but I promise that I will go with you."

What a thrilling adventure it is to live life in partnership with God! Not only do we have Him as a friend to guide us on our way and give us strength, but we have the joy of a wonderful traveling companion along the way.

Not long ago, I brought my little daughter with me to a certain town where I went for a speaking engagement. I knew that she would grow tired sitting through a long banquet, so I phoned a friend living in this community whom I had not seen for some time. I asked her if she would take care of my daughter. Immediately she responded and drove some twenty miles to be of service to me. How wonderful it is to have Christian friends on the journey of life who are always willing to give assistance at any time! And even as we receive these kindnesses from God and from others, so we should seek each day to give them to those who are about us and may so desperately need us.

TABLE TALK: *Have you ever had a friend who inconvenienced himself to do something for you? Look about you. Is there something that each member of the family might do to be of service to someone?*

FEBRUARY 19

Building Every Day

For every house is builded by some one; but he that built all things is God. Hebrews 3:4.

Every day we are building. We are constructing the house in which we are going to have to live. We are either erecting something worth while that will stand up against the storms or we are building something cheap that will fall when the winds blow.

In the history of our country there are many who have fame. Among these is Daniel Webster. In his early manhood he stood for democracy and the honest way of life. Later he traded his high convictions for a chance to run for the presidency. He changed his powerful speeches to meet the whims of influential voters, and he sacrificed his ideals to win the support of dishonest citizens.

One of his early friends was a poet, Ralph Waldo Emerson. When he saw Webster's honesty and integrity disappear he wrote this stinging condemnation, "Webster's wonderful gifts all failed, and he planted a sign on everything that was good which read: 'For Sale.'" There are many who give in to temptation. They sell their eternal values for worldliness and fame. But the results are always the same. The victory is finally lost, the house falls, for the foundation stones are not secure.

When temptations come to you and offer to buy your soul, think about the Master. His possessions in this world were few but He shared the richness of God, and that is all that He needed. When you reach a point of decision, stop to consider what things are just passing fancies and worldly pleasures. It will not profit you to buy them if the price is the sacrifice of your honesty, kindness, and love.

God has promised that He will give you all the things you need to live a life that is peaceful and happy. Take Him at His Word as you live for that which is eternal.

What kind of a house are you building?

TABLE TALK: *Discuss the temptations that come to the householders today, for example, scare-buying and hoarding. What should be the Christian's firm stand?*

FEBRUARY 20

What Is Happiness?

No man can serve two masters: for either he will hate the one, and love the other; or else he will hold to one, and despise the other. Ye cannot serve God and mammon. Matthew 6:24.

Not long ago a white haired clergyman stood in Reno watching from the side-lines as hundreds of movie fans mobbed a popular screen star. "Yes, I used to have all those once—and it is odd when you look back on it how little it means."

This man was one of the biggest stars of stage and screen back in the Twenties. Often he was mobbed by autograph hounds, he lived in a lavish Hollywood mansion, and he had his chauffeur pick up his $2,000 pay check every Wednesday.

Seven years ago be became a $120-a-month missionary to the Indians at three desolate villages in the Nevada desert. "Since then," he says, "I have known happiness such as I never knew before."

Telling about his movie experiences and the awards which he won, he indicated that with the accumulation of popularity and wealth came also the sins of the flesh. "My whole life was empty," he says. "I got on my knees. Instead of asking God to do things for me I humbly asked God what I could do for Him. I entered God's service." He now lives alone in a little village fifty miles from the town of Reno in a tiny white frame house next to his white frame church.

This minister and people who have shared his experience are really never alone. They know a presence whose friendship means more than all of the wealth and popularity in the world. Upon their soul they have discovered God's autograph. "You are My child. You belong to Me." And possessing that knowledge, they live abundantly regardless of outward circumstances.

The richest and most popular people are not always the happiest. Happiness is not created by things. It stems from the song that sings in the heart which knows peace from a loving heavenly Father who promises us all things through Christ.

TABLE TALK: *Look at the lives of some of our famous people. Divorce, scandal, excessive drinking, typify a number of them. Discuss what is missing in their lives.*

51

FEBRUARY 21

The Limitless Horizon

But insomuch as ye are partakers of Christ's sufferings, rejoice; that at the revelation of His glory also ye may rejoice with exceeding joy. 1 Peter 4:13.

There are many people who set out in life without a goal. They have no idea what their destination is nor do they seem to care. They are driven to and fro by whatever currents happen to come along. They follow the path of least resistance.

The happiest people are those who catch the inspiration of heavenly goals. With all there is to do in this world, one cannot afford to walk along without purpose just hoping everything will work out all right.

We are told that the first pioneers who climbed Pike's Peak fought a tremendous battle. So long as they could see the very top of the mountain, no matter how far it was in the distance, they had the inspiration to keep climbing. But when the peak was obscured by clouds or a mist they became discouraged and almost turned back.

Sometimes in life when the goal is hidden for a moment we become confused but if we keep our eyes upon Jesus and continue to press toward the mark His light will shine through the gloom to lead us on.

If someone were to tell you he had seen the sun rise in the west, you would probably say that he was confused to say the least. But perhaps that person had caught a beautiful vision. The Christian never sees the land of the setting sun, where the light disappears into darkness. To the heart that loves God, the end of one day is but the beginning of another. And beyond the final sunset lies even a greater land.

Do not let your dreams stop at the distant horizon. The greatest goal of all knows no boundary of space and time. For the victor's crown shall be worn in all eternity, and the love of God shall never end for the faithful soul.

TABLE TALK: *What is the importance of having an earthly goal? Discuss what relationship there should be between the earthly and heavenly goal?*

FEBRUARY 22

Show Your Colors

Ye are witnesses, and God also, how holily and righteously and unblamably we behaved ourselves toward you that believe. 1 Thessalonians 2:10.

Do you realize the example you are setting for the world today? You may think that many of the things you do are insignificant, but the people you meet in the neighborhood or in the store or in the office learn a lot from you.

Two strangers happened to get on the same streetcar and sat side by side. In a few moments they struck up a casual conversation. They talked about a number of things as they rode along. After a while one of the men turned to his new-found friend and asked, "Are you a minister by any chance?" The other man smiled and replied, "No, I am not. But why do you ask?" "Well, my friend, you have such a Christian face."

There are many ways to witness for the Master. You are preaching a sermon by the things you do and say, by a smile or a kind word, by lending a helping hand to someone in need. These kindnesses never go unnoticed even though sometimes no one is there to say, "Thanks." Remember that everything you do for others will come back some day into your own life with even greater blessing.

You should tell the world about Christ, not so much because He will be listening and will richly reward you, but because you want others to know about this greatest of all friendships which you have found. Anyone who lives without the Master is not living the real life. It is your task to prove what a difference Christ has made for you.

As others follow you today, where will you lead them? Will you show them a life that has God as protector, and a heart that is filled with the goodness and love of the Master? When someone calls out for help, will you go to the rescue? When you see someone struggling to find the way in this confused world will you be a living testimony of Christ's way?

TABLE TALK: *What changes would you make in your behavior today if you knew that someone were watching your every move, looking to you for leadership? Discuss.*

FEBRUARY 23

A Command and a Promise

Go ye therefore, and make disciples of all nations, baptizing them into the name of the Father and of the Son and of the Holy Spirit. Matthew 28:19.

In a certain church there are two windows which describe the life of a real Christian. The chancel window could be entitled "Faith." The balcony window would be named "Works." We believe that we are saved by faith alone. But faith is really never alone. For if our trust in God means anything to us we will give evidence of it in our living and in the things that we do.

The chancel window is a modern interpretation of the Christ who walks the crowded streets of life today with arms outstretched, speaking this invitation: "Come unto me, all ye that labor and are heavy laden and I will give you rest." This is the faith window. Never need we be afraid to come unto Him for His promise remains constant. "Him that cometh unto me, I will in no wise cast out." He takes our burdens upon Himself and soothes our weary spirits. The peace of soul which comes from knowing Him is a priceless possession.

The balcony window is one that pictures Christ with His loving disciples gathered about Him. He has taken them to the Mount of Olives. Forty days He has lived with them since His resurrection. They are now sure that He is the same Christ who died upon the cross. Before they had been defeated men. Now their spirit is that of men who are more than conquerors. But once more He has to leave them, and before He does He has a last word to speak. And eagerly they listen that they might carry out His command. "All authority hath been given unto me," He begins, "Go ye therefore, and make disciples of all nations, baptizing them into the name of the Father and of the Son and of the Holy Spirit, teaching them to observe all things whatsoever I commanded you." And the command is not given without a promise. "Lo, I am with you always," He continues, "even unto the end of the world."

TABLE TALK: *Have you noticed the pictures in the windows of your church? Describe some of the scenes and comment on their message.*

FEBRUARY 24

The Best Choice

But seek ye first his kingdom, and his righteousness; and all these things shall be added unto you. Matthew 6:33.

What a tremendous institution the press is in our day! What a great force it is in molding public opinion! It helps to spread happiness with its entertainment features; such as its comics, its pictures, its stories and anecdotes. It can spread truth and falsehoods through its editorials, depending upon the integrity of its staff. It gives vital information recording births, marriages, and deaths of the citizenry. By its want ads it can help a man to sell his house or buy a boat. It can tell the housewife where she can find the best brands of groceries at the most agreeable prices. It is a fascinating avenue of communication for us all.

It is interesting to think about the things for which people look first when they pick up their daily newspaper. Some people will turn directly to the sports page to see how the big names in baseball are doing. Others will turn to read what their favorite columnist has to say for the day. Little children will clamor for the funnies, and a few staunch souls will look first for the editorial page. Each one of us has something for which he seeks first in the newspaper.

Life is like that. There are choices to make. We encounter one crossroad after another along the way. We must choose at every point which way we must take in order to reach our destination. If we know what we want, the choices will usually be much easier to make. But if we do not have clearly in mind where we are headed, we can expect nothing but confusion along the way.

To seek first God's kingdom insures a complete life. It gives you the privilege of bringing your guilt to the only One who has the power to take it away. Then your soul can go unfettered to spend its will and strength in full capacity for the things that count. Everything will seem worth while because you know you are headed somewhere, and you will have a sense of well-being in seeking the first thing, the kingdom of God.

TABLE TALK: *Has there been a time when you should have taken a definite stand and did not? Discuss.*

FEBRUARY 25

Leaning on the Everlasting Arms

Now lettest thou thy servant depart, Lord, according to thy word, in peace. Luke 2:29.

Not yet forty years of age, a certain woman had had several serious operations. Through several years of severe suffering she had maintained her faith. But now she had become bitter; she could not understand why she should be called upon to carry such a heavy burden. Constantly she was asking the question, "Why did this have to happen to me?" She was ready to curse God and die.

After a period of serious depression and unbelief, God's light one day came upon her again and once more she began to smile through the pain. She became a wonderful inspiration to the many friends who would come to see her. She knew she was going to die and she had no fear of death, nor did she blame God for the intense suffering which was tearing her body to pieces. For the last eight weeks of her earthly existence she was fed intravenously and in the final days they could not even find a vein in which to put the needle. She kept growing weaker and weaker in physical strength, but stronger spiritually with God.

If you had been privileged to pay a visit to her sick room just before she was called home, you would have seen two beautiful picture windows and between them a garden setting created of multicolored flowers. These are the words she would have spoken to you, "That reminds me of the Paradise to which I am going." Then she would have smiled and said, "I have absolutely no fear. I trust the promises of God. I believe in Christ my Saviour." And then as you would observe her courageously fighting back the tears caused by the intense agony of body, you would see her close her eyes and as you listened closely you would have heard her whisper this prayer: "Mine eyes have seen Thy salvation. Lord, let now Thy servant depart in peace."

Great living by great souls like this inspires us under all circumstances to praise God. A physical calamity met with spiritual illumination will make life abundant unto the very end.

TABLE TALK: *Discuss instances in which you have seen people demonstrate real faith in their attitude toward death.*

FEBRUARY 26

The Miracle of Faith

And the Lord said unto Satan, Hast thou considered my servant Job? for there is none like him in the earth, a perfect and an upright man, one that feareth God, and turneth away from evil: and he still holdeth fast his integrity, although thou movedst me against him, to destroy him without cause. Job 2:3.

Do you know a Friend who is able to help you, come what may, and who gives you strength to face life and face it courageously? I think of a middle aged woman with a family of two boys. Oh, how she loved to live! But suddenly in the prime of life she was afflicted with one sickness after another—first arthritis, then cancer, and finally every manner of infection. But through it all she maintained the spiritual glow. Whenever I went to visit her I would always receive more than I was able to give. Her life lingered on and she suffered indescribably. Very calmly and serenely she went about making provision for her children's future education. The uppermost concern in her mind was their welfare.

Day by day her suffering became more severe. Finally one night as I stood by her bedside when she had barely enough strength to speak she gathered together her resources and smiling through the gloom she gripped my hand and said, "Pastor, tell the people next Sunday that I still believe in God."

Outward circumstances would have caused this woman to become nothing but bitter. But deep inward spiritual strength gave her the capacity to march triumphantly into the "house of many mansions." She knew that God had the power to give her eternal life. She trusted Him and her faith was rewarded.

When little disturbances mar our day's activities and we think that life is not giving us a fair deal, we should remember those who have had much greater trouble who have trusted this Friend and have always discovered the truth of His promises. Then we can say in a firm, confident voice, "I still believe in God." That is the miracle of faith.

TABLE TALK: *Point out someone you know who has borne grief and hardship well by having faith. Relate the story of Job.*

FEBRUARY 27

A Loving Partnership with God

O Lord, open thou my lips; and my mouth shall show forth thy praise. Psalm 51:15.

Whatever may be your occupation, you have an opportunity to witness in behalf of Christ your Lord. Not only are ministers called upon to give themselves in Christian service, but all of God's children have an obligation to serve Him no matter what their calling may be. What a different world it would be if Christ directed our living in every area of endeavor.

Not long ago one of our current periodicals told a story about a man who was invited by a well-known surgeon to watch a very complex operation that was about to be performed. He observed him as he went through a laborious preparation for the operation. He watched him as he scrubbed for the allotted time, and as the nurses helped him into cap and gown and rubber gloves. The doctor seemed confident, but a little tense.

Then the visitor turned to him and said, "Are you all ready now?" "Just about," he replied. Then he stopped and bowed his head for a moment. He became calm and relaxed as he led the way to the operating room. During the course of the operation his hands never faltered. He went about his duty in exact precision and uttermost confidence. When it was all over his friend turned to him and said, " I was surprised at your praying before you went in. I thought a surgeon relied on his own ability."

The doctor replied, "A surgeon is only human. He can't work any miracles by himself. I am certain that science could not have developed as far as it has, were it not for something stronger and more powerful than mere man. You see," he concluded, "I have such a living partnership with God that while I am operating I don't know where my skill leaves off and His begins."

That is the secret of living the abundant life. If you commit yourself to God and seek to do His will, you discover that you do not know where your skill leaves off and His begins.

TABLE TALK: *Discuss how a partnership with God would affect the activities of a storeowner's business; a teacher's; a politician's; a laborer's.*

FEBRUARY 28

Just As I Am, Without One Plea

But rather seek ye the kingdom of God; and all these things shall be added unto you. Luke 12:31.

An old legend contains a truth that will never die. It tells about the golden gates of heaven at which people knock. At the entrance to the eternal city there is a gatekeeper. As each soul seeks to enter, the keeper merely asks, "What is the password?"

The story goes that one man answered, "I have no password. I was great on earth and now I come to be great in heaven." But the voice within the city speaks simply. "I never knew you." Another man came and knocked and the gatekeeper asked, "What is the password?" "I have none," was the reply. "But I did many generous things on earth. I gave of my money to help take care of the poor." The voice from within answered, "I never knew you." A third man knocked upon the gates. Being asked the password he humbly said, "I am a wanderer from God and I deserve to die forever. But I heard the voice of Jesus and He asked that I only trust in His grace and love." It was then that the city echoed with a glorious answer. "Lift up the gates and let this man in!"

This is only a story, and an ancient one, but its truth is eternal! It is not enough just to be great or kind or generous—the Christian ought to be such. But there is something even more essential. Within the Christian heart there is the presence of the Saviour who directs the soul to the eternal home.

One night long ago a star shone brightly in the sky. It came to rest above a lowly manger in a small city far away. A few shepherds and wise men followed its light and in so doing they found a child whose name was Jesus, who had come to save His people from their sins.

As this child grew up into manhood, He showed a sincere and undying love for every person in God's creation. He is present even today to share His blessings with all who recognize their need of Him.

TABLE TALK: *Name some passwords which would typify a good Christian.*

FEBRUARY 29

An Extra Day

The words that I have spoken unto you are spirit, and are life. John 6:63.

A famous man once received a letter from a little boy who was just learning to write. The child concluded his note with the words, "I hope that you live all your life."

Everyone at some time or another has expressed a desire for another day to "catch up" on some unfinished business. On the extra day of leap year, how many of us actually plan to do this? Many of us regret that we have not spent our time to better advantage, that we have left little tasks undone, and that we have not been "living all of our lives." We fritter away our time busying ourselves with the incidentals while some of our essential business is put off for a better time. The extra day of leap year might well be spent in the rededication of self to the vision of purposeful living.

Life, even the longest, is short. When we realize that, we will attempt to live each day to the fullest. On his pulpit stand a young preacher placed an inscription as a special reminder to himself: "I preach as never sure to preach again; as a dying man to dying men." The minister died after three years of ministry at the age of twenty-eight. He had lived every moment with great intensity, as though it were to be his last—and also the best—moment of his life.

Raphael left a picture half completed, Sir Walter Scott left a novel without a conclusion, and Franz Schubert left an Unfinished Symphony. There was no one left to finish their work for them. An extra day, perhaps, and the products would have been complete.

Today can be the day of great achievement. What do you plan to do with it?

TABLE TALK: *Name some of the things that you have put off doing for a "better time." When do you plan to do those things?*

MARCH 1

Joyful Will the Meeting Be

And then shall they see the Son of man coming in clouds with great power and glory. Mark 13:26.

Some months ago a great soldier returned to our country. Thousands of people waited for him to come home. How they anticipated being able to see him! When he did arrive, they lined the streets to shout their welcome and they sat around their television sets to see and hear him. Though he was a General of the Army and had directed the affairs of hundreds of thousands of men, they were not afraid of his arrival, but they waited for it with eager expectation. Many made the statement that one of their greatest joys was to see him face to face.

As one thinks of the tremendous welcome that this mortal man received, we cannot help but think of another day that certainly will come for all of us who shall be privileged to meet the Master face to face. How anxious we will be to see Him and how joyful that meeting will be! But it all depends upon how we have lived before that time comes. God in His great love has given everyone of us an opportunity to become a joint heir of the One who is eternal. Each of us has the power to accept or reject that generous offer. If we say "no" to God in this world and fail to live as He would want us to, then we would be afraid some day to meet Him. If we say "yes" to God and attempt by His power to live the way He wants us to, then we shall anticipate the homecoming and the reunion with Him who is our eternal Friend.

None of us needs to be afraid of God. His love is greater than all our sin. All that He demands from us is that we daily confess our transgressions and turn to Him for forgiveness and pardon. And when we do, we will live in the light. We need fear no darkness, for even though we must walk through the valley of the shadow of death, God will still be there as our Friend to lead us on to the summit and into the "house of many mansions."

TABLE TALK: *Call to mind great people in whose presence you have been and how happy the experience was. Picture as the greatest privilege the meeting with Christ.*

Are You Willing to Pay the Price?

Blessed is the man that endureth temptation; for when he hath been approved, he shall receive the crown of life, which the Lord promised to them that love him. James 1:12.

A little boy stood before a candy counter. In his hand he clutched tightly a single penny. The boy moved his hand over the glass, first pointing to some caramels, then to some licorice, then to a piece of bubble gum, and then to a little red sucker. The boy's father stood beside him wondering what his choice was going to be. It would not have been such a big problem for the little lad if he had five pennies, or four, or even two. But he had only one and it made a big difference how he spent it.

The father mused to himself and thought how much life is like that. It would have been so different if God had given us five, or four, or even two lives; but there is just one to spend and it is so important what we do with it. The bargain counters seem littered with goods. Some are wrapped with expensive trimmings and the glittering seems to attract our attention. Sometimes when we pay the price and purchase them we discover that under the fancy wrappings is very little worth while.

There are other things which do not look so attractive, but are of supreme worth and what folly for people to be unwilling to pay the price! For example, there is one thing above all others. It seems expensive. In fact the price is so great that it far surpasses the combined price of all these other things, such as fame, fortune, and success. On this box is a cross, and as you lift the cover you discover that chained to it is a crown, so that you cannot have one without the other.

There was a rich young ruler who was once attracted to the Lord and to what He had to offer. He wondered about the terms of the bargain. But the Master discovered this man's weakness and named the price it would cost him to follow Him. It was far too great, and as far as we know this man remained separated forever from the spiritual Kingdom. He was so attracted to the tinsels of the world that he refuses to leave them.

TABLE TALK: *What choices must you make as a Christian? What must you reject? Is it always easy to be a Christian?*

MARCH 3

This Is Mine

As thy days, so shall thy strength be. Deuteronomy 33:25.

The setting is in the Negeb desert in the southern part of the state of Israel. To reach there, one travels through old settlements that have been bombed out by war. Destruction is seen on every hand. In contrast is the activity of a people with a will to rebuild.

I was standing in a bombed-out village one day where not a wall of any home was standing. Near by, another settlement was being constructed to take its place. Walking through the rubble, I heard whistling and suddenly I saw a young man about thirty years of age picking up some sticks and stones. He was gathering together some of the remnants because he was one of the new settlers who were helping in the rebuilding process. As I entered into conversation with him I discovered that he had traveled over much of the world and in many places had been the victim of persecution. Some nights he was afraid to go to sleep for fear that his life would be taken. Now he found himself in this new land with little of material worth but with a strange song in his heart. I asked him how he could be so happy for he seemed to have so little for which to be thankful. He looked at me and smiled and then pointed to the barren ground as he said, "This is mine!" Only then could I understand the deep feelings in his heart. What if he had to sleep on the bare ground with only a tent overhead? That mattered little to him for he had the assurance of knowing that his home was now in a place where he could be secure and where he no longer had to live in fear.

Whenever I have thought of that incident I have been reminded of how much we Christians have for which to be thankful. Perhaps we do not have as many material blessings as we may desire. But think of the security! We build on the Rock of Ages! Christ died for each one of us and we can point to the cross as our foundation stone and say, "This is mine!"

TABLE TALK: *"Count your many blessings, Name them one by one"* is a familiar song. Discuss and enumerate all the privileges you have by living in a Christian community.

MARCH 4

I Have Wings

If ye have faith as a grain of mustard seed, ye shall say unto this mountain, Remove hence to yonder place; and it shall remove; and nothing shall be impossible unto you. Matthew 17:20.

Perhaps the greatest enemy of mankind today is fear. In childhood we are afraid of the dark and when we become men that fear remains, asserting itself as the storm clouds gather on the horizon. We say we have faith and yet we live contrary to our profession, and as a result, the lustre of life departs. "What is the secret?" we ask of those great souls who seem to retain their confidence regardless of the outward circumstance.

Perhaps we can learn a lesson from the little bird perched one day on the end of a branch of a tree. The wind was blowing violently and the branch was swaying to and fro. But in spite of this fact, the bird was singing a beautiful melody. Suppose for a moment that the bird were able to speak. You might well ask, "How can you be singing and maintain such complete calm in the midst of the storm? What if the branch should break?" The bird would reply: "I have wings!"

The Master often referred to the creatures of His heavens as examples of trust and faith. They are not concerned about the changing seasons for they have been given the capacity of knowing the direction they should go through the uncharted skies, which are their highways. They have no markers or maps to guide them on their way, and yet God has endowed them with the capacity to reach their destination.

If this is true of the lower creatures of creation, how much more must it be true of those made in the image of the heavenly Father. Certainly if we, His children, live close to Him, He will give us the absolute assurance that He knows the way that He is leading us, and that ultimately we will be conquerors of any problem we might have to face. We, too, have "wings," wings which will enable us to soar over the mountains of troubles. And some day we know they will carry us to our eternal home.

TABLE TALK: *Discuss instances of how sometimes you have been afraid of what was going to happen and how foolish it seemed afterwards that you were so concerned.*

MARCH 5

You Are Drawing a Picture

By this shall all men know that ye are my disciples, if ye have love one to another. John 13:35.

One day a father discovered his boy attempting to draw some kind of a picture. "What are you making, my lad?" he said. "I am drawing a picture of God," the son replied. "But nobody knows what God looks like," answered the father. "Now they will," responded the boy.

Because of the power of God that is within you it is possible to so live that people will know what He is like. "By this shall all men know that ye are my disciples," the Master said, "if ye love one another." Every once in a while some great soul has come upon the stage of life who by his walk has given us a clearer picture of God. One reason for all of the misery and hatred in the world today is that so many of us have failed to do our part in the drawing of the picture. Some are greater artists than others. But each of us has the capacity to add something to the drawing. Our difficulty is that if we cannot paint the whole picture we do not want to paint any part of it.

Can you imagine how different this world would become if every person who calls himself a Christian would seek each day, by the way that he lives, to portray to his fellow men the kind of a God he worships and loves?

What a thrill a pastor receives when someone comes to him and says, "I want to join the church because if Christ can make a person as happy as this friend of mine, I want to give Him the chance to make my life like that, too."

Always remember that people are looking at you as an example of the cause you represent. You may lead others to God or away from God, depending on the way you live and the things you do. You may never realize how great an influence you have really been. Therefore, live each day so close to God that you cannot help but reflect His spirit as you walk down the highway of life.

TABLE TALK: *Discuss what specific things you can do to make people know that you are a Christian and that you really love God.*

MARCH 6

Do You Know the Pilot?

Teaching them to observe all things whatsoever I commanded you: and lo, I am with you always, even unto the end of the world. Matthew 28:20.

I was riding in a plane one day when suddenly it was tossed about by a terrible storm. Across from me, sat a man dressed in an officer's uniform. I engaged him in conversation and discovered that He was a pilot who had spent a countless number of hours in the air. I started to talk about the storm and the possibility of our making a safe landing. How reassuring were his words! He said, "I have known the man who is piloting this ship for a number of years. He is one of the very best and I have complete confidence in him."

As he spoke these words to me, I could not help but think of a prayer that has often come from my lips: "Jesus, Saviour, pilot me over life's tempestuous sea." I thought of how reassuring it is to know personally the Pilot of my life and to have such complete confidence in Him.

It is only when that faith falters that there is room for fear to creep into our lives, for no matter how severe the storms may be, no matter how heavy the burdens, or strong the temptations, if Jesus is with us directing our course and assuring us of His presence, we know that we will be safely directed to our destination.

If I should have had to pilot that plane through the storm that day, I would have been afraid. Tragedy would have resulted because of my lack of knowledge in that particular sphere. There are many times in our lives, too, when we do not have the power to become victorious in conquering a certain obstacle. But we never have to be afraid if we have the confidence that the Master is the Captain of our lives, and if we become assured that His power will be ours.

TABLE TALK: *Discuss ways in which Jesus can become more real to you as you meet the problems of each day.*

MARCH 7

Assets Unlimited

Know ye that the Lord, he is God: it is he that hath made us, and we are his; we are his people, and the sheep of his pasture.

Psalm 100:3.

During the last war a picture was published of a refugee child. Her clothes were torn and tattered. You could readily understand why she looked so lonesome. She had been uprooted from her home scene. She was an orphan, having neither father nor mother. Now, surrounded by strangers and having nowhere to go she was saying, "I am nobody's nothing. I am nobody's nothing!"

In contrast, another little child, living in America, had just returned from her first day at school. That evening when it came time for family devotions she was heard to say, "Thank You, God, for books to read in, pencils to write with, and teachers to help us learn things. Thank You, God, that I could be born."

Take a look at your own life and think of how fortunate you are compared to many other people throughout the world. As we take inventory, we begin to realize how many blessings we receive each day at the hand of God, and also the blessings that we have inherited from those who have lived before us.

Think how fortunate we are to be born in a country where someone has built for us our schools, our churches, and our hospitals. Someone else has built roads, and bridges so that we can travel safely from place to place. Our parents have surrounded us with love, and we feel secure because we belong to somebody.

Think how dependent we are upon each other. The postman brings us our mail, the newsboy delivers the daily newspaper, and the storekeeper brings us our groceries. We have many privileges today that our forefathers never thought of having. Even though the days may seem to be dark, let us look at the bright side of living, and pray: "Thank You, God, that I could be born."

TABLE TALK: *Mention instances of people you have been dependent upon today to make living more enjoyable for you. Discuss your responsibilities to others.*

MARCH 8

Live Like the Master

Therefore all things whatsoever ye would that men should do to you, do ye even so to them. Matthew 7:12.

For many years a plantation owner had admired the Negro woman who was in charge of the estate. During all this time she had given her life in unselfish service to her master. Besides being very capable in her work, she spent her meager earnings to help raise the orphans of this wilderness community. Her work for those less fortunate than herself impressed her master so much that he built her a little house right in his own yard. It was a very humble but immaculate cottage. Pretty new furniture filled each room. Into this house moved the Negro woman and her orphanage.

To the horror of the plantation owner, the very first thing this Negro woman did was to invite into her shiny new home the most disreputable Negro woman in that part of the country in order that she might nurse her back to strength and virtue. The master turned to his employee and asked, "How could you ever take that creature into your pretty new home?" She looked at him with eyes that shone as lights of mercy and love as she softly answered, "Jesus did!"

Sometimes we wonder as we stop to count our many sins and discover how short of the ideal we have come, how we can possibly get into the glorious heaven beyond. In our own strength it is impossible. Nor will we reach our destination because of our own merits. The blood of Jesus cleanseth us from all sin and because of Him we are redeemed in the sight of God. The Great Physician will nurse us back to health and virtue. Finally when Judgment Day comes we can be sure that we will not have to stand alone. Beside us, pleading the case in our behalf, will be the Presence!

In His house are many mansions with room for all the orphans and sinners of the world. He has prepared a place for everyone. In love and mercy Jesus will take you there.

TABLE TALK: *Would you take strangers into your home to nurse them back to strength and virtue? Do transients ever come to your house begging for food? What do you do?*

MARCH 9

A Habit Like a Cable

Thou wilt guide me with thy counsel, and afterward receive me to glory. Whom have I in heaven but thee? and there is none upon earth that I desire beside thee. Psalm 73:24-25.

Do you remember learning these lines in school: "Habit is like a cable; you weave a thread of it each day until at last it becomes so strong you cannot break it?" It would be wise indeed if each day you recalled this statement.

It applies first of all to our bad habits. We are tempted to do something wrong and it seems so insignificant, so we yield to the temptation and commit the sin. And then it becomes much easier to yield the second and the third time. And if we continue to persist in doing it, we discover that it is just like a cable—it becomes so strong that we cannot break it. We become so rutted in the way that we travel that we cannot possibly take any other pathway. How dangerous it is therefore, to weave the thread of a recurring bad habit into the very cable of one's life! Eventually and always, it means spiritual death.

Out of the Orient comes a story of a plant which is delicious to eat but has no food value. It is called Nardo. The dangerous thing about this plant is that it satisfies the appetite and, if one persists in eating it he will ultimately die of starvation. Likewise a person who gives in little by little to the habits of sin will ultimately be hopelessly chained to them.

"A habit is like a cable; you weave a thread of it each day." Think what would happen if you concentrated upon goodness, if you would develop the habit of reading God's Word, of frequently talking with Him in prayer, of lending a helping hand to someone in need, of speaking an encouraging word to someone in trouble, of defending someone who is being persecuted or criticized, or being just Christlike in all your words and deeds. "A habit is like a cable; you weave a thread of it each day until at last it becomes so strong you cannot break it." It is possible under God to build a life that nothing can destroy!

TABLE TALK: *What little bad habits do you have that should be broken? What good ones should be strengthened by practice?*

MARCH 10

The Great Physician Can Cure

But when he heard it, he said, They that are whole have no need of a physician, but they that are sick. Matthew 9:12.

Sickness often strikes a family quite unexpectedly. For many years we have enjoyed good health. But suddenly illness comes, perhaps just for a short time, or maybe for weeks or months. Ready to give us care and treatment is the doctor. We call him any hour of the day or night, and rely upon him to make us well. We Christians also know the Great Physician who stands always ready to heal our aching hearts and to make our souls well. Someone has suggested that suffering may become for us something like a school where we can learn great lessons. For even out of evil, good can come, if one seeks a way.

Doctors tell us that when we get sick our bodies take on new strength to overcome the germs which threaten to invade. When we are cut or bruised healing particles within us go to work at once to protect the injury. If the sickness is prolonged the temperature of the body rises as these defenders strive to drive out the unhealthy invaders.

Often the treatment of physical illness will help cure an accompanying spiritual illness. The time spent recuperating gives one a chance to think, to meditate, and to renew the spirit. When we are hurt or bruised by sin or evil, God sends healing power to our assistance. He has promised that life will not be too troubled for us if we will trust in Him and depend on Him for our strength. God is always ready to supply us with the power which will enable us to endure.

Let us never forget the invitation that has been given us to call upon the Great Physician for comfort. In Him is the soothing balm to heal the wounds of a sinful soul and to give us the vitality of a blessed Christian life. Greater than all the sin and suffering of the world is the love of Almighty God.

TABLE TALK: *What have you learned during some illness you have had? Did it give you a new outlook on life?*

MARCH 11

I Will Not Be Afraid

Fear thou not, for I am with thee; be not dismayed, for I am thy God. Isaiah 41:10.

One evening a little girl climbed up into her father's lap. Looking into his eyes she fearfully asked, "Daddy, is the devil bigger than I am?" "Yes, my darling," he replied, "much bigger than you." A second time she questioned as she looked at her father hopefully, "Daddy, is the devil bigger than you are?" "Yes, my dear," he answered, "much bigger than I am." Then she said, "Is he bigger than God?" "Oh, no, my dear," the father replied, "God is much bigger than the devil." Reassured she smiled as she said, "Then, Daddy, there really isn't anything for me to worry about as long as I love God, is there?"

The faith of that little girl can be ours. There really is nothing to worry about as long as we know that God is bigger than any evil, that He is stronger, more powerful, and able to overcome any enemy that we might have to face as we walk the pathway of life. That is, there is nothing to worry about if we keep going God's way and He remains our partner wherever we may be.

Only when we allow sin to separate us from our heavenly Father do we need to be concerned about any fears that may lurk in our pathway. For if God is with us and if His everlasting and all-powerful arms surround us, we are assured of the strength that will make us conquerors. God is greater than any evil. His is a love that will never let us go.

As we live each day, let us turn to the ever-present Christ and say, "I want you to take me by the hand and go with me wherever I go today, and I promise You, God, that I will not go any place nor do anything that will make me ashamed to take You with me." Hear His answer: "Fear thou not: for I am with thee; be not dismayed; for I am thy God."

With the assurances which God gives us we need never feel afraid. We never walk alone.

TABLE TALK: *Discuss together any instances you may recall of how the knowledge of the presence of Christ has strengthened people in time of difficulty and temptation.*

MARCH 12

Always More Than Enough

Thou preparest a table before me in the presence of mine enemies: thou anointest my head with oil; my cup runneth over.
Psalm 23:5.

I went into a restaurant not long ago and ordered a cup of coffee. Instead of bringing me a cup already poured as is usually done, the waitress set before me an empty cup. If I had not trusted her and had walked out before she had come back I would have seen nothing but that empty cup and my thirst would not have been quenched. But her act in placing it before me indicated to me that she would come back, and that she would fill it to my satisfaction.

Many of God's children go through life with an empty cup because they have not the patience to wait until they are served. God has made us a promise which He has proved He will keep. "Ask and it shall be given you." Our part of the bargain is that we have confidence to believe that He will grant us our requests. If we doubt Him as many of us do, we are left with an empty cup!

Those who wait upon the Lord are more than filled to satisfaction. The Psalmist describes it this way: "My cup runneth over. Surely goodness and mercy shall follow me all the days of my life." Each one is given according to his capacity. Some receive more than others, but the promise is that all of us shall be satisfied. And we shall be judged only in proportion to what we have given. The one talent man is not expected to return as much as the ten talent man, but he is expected to produce in proportion to that which he has.

Let us remember that the loving hand of God provides for all of His children. There is no hungering and thirsting from the spiritual point of view if we make our requests known unto Him and are confident that He will hear us as we pray. The cup of your life will never be empty.

TABLE TALK: *What have you asked of the Lord? What was His answer? What has the Lord provided for you?*

MARCH 13

All the Way He Leads Me

I will instruct thee and teach thee in the way which thou shalt go; I will guide thee with mine eye upon thee. Psalm 32:8.

One day a young father was teaching his little boy how to cross the street. First he had taken his little lad to the end of the block and had there told him how he must look carefully in both directions to see if any cars were approaching. As the little boy practiced, the father watched intently from the sidewalk, and gave him instructions as to how to gauge his crossings. After several such instructions the little boy had graduated from a single street crossing to an intersection.

On this particular day the lad had not two directions in which to look but four. That had its complications of course. At first the father took the lad's hand and walked with him across the street to show him just how it should be done. Then he took his position back on the sidewalk and let the boy go on his own. The father stood there tensely poised in case an emergency should arise.

The boy would stand on the curb and ask, "Daddy, is it all right for me to go now?" Then the wise teacher would say, "That is for you to decide, Sonny." At first that seemed to weaken the lad's spirit, but then he braced himself in the thought that his dad had faith in him to go on his own judgment.

This is a parable of life. We have a heavenly Father who will lead us all the way. This is His promise: "I will instruct thee, and teach thee in the way that thou shalt go." He has given us the will and the determination but He wants us to grow up, too. He wants us to learn of Him so that we will make right and safe decisions for our journey through life. But at the same time, like the father who was teaching his little lad that morning, our heavenly Father will also stand by and give us direction and help if we will only call upon Him. For we can have the assurance that our Saviour will lead us all the way.

TABLE TALK: *What decision have you had to make in which God's teaching helped you to choose the "right way"?*

MARCH 14

Forgiveness Bridges the Chasm

How many are mine iniquities and sins? Make me to know my transgression and my sin. Job 13:23.

A woman came to a minister carrying in her hands a mound of sand heaped high. "This," she said, "is the multitude of my sins. So many that I cannot count them." The minister spoke calmly to her. "I am sure that each one of us has within his life sins which number this many and even more. But may I ask where you found the sand?" "Down by the ocean," she replied. "Then take it back to the shore and pile it high near the water's edge. Stand back and watch what happens to it as the tide comes rolling in. It will all be swept away."

As we look back upon the hours of each day we see all the wrongs which we have committed. Pride and selfishness have filled our lives. But we know we can bring these countless sins to the foot of the cross and they will be washed away, just as surely as the tide takes away the mound of sand. The Master knows our shortcomings and he anxiously waits to offer His forgiveness to every sinner who comes in humility and penitence seeking to rid himself of these dark blots. Jesus takes the burden of sin from our weary shoulders and sets us free so that we may again walk upright, facing the new day with strength and courage.

And how many times will the Master forgive you? He has never counted the times that you have knelt at His feet asking for another chance. And neither can you buy this forgiveness with the dollars you have in your own pocket. The price has already been paid. It has been paid with the suffering on the cross and it is free to the humble and penitent sinner.

Forgiveness bridges the deep chasm of sin. It is an act whereby the Master carries us to the other side where there is a new and brighter beginning and where the road to eternity leads on.

TABLE TALK: *Analyze your actions of the past week. Have you wronged anyone? Have you sought forgiveness?*

MARCH 15

Build Carefully

For we are God's fellow-workers: ye are God's husbandry, God's building. 1 Corinthians 3:9.

Have you ever watched skilled carpenters constructing a building? Perhaps you have noticed how carefully they work to see that each piece of lumber fits exactly as it is supposed to. First, they take the correct measurements and then they saw the boards to the right length. With a keen eye they can usually tell if the board is straight and even. But if they want to make perfectly sure they use a square or level. Sometimes they find that there are places which are just a bit too high or too low and so they plane the board until it is just right.

Each one of us is building a life. We are creating a reputation of one kind or another. We are seeking to build a foundation that will stand firm in future days. If we are skilled at this business of building a life, we look carefully at the thoughts, words, and deeds that go to make up each day's living. Carefully we consider whether or not they will fit into the structure as they are supposed to. And if we want to be real sure we test them with a level, the level of God's Word.

God's love and mercy are ever present. All we need to do is to drink of the satisfying and eternal stream. If we try to take with us our own supply of strength and courage, we will not travel life's journey very far before we discover how insufficient it is to meet the needs of the day.

But when we drink of the living waters we find that our thirst is quenched and we have new faith and hope. There is nothing more wonderful than to know that God is able to supply us with His forgiveness and the power of worthier living. Laboring with God you are building a life. Build carefully!

TABLE TALK: *Suppose you were to build a small chapel. Think of all the things you would consider in planning and building it. Relate it to the building of a life.*

MARCH 16

"Yes" or "No"

And this is the promise which he promised us, even the life eternal. 1 John 2:25.

There are many things about the powers of God which we cannot understand, but we should not let our ignorance keep us from using and sharing them. When we see an electric light burning, not many of us know why or how it manages to give off light. In spite of this fact, when it gets dark, we just turn it on to let it shine. If we used only those things we understood, our lives would be very backward indeed.

When the hours of the day look dark and cloudy we can call on the Master and the light begins to shine. New hope comes into our lives. We cannot explain the power, but we do not have to. We know it is there because the clouds disappear and once more there is the sunshine which fills our hearts.

If you do not use God's power it does not mean that it has disappeared or faded away. His Almighty strength remains. But if you choose to ignore it you go on your way alone. Perhaps at some time or another you have asked to borrow your neighbor's lawn mower or garden hose and he has very willingly told you to help yourself. Being your friend, he offers you the opportunity to use anything that he has. The door is always open.

God has given you the same kind of invitation. Whenever you need His help He is ready to share it with you. The door to the storehouse of His wisdom and power is always open. All you have to do is to talk to the ever-present Christ and say, "Lord, take my life and make of it something good and useful." Then you have tapped the fountain of His Almighty power.

God's hand reaches down to you today, and He anxiously waits to lead you up the high road to triumphant living. It is for you to say, "Yes" or "No." Your answer determines your destiny.

TABLE TALK: *Have there been times of trouble when you forget God's invitation? Discuss whether it is possible for you to "go it alone."*

Love Conquers All

And the Word became flesh, and dwelt among us, (and we beheld his glory, glory as of the only begotten from the Father), full of grace and truth. John 1:14.

General Wallace was a soldier and an expert diplomat. A very educated man, he knew how to get the very most from his fighting forces. One day a friend suggested that he write a book and the suggestion intrigued him. But what should he write about?

His friends told him that if he wrote a story with the life of Jesus as the background, the book would be sure to be a success. General Wallace accepted the challenge, and he began to read and study about this man Jesus. He read books of every description—fiction, history, doctrine, and of course, the Bible. He even made a trip to Palestine and the Near East so that he might have an insight into the countryside and conditions where Jesus had lived. After years of research, General Wallace wrote his book. He called it *Ben Hur* and it became a classic of the ages.

But when he had finished the book, he began to discover that he had written this great story only with his pen and not with his heart. He realized as never before that the life of Jesus was more than the biography of a man who had walked the pathways of Palestine. Wallace discovered that he himself could know this Christ as his own Friend, as the One who would teach him the way to live. And so he came to be known as more than just the author of a great book; he became a sincere Christian.

The glorious message, which is the same for each generation and for all people, is this: God is love and love can conquer all. If we would open our hearts today, they would be filled with a peace that is greater than all worldly struggle and our lives would be filled with songs of praise and adoration to the King of kings.

It is possible through faith to be in partnership with one who has the power to lead you through all earth's difficulties into the glorious land of forever with God.

TABLE TALK: *Suppose you had to convince someone that Jesus was more than just a man. What would you say?*

God Forgives and Forgets

And whensoever ye stand praying, forgive, if ye have aught against anyone: that your Father also which is in heaven may forgive you your trespasses. Mark 11:25.

In a certain home there was a beautiful vase that had been handed down from generation to generation. Whenever company came the mother, with great pride, would show the guests this valuable possession. The children were taught to be very careful lest by accident the treasured possession should be toppled over, and broken.

One day Tommy was running about the house playing cowboy. He became a little too enthusiastic and, quite by accident, of course, knocked the vase over, and it fell to the floor broken in many pieces. Naturally the mother was very disturbed and said, "Tommy, you are going to have to go right to bed without any supper, but before you go to sleep, I want you to pray God to forgive you for being careless and breaking Mother's vase."

With tears in his eyes, Tommy retired to his bedroom to do as his mother had commanded. He said his prayers, felt assured that God had forgiven him, and then fell fast asleep.

He awakened in the morning as happy as he usually was on any day and as he came down for breakfast his mother said to him, "Oh, Tommy, why did you break Mother's vase yesterday?" The little boy was puzzled and began to cry as he said, "Mother, God has forgotten, haven't you?"

How grateful we should be that we have a loving heavenly Father who is willing, not only to forgive our sins, but also to forget them. His promise is that He will separate us from them as far as the East is from the West. So often we say of each other, "I will forgive him, but I will never forget what he has done." How grateful we should be that God is not like that. His is a love that let's us awaken every day confident that He has not only forgiven the mistakes of the past, but that He has completely forgotten them.

TABLE TALK: *Mention ways in which you can be more loving in your attitudes toward people when they wrong you in some special way.*

The Glory Road

If we confess our sins, he is faithful and righteous to forgive our sins, and to cleanse us from all unrighteousness. 1 John 1:9.

Are you on the glory road? It is a highway that has been built by love. All may travel on it who believe this promise: "If we confess our sins, he is faithful and righteous to forgive us our sins and to cleanse us from all unrighteousness."

So often we have false notions about God and what He is like. This is a description by a man who knew God: "I came crawling to Him on my hands and knees in deepest penitence. What did He do? Did He rebuke me? God knew I had had plenty of that. Did He criticize me or give me all kinds of advice? No, He knew that I had had enough of that, too. What He did do was to put His loving arms around me and hold me. Then I stood up a new man and have had a song in my heart ever since."

The glory road is the way of the loving heart. The prophecy was that there should be a highway, and one day the dream in the heart of God came true. The Master announced His intentions: "Behold, we go up to Jerusalem." The construction was to begin. A great cost was to be involved. He must suffer persecution, rebuke, and denial by His best friends. But this did not stop the divine Road Builder in attaining His purpose. He kept building the highway even though it led up a hill, and even though He had to carry on His own shoulders the cross which was to bridge the final chasm and complete the glory road from earth to heaven.

When upon the cross He uttered the words, "It is finished," new hope could come into every human soul. No longer need God's children fear the consequence of sin or the penalty of death or separation from the Creator. For now once more God and man were one through Christ.

Are you on the glory road? It is the road built by the great God of the loving heart and it extends right from your heart and bridges all gulfs between you and heaven.

TABLE TALK: *Think of instances when God's love has been a bridge over hardship. Can you think of anyone whose faith in God has become stronger during a hardship?*

Go and Sin No More

Though your sins be as scarlet, they shall be as white as snow; though they be red like crimson, they shall be as wool.

Isaiah 1:18.

A little boy had become increasingly bad. Though his father tried to reason with him, he could not make him improve. Finally, he tried the method of taking him to the woodshed, but even physical punishment did not seem to influence the boy to do right. Finally, one day in almost utter desperation the father tried a new approach. He said, "Come with me." As they walked out the back door the boy shuddered to think of what might be in prospect. He was much surprised to hear his father speak these words: "Son, there is the woodshed and you see I have placed a new door leading into it. There is not a single mark upon it. Now the next several weeks I am not going to punish you, but instead each time you do wrong, I am going to drive a nail into the door." The boy was much pleased with this new technique and he went whistling on his way.

After a few days had passed, the father called his son aside and took him into the back yard and said, "Son, now look at the door." Much to the boy's dismay, it was full of nails. Finally, realizing how bad he had been he said, "Father, is there anyway I can get those nails out of that door?" And the father replied, "Yes, Son, each time you do something good, when before you have done something bad, I will remove one nail."

Again a few days passed when once more the father brought the lad into the back yard. "See, Son," he said jubilantly, "you can do it. All the nails are gone." The little boy looked and then began to cry. "Daddy," he sobbed, "the nails are gone, but the marks are still there."

Though we should never forget that we may have to pay in a sense for the sins we commit, let us always remember that if we have faith in Christ our Saviour, even the marks in the door are covered over by His redeeming love and mercy.

TABLE TALK: *Point out examples of people who have sinned and who, though they have been forgiven, still have to suffer physical effects for their wrong doings.*

MARCH 21

Rejoice in the Lord

I will declare thy name unto my brethren: in the midst of the assembly will I praise thee. Psalm 22:22.

Our God does not live in some faraway heaven seated upon a glittering throne, commanding his empire of slaves. Our God stands beside us in every tribulation, sharing our apparent defeats and turning them into ultimate victories. He goes before His Christian army, leading the way into battle, comforting us in our tears, and rejoicing in our victories. He stoops low to touch the heart of those who follow Him and with His everlasting arms He carries the repentant sinner to His place of eternal rest. This is our God to whom we give thanks.

According to an old legend all the angels of heaven were once called together and the great Creator asked them if they were pleased with the newly created world. Some had minor suggestions about what might be added. But a certain angel gave this reply. "There is only one thing lacking. That is the sound of praise to God." And so the Creator added music to the world. He gave voice to the birds. He made the sound of wind, and the rolling ocean, and he planted a melody in the hearts of men.

You should be singing that melody today! It will help you to forgive those who do you harm. It will give you hope when everyone else has given up. It will make it possible for you to bear all things.

The thousands of people who heard the great Jenny Lind wondered at her marvelous ability. She never failed to thrill an audience with her beautiful voice. But she took little credit for herself. "When I sing," she said, "I sing to God." She virtually forgot the people who listened to her as she looked into the Master's face and sang her songs of thanksgiving.

There is nothing greater in life than to know that the Master stands beside you with His hand upon your shoulder promising you blessings for ever and ever.

TABLE TALK: *Tell of the effect music has upon each of you. How can it be an "international language"?*

MARCH 22

Are You a Lamplighter?

Again therefore Jesus spake unto them, saying, I am the light of the world: he that followeth me shall not walk in the darkness, but shall have the light of life. John 8:12.

There is a childhood memory that many of us will never forget. It happened in the days when there were gasoline lanterns on each side of the street. The city would hire a lamplighter who each night would walk down the street carrying a lighted torch in his hand. First, he would light one lantern, and then he would cross the street and light another. And the memory that remains is this: Wherever the lamplighter went, he left a lighted pathway behind him so that people who followed him would no longer have to walk in darkness but would safely see their way home.

The Master once said, "I am the light of the world: he that followeth me shall not walk in the darkness." Wherever He went, He became a lamplighter. He would talk to people whose lives had been darkened by sin. If they became penitent, He would forgive them their sins and light candles of hope in their hearts. He would talk to people who were afraid, and would make them confident as He lighted the candle of faith for their future. He would talk to people who were lonely, and would assure them of His presence with them always as He lighted the candle of love which made them confident that He was their friend.

The Master has meant that we should be lamplighters, too. Each day we meet people who are sad and lonely, and who are weary and distressed. Perhaps a smile or an encouraging word or a Christlike understanding of their problems is all they need to be given the lift that will help carry them through.

Why not resolve to be a lamplighter so that each day that you live you can feel that, because of the power and influence of Christ in your life, you have been able to be a blessing to mankind. You *will* if you follow Him!

TABLE TALK: *Point out people you know who are always doing kind and good things for others. What can you do as a "lamplighter"?*

MARCH 23

Tomorrow Greater Still!

Be thou faithful unto death, and I will give thee the crown of life. Revelation 2:10.

Do you remember that story of the old monk who was supposed to have found the crown of thorns which had been placed on the head of Jesus? He took the ugly-looking crown to chapel one night and placed it upon the altar. Very early the next morning, when he went to this place to pray, the sun was streaming down in all its glory upon that simple, rough-hewn altar. There he noticed that the crown of thorns had lost its ugliness. Miraculously the thorns had been transformed into beautiful roses blooming in all their glory in the sunshine of a new day.

For a moment in life, the distant horizon may seem darkened. However, with the dawning of another day, the sun appears more majestic than ever before. God has made us no idle promises. Jesus meant what He said, when He gave us the assurance, "I am the resurrection, and the life." He sounded the trumpet of victory which keeps echoing through all time. He lived and died and lived again to prove to us that He is the way of salvation and the fulfillment of God's faithful promises.

Our heavenly Father's plan is not just a code of right and wrong. It is not just a blind happiness that blots out the reality of life. God gives us the power to win, and the strength to conquer—yes, to conquer even death. We live each day with the Master confidently being assured that tomorrow will be greater still. If we live faithfully we know that some day we shall hear Him say, "You have fought a good fight. You have kept the faith. This crown of righteousness is yours."

God's truth and love will live on forever. To share in His eternal kingdom is your privilege if you will earnestly say, "Lord, here I am, sinful and ashamed, but I need you."

TABLE TALK: *Does the weather have any effect on your spirit? What can bring the sunshine even on a cloudy day?*

MARCH 24

Faith Will Make You Whole

And Jesus answered and said unto them, Verily I say unto you, If ye have faith, and doubt not, ye shall not only do what is done to the fig tree, but even if ye shall say unto this mountain, Be thou taken up and cast into the sea, it shall be done. Matthew 21:21.

Never will I forget the first time that I visited her. She was a comparatively young woman who had started life with much zest in living and it seemed to hold so many possibilities for her. Then suddenly, one tragedy after another struck her and the result was not only a broken home but also a broken body. Badly crippled with arthritis she was confined to her bed and now it appeared that she might become broken in spirit, too. I shall never forget her words: "I am not any good to anybody now. I might as well give up."

This young woman is not the only person who has found herself in that predicament. Have you never felt that life was going to tumble in? The beginning of the pathway had seemed so pleasant and you desired so much to be on the road to victory without the possibility of sickness or sorrow—without any of these crosses to face. But suddenly they surrounded you and hemmed you in. You said to yourself: "Oh, what's the use? If I could just get away from it all."

But this young woman changed her philosophy and when the change took place within it altered the outward circumstance, too. And it all happened because of the power of Almighty God. She resolved to face her situation with the faith to believe that she was in partnership with the Eternal. And when that faith came to her the miracle happened.

She is no longer a helpless victim confined to her home. She is going about in a wheel chair using what strength she has to help with the household duties. But the greatest miracle is the change in her spirit. God's presence is in her living. The same Friend can give you courage for each day.

TABLE TALK: *Discuss together how God's message may have new significance when illness and hardship come and when we have more time to think.*

MARCH 25

Leave the Lowlands

The Lord knoweth how to deliver the godly out of temptation. 2 Peter 2:9.

A detective, investigating a shooting affair in a certain restaurant, asked a man who was thought to have been a witness in the affair, "Where were you sitting when the first shot was fired?" "Right next to that window that was shattered," the customer answered as he pointed to the place. "Where were you when the second shot was fired?" The man gave the detective a blank look. "What second shot?" he asked. It was evident that he had not waited to hear it.

There is a good lesson in this little incident. At the first sound of danger, the man immediately got out of harm's way. He did not linger to be tempted by the excitement. He thought more of his life than that.

We live in a world in which each day we face sin and temptation. Too often when the danger comes we linger and allow ourselves to get into trouble. If we would turn our backs and quickly leave the region where the temptation occurs, we would be much wiser.

A very remarkable woman, who today is happily serving her Lord, was raised in a Christian home but when she got into the world lingered too long around the sins that so easily beset us. She became separated from the church. One Christmas Eve, for no apparent reason other than a deep spiritual hunger that must have kept persisting in her soul, she and her husband attended a service in a community church. There they heard the story of how it was said concerning the Babe of Bethlehem that His name should be called Jesus because He was to save His people from their sins. That evening was an important crossroads for this family and a significant moment in the life of that congregation. For here two souls came home from the far-off country. During the subsequent years both of them have been towers of strength in the kingdom work. Grace gave them power to leave the lowlands and dedicate their lives to God.

TABLE TALK: *Discuss what each of you thinks is the biggest temptation in the world.*

MARCH 26

Never Alone!

All that which the Father giveth me shall come unto me; and him that cometh to me I will in no wise cast out. John 6:37.

During the last war a doctor was called into service and shipped over to faraway Africa. He missed his home life very much. He was the father of two children, and had spent much of his leisure time playing with them and trying in various ways to entertain them. Now he was far away and very lonely.

"The weather is very hot here in Africa," he wrote his pastor. "In fact during certain hours of the day it is impossible to stay out in the sun. How often I have wished that I could be back home to walk with my children down to the corner drugstore and buy an ice-cream cone!"

"I don't want you to think that I am complaining for I have so much for which to be grateful. As I was lying in bed the other night I was thinking of my many blessings. Above me were four canopies: First, was the canopy of netting protecting me from the mosquito carrying the virus malaria germs, and I was grateful for that; then there was the canopy of the tent protecting me from the rain and the elements of nature, and I was grateful for that; then there was the canopy of the darkness of the blackout protecting me from the raiding enemy, and I was grateful for that; and finally, there was the canopy of God's guardian angels keeping watch over His children in faraway Africa and reminding them that no matter where they would go they would never be alone, and I was most grateful for that!"

We would do well if each day we would substitute the time that is spent complaining for an inventory period when we would count our blessings and discover how good God has really been to us. Even the poorest are rich indeed as long as God is on their side. No one need be excluded from the abundance of His mercies, for His promise is always the same: "Him that cometh to me I will in no wise cast out." The door is open for you!

TABLE TALK: *Count how many times you have complained today—about weather, work, etc. Resolve the next time you start to complain to substitute words of thankfulness and happiness.*

MARCH 27

We Belong to God

For God so loved the world, that he gave his only begotten Son, that whosoever believeth on him should not perish, but have eternal life. John 3:16.

"Ye shall be my sons and I shall be with you and live with you forevermore." This is the promise our heavenly Father has given us. Life is a thrilling adventure when in the soul there are blue skies smiling today and a far-off horizon beckoning us on, but life, for some, is foreboding with dark skies.

We do not know what life holds for any one of us in the way of physical suffering but we know, if we believe and trust in God, that no matter what comes, He will give us strength to believe and to lead us gloriously through it. God gave Paul sufficient power to bear his thorn in the flesh so that he could become a flaming evangelist in spite of his physical suffering. Our hope is based on the fact that no sacrifice has ever been too great for God to make for us. The giving of His Son proves that.

In the days of the horse and buggy there was a farmer who had come to town with a load of hay. As he was about to go into the store, he noticed that his horses had become frightened and had started to dash away. He grabbed the bridle and ran side by side with them down the street, trying to control them. When they finally came to a stop, they reared up and came down upon him crushing him beneath their weight. One of his friends knelt over him and said, "Sam, why did you risk your life to save that load of hay?" The last dying words he gasped were these: "Go look in the hay!" When they did, they found a little blond-haired, sleeping boy, the farmer's son. There must have been times when the angels in heaven came to God and said, "Why do you hang on to the reins? Why did you let Your Son die?" And God's reply must have been, "They are My children, and no sacrifice is too great to save their souls."

TABLE TALK: *Discuss stories you have heard about fathers and mothers sacrificing for their children. Who is sacrificing for you today? The soldiers? S c i e n t i s t s? Teachers? Discuss whether sacrifice is worth while (a) for the person sacrificing (b) for the persons for whom the sacrifice is made.*

87

MARCH 28

Hope for a Better Tomorrow

Forgetting the things which are behind, and stretching forward to the things which are before, I press on toward the goal unto the prize of the high calling of God in Christ Jesus.
Philippians 3:13-14.

A middle-aged man stood before the judge in a courtroom. The wise old jurist peered over his glasses at the file which lay on his desk, scanning the pages one by one. Then he sat back in his chair and looked squarely into the face of the accused man. "My friend," he said, "you have stood before me like this many times. You have stolen a car, taken money which didn't belong to you, and broken into houses. I wonder if you ever feel sorry for the wrongs that you do." "Yes, your honor," replied the accused, "but somehow I keep on doing them."

The old judge had seen hundreds of thieves and criminals, but he had never lost faith in the ultimate goodness of mankind. A sense of compassion came over him as he listened to this criminal. "We have tried everything to help you. We have seen that you have been given money for things that you need. We have gotten you a job. We have put you in jail as punishment. But one thing we have never tried: You have never been just forgiven. So now go on your way with a new start and see how much good you can do in your life." The heart of the condemned man was warmed by these words and he made and kept the promise that from henceforth he was going to choose the high road in living.

Not many words have greater meaning than the simple word forgiveness. It reminds us that our friendship is not broken and it gives a hope for a better tomorrow.

Years ago there was a man hanging on a cross on Calvary's hill. The sky was black. A crowd of people stood around a rough-hewn cross. The man upon it began to pray for those who were torturing Him, "Father, forgive them, for they know not what they do." He is offering that same prayer on our behalf before the throne of grace this day.

TABLE TALK: *Discuss what punishments you think are most just and would do the most good for offenders of the law.*

Mind the Light

While ye have the light, believe on the light, that ye may become sons of light. John 12:36.

A boat was floundering off the shore. A storm was raging high. The rescue squad was alerted. The captain said to the men, "Launch the boats." But one replied, "Sir, the tide is going out. We may be able to reach the boat but we will never get back." "Launch the boats," the captain repeated. "We have to go out. We don't have to come back "

In that spirit of courage the Christian must live. Christ counted not the cost and neither must those who follow Him. The Master faced His Calvary and Jerusalem without wavering His step. Steadfastly He marched toward His goal fully aware of the fact that He was facing certain death, but likewise convinced that the apparent defeat would result in ultimate victory.

Never in the world's history has the darkness been more black than on Good Friday, and never did the sun shine more brightly than on the first Easter, three days later. "I am the light of the world," Christ declared, and as such He promised always to be with His children. We must be faithful to the trust He has placed in us and hold high His light before men.

A young couple, happily married, moved to a little island upon which was located a lighthouse. At first it was quite lonely but soon they became accustomed to the location. They both loved their work as they were privileged to help guide the ships along safely to their destination. One day the husband became ill. They came from shore to take him to a hospital and as the boat was pulling away, these were his parting words to his beloved wife: "Mind the light! Mind the light!" After several days of anxious waiting, the boat returned and the wife knew from the look on the face of the one that greeted her what had happened. Left alone, she resolved that she would make good the trust that her departed loved one had placed in .her. She would remain to "mind the light."

"Mind the light" is Christ's word to us today.

TABLE TALK: *How are you to go about following the command: "Mind the light"?*

Thou Art Free

But the Lord hath been my high tower; and my God the rock of my refuge. Psalm 94:22.

When slavery was common in our country, a kind and gentle man was visiting the market place. There upon the auction block, he found a young Negro woman who all her life had known hardship and grief. Bidding the highest price, the man took the woman and brought her to his near-by estate. There he showed her his large and beautiful plantation. Then the woman bowed low to the feet of the owner and said, "I am your slave. What will you have me do?" Quickly the man answered, "I have not bought you to keep you in slavery but rather, to set you free." Astonished at the words which she heard, the woman broke into tears: "Please then, let me serve you forever."

Christ died on Calvary to set us free from the slavery of our sins. If this act of love means anything to us, it should cause us to turn to Him and say, "Because Thou hast set us free, we will serve Thee forever."

Have you ever observed the happenings in a great harbor like the one in New York City? There, an endless number of ships keep coming in and going out. They drop anchor for a short time while they pick up new cargoes and make necessary repairs. But soon they leave again for ports across the world. Perhaps we have always thought of a harbor as a place where the ships come to rest. But now we can understand that it is also a starting place, a place from which they begin a new journey. No ship goes out empty. Each one carries supplies that are needed in some part of the world.

In Christ we Christians find refuge, a haven from a restless world. But we also find in Him a source of strength and courage, and share with Him a life of joy and happiness. We go out on the many journeys of life to bring the good news of salvation wherever it is needed in this troubled world. Christ offers us a place where we may begin anew to live a life that is devoted to Him and engage in service to enrich the lives of others.

TABLE TALK: *We have been set free in America. To whom are we obligated? What are our further responsibilities?*

MARCH 31

Stand Up for Jesus

Suffer hardness with me, as a good soldier of Christ Jesus.
2 Timothy 2:3.

A soldier recently wrote in a letter home of a battle-front church service in Korea. He told of the day—it was sunny and warm with just a little breeze. The service was held in a rice paddy. The chaplain placed a small bronze cross on the hood of his jeep and that was the altar.

These are the exact words of the soldier boy: "I took communion at the end of the service. It made me feel good and strong. The service was very nice. We, of course, stood the entire time but none of us were tired. Sunshine overhead and a babbling brook nearby made as beautiful a setting as any cathedral I have ever seen. We sang hymns, had responsive readings, the chaplain read from the Scriptures, and also preached a sermon. One song which I particularly enjoyed was this: 'Stand Up, Stand Up for Jesus.' Even in far away Korea there are many opportunities of witnessing for the Master."

As today we think of the comforts of our homes and of the beauty of the church in which we worship, let us remember the privileges which we have, and the soldier boy in a faraway land grateful for the opportunity of worshiping God, even though our worship must take place in a day of war. We who live in a land of peace should ever be mindful of the responsibilities which are ours. God has blessed us. May we show our thankfulness by willingly testifying to others concerning the faith which is ours.

Each day you have a chance to stand up for Jesus. Remember He is the best friend you will ever have. The way that you live shows how you value that friendship. Never do anything to disgrace His name, and then your friends will know by the way you act and speak that you are a part of His company.

"From victory unto victory, His army He shall lead,
Till every foe is vanquished, and Christ is Lord, indeed."

TABLE TALK: *Discuss ways that you can live and things you can do whereby people will know that you are a friend of Jesus.*

APRIL 1

The Road of the Loving Hands

Whosoever shall seek to gain his life shall lose it: but whosoever shall lose his life shall preserve it. Luke 17:33.

There are too many "Palm Sunday Christians" in the world today. There are those who would glibly shout their hosannas in one moment and be ready to deny or crucify the Master the next. They are like flowers without roots. They bloom beautifully for a short time but quickly wither away because they are not planted deep enough in good ground.

To be consistent in our living we must not only pray but must help God make our prayers come true. A certain father in his devotions would always pray, "Lord, take the cobwebs out of my life." He prayed this prayer so often that finally it caused someone to remark, "I think it would be a better idea to get rid of the spider." We must always remember that God expects us to co-operate with Him in helping to eliminate the cause of the sin in our lives.

When we have received forgiveness and have felt the glory of a new beginning, the experience should cause us to live our faith consistently. It should make us want to be more than "Palm Sunday Christians." We will be wanting to practice our Christian faith every day in all that we do.

No finer tribute to anybody can be given than the one by a little boy about his father. The lad was sitting on the curb outside of his home. A man came by and said, "Is your dad at home?" "No," the boy replied. The man asked, "Well, do you know where he might be?" The boy quickly answered, "Well, I don't know exactly, but you might go look in the hospitals where there are sick people or you might look for places where there are people in need. For this I know, that you will find my father helping somebody."

The glory road is the road of the loving hands. A consistent faith will be in constant service in helping others. "Whosoever shall lose his life shall preserve it."

TABLE TALK: *Discuss the need for "year-around Christians." Why must religious practice be constant?*

APRIL 2

Which Way?

The Lord redeemeth the soul of his servants; and none of them that take refuge in him shall be condemned. Psalm 34:22.

Many years ago, in a small village in France, there lived a certain family. They appeared to be average, being neither rich nor poor; and they had two sons, one named Charles and the other, John. When they were young, the boys went to the same school, they played on the nearby hillside together, and they carried water and ran errands for their mother. Later, they left the little village to make their own way in the world and each of them went on to further schooling. It was then the lives of these two brothers began to separate.

John studied and worked hard. Charles preferred to skip classes and have a good time. As the years passed on John became famous as a great leader of his day but his brother was a forgotten man. One day in the squalid section of the city, a beggar was found dead on the street. All any one knew about him was that his name was Charles and that he had no friends. Some years later the news of another man's death was announced to the world. His name was John—John Calvin—the man who put into writing some of the greatest religious thoughts in his century, and who led hundreds to Christian faith.

Why did one brother become a lowly street beggar and the other a great Christian leader? Certainly it was not the home or the education or the opportunities in life. For in these respects each had the same chance for success. The answer is that one chose a good life, though it was the difficult way, while the other chose the way that looked easy but was filled with nothing but selfishness. The choice which each made determined the difference.

God sets before each one of us a life. Each day we stand at the crossroads and choose which way we shall go. We plot our own chart, for God cannot force us along the pathway of salvation. We make that decision ourselves. But today the Master is beckoning us along the narrow way which leadeth unto life.

TABLE TALK: *Think of families you know whose children had the same opportunity. Point out how their paths differed.*

APRIL 3

It Makes a Difference

And whither I go, ye know the way. John 14:4.

A woman was taking her first ride on a Pullman train. When she had found her place, she stopped the conductor as he passed by to have him examine her ticket. She asked him this question: "Are you sure this train will bring me to my proper destination in the morning?" "Of course," he replied, "This is the train that takes you to the place marked on your ticket." A second time the conductor came by and she asked him the same question and received the same answer. A third time the same story repeated itself, and finally in utter dismay, the conductor said, "I told you, lady, that this train will take you to the destination you are seeking. What are you getting so excited about?" The lady replied, "Mister, it will make a lot of difference tomorrow morning if I have gotten on the wrong train tonight!"

The woman was absolutely right. Her action should remind each one of us to look at ourselves and the way we are living. Many of us seem to forget that today we are building the house that we are going to have to live in tomorrow. The habits that we form today, the character that we mold, and the direction of life that we take will determine our degree of happiness in the tomorrow that each one of us will ultimately have to face.

It will make a lot of difference tomorrow morning, if we get on the wrong train today. The results will be apparent when it is almost too late to do anything about it. Each day we are faced with choices. When we come to the crossroads, let us be sure that we take the road that will lead to the destination that marks a forward point in continuing abundant life. So often people have made the wrong choices, and as a result, have suffered endless agony. Christ is willing to help us make the right choices, so that each succeeding moment of living may be more victorious than any that has gone before.

TABLE TALK: *Discuss instances of people who by making wrong choices in life have suffered tragic consequences.*

Our Guide Goes First

And when the chief Shepherd shall be manifested, ye shall receive the crown of glory that fadeth not away. 1 Peter 5:4.

When mountain climbers start out on their journey, the poorest climber is most generally given the safest place. The skillful guide goes first and each of the climbers is tied to a strong rope. If anyone should fall, the experts, and the more experienced climbers higher up take a secure hold, and keep the hold until everyone is safe on the trail again. Then once more they continue on toward their destination, the very top of the mountain.

If we hold fast to our guide in life, He will never let us fall into the valleys below. Our skillful guide goes first. He charts the way. If we should stumble His strength stands firm and His ever loving arms reach down and carry us to a safe position on the high road again, and we are enabled to continue our climb to the mountaintop experiences of life.

As the Good Shepherd, He gently cares for His flock, shielding them from the storms and safely guiding them to the green pastures on the distant hill. If one of them should go astray, He goes out to find it and carries it back in His arms. He will never leave us, for no matter how fierce the storm or how dangerous, He never forsakes His own.

Christ's victory on the cross can be shared by you today. On Good Friday long ago the dream of having a great earthly King faded in the hearts of many. On Easter Morn the world came to realize that this Son of God was even more wonderful than His closest friends had imagined. He had proved Himself to be the King of kings, and the Lord of lords, whose love was to reach around the whole world. That which at first seemed to be defeat was in truth the greatest triumph of all ages. It is a victory that not only occurred on that first Easter Day, but which happens every day as you take the Master's strength and conquer temptation and the ways of the world. For then you share the Resurrection experienced. Then you are really alive.

TABLE TALK: *Retell what Christ said about the Good Shepherd and the lost sheep. Matthew 18. Describe the pictures you may have seen of Christ with His sheep.*

APRIL 5

Try Singing

O give thanks unto the Lord; for he is good; for his loving-kindness endureth for ever. 1 Chronicles 16:34.

A young boy who had had a lot of misfortune in his young life, was as brave and as cheerful as anyone could be. One summer day, he and his playmate were climbing a tree in the back yard. As the lad tried to go just one branch higher, his foot slipped and he fell to the ground. The doctor said that it meant another session of long days in bed.

One morning as his mother was going about her housework she thought she heard a low whimper coming from the lad's room. She hurried to his bedside anxiously. "Did you call me, Jimmy?" she said. "No, Mother," came his quick reply, "I wasn't calling you. I just thought I would try singing a bit."

Maybe that is what we need more of today. We need to try singing the songs of happiness and thanksgiving in spite of our troubles. For there can always be joy within regardless of the circumstances without, if only we remind ourselves of God's presence in our hearts.

When you are tempted to complain, why not stop to consider the blessings which are yours? One winter night a little girl and her father were walking along a snow-covered street. All of a sudden the little girl looked up into the clear sky and said, "Daddy, I think I will count the stars." And she began one, two, three, pointing as she went along. Then suddenly she stopped and with a look of amazement on her face she said, "You know, Daddy, I never knew there were so many stars."

Someone has said that if you took time to give thanks for all the good things that come your way, you would not have time to be disheartened and sad. Why not count the blessings that God has given you? Add them together day by day and you will soon stop and exclaim, "I never knew there were so many things for which to be thankful." "He is good, for His lovingkindness endureth forever."

TABLE TALK: *Make a verbal list of your hardships or worries; and then name your blessings. Which list outweighs the other? Remember the love of God will balance all scales.*

APRIL 6

Seeing with the Eyes of the Soul

For whether we live, we live unto the Lord; and whether we die, we die unto the Lord: whether we live therefore, or die, we are the Lord's. Romans 14:8.

There is a little girl by the name of Carolyn. Her fate is either a life without sight or no life at all, and the decision must be made soon by her mother. The child has cancer in both eyes. Two specialists have recommended that Carolyn's right eye be removed immediately. The mother hesitates about making up her mind. "I don't know," she weeps. "I can't decide a thing like that. I keep hoping for a miracle. Maybe the Lord will take a hand and save her from the darkness."

Of course there is one miracle that the Lord has always promised to perform. It is the giving of inward power sufficient for outward strain. He is always willing to save any soul from darkness. He will always give spiritual eyesight to His children. And that is far greater than any physical miracle that can be performed.

The mother of a household had taken the journey to heaven. She was a woman of great faith. She, too, was suffering from an incurable disease. But in talking to her, one could never detect it. Her smile through pain was an inspiration that is unforgettable. She was a great soldier of the cross and she knew that nothing could ever separate her from Christ, not even great tribulation. She knew that whether she lived or died she belonged to the Lord. Such great souls, living their day upon the stage of life, make us so sure of Almighty God and His faithfulness in keeping the promises He has made.

This same faith can be ours. There will always be physical pain, sickness, and death, because there will always be sin. There will always be spiritual sight, victories, and eternal life because we believe in Christ our Saviour. We can overcome anything when we see with the eyes of the soul.

TABLE TALK: *Talk about people you know who in spite of physical handicaps and sickness yet are evidencing a triumphant faith.*

97

APRIL 7

We Know There Is a God

And the Lord make you to increase and abound in love one toward another, and toward all men, even as we also do toward you. 1 Thessalonians 3:12.

I was once attracted to an article in the newspaper with the title, "Why I Know There Is a God." I read the story of how on a certain Saturday morning a mother and her four children were without a home. By evening she had a new modern four-room cottage, erected by eighty-five men who donated their time and labor. Funds for the materials came from the donations of hundreds who had read a newspaper account of this woman's struggle to keep her family together after their home had burned down. Now all the work was completed except painting and a few interior details. The church group which backed the project indicated that enough money would be left over to buy some furniture.

It is readily understandable why the headline writer had used this title: "Why I Know There Is a God." For only He could persuade people to be so unselfish and thoughtful of their fellow men. His is the only power that is able to change our selfish lives into loving examples of what He wants us to be.

Without God we think only of ourselves and of doing those things that will make us happy. We have little concern for our fellow men, for we feel that they ought to be able to take care of their own lives. We pass by their suffering and hardship, excusing ourselves by saying that we have problems too, and that no one else is bothering himself about these.

What we forget is that the greatest Good Samaritan of all never saw human need without stopping to minister to it. What we also forget is the fact that we will not help Him build His kingdom here on earth unless we follow in His footsteps by being helpful to those who need us day by day. Let us remember that even a little act of kindness may bring a great blessing to some life.

TABLE TALK: *Point to examples of people who have had great difficulty but who were helped tremendously because of the loving efforts of some of their fellow men.*

The Life That Faith Builds

And Jesus . . . saith unto them, Have faith in God. Mark 11:22.

This is the story of a life that faith built. It concerns a woman who came to the Midwest to forget about her earlier life. She had been married and her home was broken because of divorce, and she was left to raise two small children. She graciously accepted her fate, and in coming to the new community, immediately looked for a church home. Her whole life was now centered in her two children, and she wanted nothing but the best for each of them.

One day the pastor of the church which the family had joined, was called to the city hospital. Here he was informed that the boy was suffering from severe burns. He had been working in a filling station where an explosion had taken place, and a door had shut tight, trapping him inside. When he was able to escape, he was nothing but a flaming torch. After several days of anxiety, the boy was called into the Great Beyond. Yet the faith of the mother remained firm.

Not many years later, the daughter in the family was taking the car to town. She backed it out of the garage, and then got out to shut the doors. She had forgotten to set the emergency brakes and the car ran over her, crushing out her young life. But even now, the mother's faith did not waver. She still believed in God. Although she was now alone, as far as an earthly family was concerned, she remained confident that God was still her Friend and Helper.

The pastor of the church moved to another location. The mother who had been burdened with all of this adversity came to visit him one day. This was her greeting when they met: "The Lord is good and His mercy endureth forever."

The promise of God still holds. "If ye have faith." "To them that love God, all things work together for good."

TABLE TALK: *Discuss people you know who have experienced hardship and sorrow which might have tempted them to lose faith, but who remained firm. Discuss how God's strength has enabled you to rise above everything.*

APRIL 9

You Can Always Come Home

Today if ye will hear his voice, harden not your hearts.
Hebrews 4:7.

The "Personals" column of a daily newspaper carried this message from a wife to her husband. "I love you, and I will forgive you if you will just come home." One can well imagine the story behind that statement. Here was a family whose home life had been broken by sins that had been committed. The separation was more than the wife could endure. And so, out of her great love, she was willing to receive back the one who had caused the great heartaches.

The divine love is beyond human imagination. Whenever we find ourselves in a far-off country because of sins we have committed, we should remember that there is a loving heavenly Father who stands at the gate waiting for us to return. He speaks to us, His children, "I love you, and I will forgive you if you will just come back."

No man has ever sinned beyond the point of redemption, except he who has so hardened his heart that he cannot any longer hear the voice of God. The love in the Father's heart is greater than all the sin of the world. With confidence we can come to Him knowing that He is good and His mercy endureth for ever. But once we have been forgiven, we must remember that he expects us to live a more noble life. In His great plan of salvation He does not take us from the world but leaves us in it, standing as soldiers of His, fighting for the cause of righteousness.

Have you ever seen a water lily as it glows in all its beauty in the bay of some inland lake? It has a story to tell. As it rises from the muddy depths of the water in which it grows it keeps its head closed and blooms into its fullest beauty only when it rises above the water and points its head toward the shining sun. So we, God's children, will stay on the narrow way that leads to life, only if we close our eyes to the things that lead us away from Him and open them to the things that lead to glory.

TABLE TALK: *Our love cannot be taken for granted. Discuss how we can express our love toward each other.*

APRIL 10

All Are Brothers

Inasmuch as ye did it unto one of these my brethren, even these least, ye did it unto me. Matthew 25:40.

It was supper time on a college campus. The students were moving steadily into the cafeteria. They formed a long circling line as they waited to pick up their trays and move down the aisle to select their food. There was the usual chatter and banter that are a part of collegiate life, especially at the end of the day when things have a way of taking on an air of relaxation.

But in the midst of all this youthful exuberance, a shadow fell. Something happened which sent something like an electric shock through the whole line of students. A few people had noticed that the door to the outside was opening, but very slowly. Presently an old man trudged in. He was stooped and gray. His clothes were noticeably tattered. He just stood there as if his feet were frozen to the spot. He looked about rather gropingly, obviously not knowing where to turn or what to do. Soon students throughout the line were nudging one another as they looked at the stranger. Their voices grew hushed. There seemed to be a flashing reaction, "He is such a misfit here."

Doris had no flair for the dramatic whatsoever, but she took the center of the stage now. She was much admired on the campus. She had a real enthusiasm for living. Her faith was not just a Sunday-go-to-meeting pose. It was real. She stepped out of her place in the line, walked over to the old man, took him by the arm, directed him into the line, paid his bill, and then sat with him while he ate.

The campus did not soon forget the incident, and we believe the Lord remembers it still. In fact there were many who observed Doris, as with no trace of condescension she carried on conversation with this old man, who were sure that they saw a Presence and heard a voice say: "Inasmuch as ye did it unto one of these my brethren, even these least, ye did it unto me."

TABLE TALK: *A thoughtless crowd often ridicules the unfortunate. Perhaps there is a clique in school, or a "high society" club, of which you know. Discuss the danger of such groups hurting others by forgetting the worth of each individual.*

APRIL 11

Life Is Like a River

He that believeth on me, as the scripture hath said, from within him shall flow rivers of living water. John 7:38.

There is nothing more beautiful than a river winding its way through the countryside, giving life to the flowers, the grass, and the trees along its banks. There is nothing more beautiful than a river, if it stays within its boundaries and follows the proper course. There is nothing more destructive than a river when it decides to cast aside the restraints, leave its proper channel, and flow just anywhere.

That is exactly what the Root River decided to do one day. Many families were victims of the flooding water. For example, it entered into the home of the Lloyd Parkers. "Water swirled over our kitchen stove and then some," said Mrs. Parker. "It crept over the keys on our piano." The Parkers and their four children looked out the window to see chicken brooders floating past. The road leading to their home began washing away. Finally the Red Cross came and saved them.

Life is like a river. There is nothing more beautiful than a life on the highway that leads somewhere, staying within bounds, and being a blessing to all with whom it comes in contact. There is nothing more destructive than a life that chooses to cast away the restraints and to live as it pleases regardless of the consequences to others.

The swamp is forever a curse. It has no channel. It goes wherever it pleases. Too many lives are like that. But a river following its proper course is forever flowing. It is going somewhere. Steadfastly it sets its face to the open sea for it knows that some day that will be its destination.

Life with a purpose leads you to the destiny of an eternal future! Has your life been channeled in the proper course? Let God help you plan your way.

TABLE TALK: *There are some precautions which can be taken to guard against a flood. What are some spiritual precautions?*

APRIL 12

Unfinished Business

We must work the works of him that sent me, while it is day:
the night cometh, when no man can work. John 9:4.

In several of our states the legislature is bound by law to
keep its business within the period of ninety days. Many times
this is a difficult thing to do and as a result, when time runs
short, the clock is stopped and business is transacted for a period
of several days after the legal session is ended. According to
the clock which the legislature goes by however, they are still
within time limits. The practice itself seems ridiculous, but
nevertheless it has grown considerably over the years.

Some people live as though they will be able to "stop the
clock" in case they cannot get all of their work done and all the
preparations made before this journey of life comes to an end.
But in the spiritual world we cannot arbitrarily decide that this
day shall not end until our work is done. Time passes on relent-
lessly. We must work "while it is day: the night cometh, when
no man can work." Unfortunately many do not realize that it
is impossible to "stop the clock" of life and thus they lose the
benefit of all of God's promises.

If we meet the tasks of each day courageously and work to
the best of our God-given ability, always remembering to live
close to Him, we will never have to be afraid that when the end
comes we shall be unprepared to meet Him because of unfinished business.

A father and his five-year-old daughter were out riding one
day when the little girl asked if she could not take hold of the
wheel and steer the car. Finally the father consented and eagerly she put her two little hands upon the wheel and tried to steer.
And apparently she was successful. But soon she discovered
the reason why. The father also had his hand upon the wheel
and he was helping her to drive. She exclaimed, "Daddy, you
have your hand upon the wheel, too, haven't you?"

It is such a confidence we may have in God.

TABLE TALK: *Perhaps you have known of someone who
accepted God only when the end was near. Comment on how
more abundant his life would have been if he had done so earlier.*

103

APRIL 13

There Is Work to Be Done

But what think ye? A man had two sons; and he came to the first, and said, Son, go work today in the vineyard.

Matthew 21:28.

There is a mechanical engineer who claims that in years to come he will be able to focus his camera on the past and take pictures of great historical events of the past. He says that last year he took a photograph of an event that happened in 1928. His instrument, a product of twelve years of research, is based on the theory that every event that has ever taken place still leaves its trace somewhere in the form of energy rays. He claims his apparatus can catch these radiations of the past and register them on photographic plates.

Another scientific writer says that he believes it to be beyond the realm of possibility. But one thing we do know—it is possible for God to call to remembrance everything we have ever done. The all-knowing Father is able to hold in memory all the sins we have ever committed.

But how grateful we should be to know that He is not that kind of a God. This is His promise: "I will forgive your transgressions and will remember them no more." This promise certainly merits the full devotion of our lives. We must prove to this loving God that we appreciate what He has done for us.

We must ever remember that He has no hands but ours to do His work today. All of us are capable of doing something. Suppose you did some kind deed that would make two people happy this day, that would be 730 in the course of a year. And suppose you lived forty years after commencing this course of action, you would in your lifetime, have added to the happiness of 29,200 people. And your acts might in turn inspire others to do the same.

Then, though a camera would not catch the events as they happen, the results of the added good in the world would undoubtedly be evident in the events of the world. The command is this: "Go work today in my vineyard."

TABLE TALK: *What have you done today to make someone happy? Do you give more happiness than unhappiness?*

APRIL 14

No Cross—No Crown

For narrow is the gate, and straitened the way, that leadeth unto life, and few are they that find it. Matthew 7:14.

There was a picture of the Mississippi River in a daily newspaper one spring, and over it was this caption: "River All Broken Up over Spring." The story went on to relate that the mighty river had begun to shed its coat of ice in earnest. The people of the community were happy and glad, because signs of spring are always welcome after a long and severe winter. But if spring were to come in all its beauty, blocks of ice would have to break up and melt away—that is the law of life.

You have to pay a price for everything that is worthwhile. This applies to the material world and to the spiritual as well. About the life of the Master it could be said, "No cross—no crown." And the same applies to all who follow Him.

A man was once traveling to his destination by plane. It was early in the morning and he was the lone passenger aboard. The pilot invited him to the cabin to watch the landing. Soon the destination was sighted. The city was all aglow with its thousands of lights burning brightly. Street after street was marked with them. The pilot pointed to a certain spot and said, "That is the airport." He directed the plane very gracefully toward the field, and during this whole time, he was in direct communication with the airport. Far ahead was the runway to which he had been directed. There seemed to be a million lights below, and many lighted ways. But there was only one way the pilot could go and that was to follow the two rows of lights that marked for him a single runway. He was heard reporting to the man in the control tower his descending altitude, "100 feet, 75 feet, 50 feet." As the plane headed down to safety on the runway ahead, this thought came to the watching passenger, "Narrow is the way." The pilot had followed directions, he had been obedient to the commands, and the result was a happy landing.

For happy landings in life we must meet God's conditions.

TABLE TALK: *Suppose you want to do something wrong, are you willing to pay the price of punishment? For something good, are you willing to pay the price of sacrifice?*

APRIL 15

Thanks Be to God

Better is little that the righteous hath than the abundance of many wicked. Psalm 37:16.

A few years ago an adventurous man started out to walk all the way from San Francisco to New York City. It was a long rugged trip as you can well imagine. When he finally reached his destination everyone wanted to know all about his unusual journey, but they were especially interested to learn what he considered the most difficult part of his long walk. It was not, he said, climbing over the Rocky Mountains, the crossing of the hot deserts, or passing through the busy cities: the thing that almost defeated him was the sand that got into his shoes.

Oftentimes the most trying problems we must face are not the earth-shaking ones, but the little insignificant things that bring discouragement and despair. The big problems of life seem somehow to arouse our courage, but the small everyday worries sometimes pile up and finally defeat us. Little grains of envy, or of doubt, can cause us more trouble than anything else.

Though little bad things can make life miserable, little good things can make living wonderful! But so many of the riches that come from God are easily overlooked and taken for granted.

There was an old woman who lived in a very nice house just across from the park. Frequently she could be found sitting in a rocking chair watching the cars going by, enjoying the beautiful flowers that surrounded her. But her money began to dwindle and she had to move to another location which was not nearly as beautiful. Uncomplainingly she kept her strong faith in Christ, and as she sat in her rocking chair at a small dingy window, she would say, "I am so thankful to God that I have such a wonderful view of the sky."

Listening to the song of one tiny bird, glimpsing a delicate flower, seeing a smile on a child's face—are these not enough to cause us to give thanks this day?

TABLE TALK: *Discuss the things you have about you which give cause for giving thanks. Resolve that you will be mindful of your many blessings.*

APRIL 16

Even One Is Important

I say unto you, that even so there shall be joy in heaven over one sinner that repenteth, more than over ninety and nine righteous persons, who need no repentance. Luke 15:7.

There was once a lad by the name of Johnny who did very poorly in school. He studied as little as he could, and when it came time for an examination he cheated just enough to get by. The teacher kept a record of each of her students, and one day she called Johnny in to talk to him about his work.

Much to his surprise, the teacher had only kind and encouraging words, and Johnny promised that he would try to do better. He worked hard and his marks steadily went higher until finally he had proved that he could be a studious and honest boy.

The time came for the end of the school year. An invitation went out to all the parents to visit their children's rooms to see the work which they had been doing. Johnny knew that his teacher would have all the record books out and he was heavy hearted as he thought of his mother seeing the disgraceful marks made in his early record. He thought of how disheartened she would be. When the visitors went through the rooms, he watched his mother as she finally came to his book. She picked it up and as she looked through it, she smiled and told her son of how proud she was of his accomplishments. Then Johnny got the courage to look at the book himself. It was then that he discovered that the kind teacher had torn out the pages which showed his bad marks and only the records of his improvement and hard work were still there.

God is a great teacher in the school of life. There are many times when our records are not as good as they should have been. In spite of the fact that he does not like our mistakes He has in His heart an undying love that forgives the penitent soul. As sure as each new day brings the rising sun, so sure are we of the promise of our merciful Saviour. To God each one is important and there is much joy when a strayed one returns.

TABLE TALK: *Have you ever resolved to "turn over a new leaf" and try to do better at some task or break a habit? What was the result?*

APRIL 17

We Are Never Alone

Behold, the hour cometh, yea, is come, that ye shall be scattered, every man to his own, and shall leave me alone; and yet I am not alone, because the Father is with me. John 16:32.

When Christ comes into your life it is as if the sunshine had been let in. With His presence in our lives, it is always springtime. Each day is more glorious than the one that has passed. There is a constant unfolding of glory and blessings, for the Master gives a new and greater meaning to the hours of every day. That is why we are foolish when we serve Him only on Sundays. We miss all the blessings that could be ours if we walked and lived with Him day by day.

We need to capture the truth that God is really love, and that there can be no true living apart from Him. As children, we know what it means to have parents to whom we may tell our troubles. How willing they are to soothe our heartaches and cheer us up! One man, now grown up and successful in life, once took time to sit down and write about all the things his mother had done for him. He wrote about the many times that he had been downhearted and sad, but how each time his mother was there to love him and care for him. No matter how many things he did wrong, Mother would always forgive him and encourage him to do better next time.

We should remember that our God loves us much the same way, only with even greater devotion, and though each day we do many things which make Him sad, He is always willing to give us another chance to be better. No matter what happens, we can always be assured that He cares for us and loves us.

There are too many of us who are trying to sail this way of life alone. Perhaps even now the storms of life are frightening. We may be on the high seas and think that all hope is gone and that there is no way of escape. But wherever your little boat may be on the voyage of life, there is One who is ever present, willing to take control and assure you of victory.

TABLE TALK: *Have you ever gone to God and laid all your troubles at His feet? What reassurance were you given?*

APRIL 18

Put Life into Living

Simon Peter answered him, Lord, to whom shall we go? thou hast the words of eternal life. John 6:68.

One day Jesus turned to the disciples and said, "Would ye also go away?" Simon Peter answered Him, "Lord, to whom shall we go? Thou hast the words of eternal life."

Many people reach the point where they just get tired of living and they think they would like to run away from it all. Where would you go? What choices face you? What philosophy would you follow?

Well, you can believe that life is a joke that has ceased to be funny. You could take that direction in your thinking. Then there would be no meaning to your existence. It would lead you to the conclusion that if there is an almighty power, all He is trying to do is give you a "bad time." Certainly it would hold no hope for the future.

You could take the way that would lead to the belief that life is a jail sentence for the crime of being born. Following that way, the burdens of life would hem you in. There would be no way of escape. You should be doomed to life imprisonment.

You could take the way that would lead you to believe that life is a disease for which death is a cure. But how could that satisfy? It would mean that life consists of nothing but suffering and that death will mean only the crumbling of an earthly tabernacle, with no soul to live on forever.

Consider the other alternative, a faith in a God who says, "I came that they may have life, and have it abundantly." We need to remember these words. For the real object of life is partnership with God here and a continuing fellowship in the hereafter. Then life would not be one of despair, or of imprisonment, or of suffering. Life with faith is a life worth living.

TABLE TALK: *Can you think of people who have some of the philosophies mentioned? Are they happy? What has happened to their lives?*

APRIL 19

There Is Always Hope

And forgive us our sins; for we ourselves also forgive every one that is indebted to us. And bring us not into temptation.
Luke 11:4.

A minister was counseling with a man one day, trying to convince him that he should take a different course in his living. There were several children in the family who were being raised under very adverse circumstances. The mother was desperately struggling to hold the home together. She tried to convince her husband of their need to live closer to the way of God. As the minister was trying with the help of God to convince this man, he turned to him and proudly and defiantly said, "I don't think I have ever done anything wrong."

In spite of his self-righteousness, life has not given this man the happiness which God intended for him. For today he suffers a great loneliness, separated not only from his family, but also from God.

Consider the case of another. He, too, sought out his pastor for counsel and advice. With tears streaming down his cheeks he told of a sordid life in sin. "I live in fear," he said, "the fear of being caught. Never did I have a real night of peace. It is the worst hell that anyone could be called upon to endure. But I am glad it is all over now. Pastor, is there any hope for me?" The minister assured him that God was willing to forgive and offer him another chance to live a good life.

In the days that followed he not only attended his church regularly but daily communed with God in prayer and learned of Him through the reading of His Word. And the result has been a life that has been transformed by the power of the Almighty. He is now a radiant soul, whose living testifies that the mercy and love of God endures forever for the humblest sinner who comes in penitence to the throne of grace.

God calls you to repentance, promising forgiveness and more abundant life. Will you answer that call?

TABLE TALK: *Can you recall instances when a home was broken because a member would not admit a mistake?*

APRIL 20

The Cost of Discipleship

Then said Jesus unto his disciples, If any man would come after me, let him deny himself, and take up his cross, and follow me. Matthew 16:24.

Everyone likes a bargain. The crowded store on a Sale Day attests to that. Sometimes, even, you go into a store in search of a saving, and ask, "Can't I have it for a little less?"

So many attempt to bargain with God. We turn to Him and say, "If I just give up this part of me, is that not enough?" And God replies, "The price is marked. You cannot change it. You take it on those terms or you will never derive the benefits which come from receiving it."

God does not ask that you undertake dangerous missions to testify for him in order to receive his goodness. Christ has paid the full price of redemption. What then, does he ask of you? He does not demand a life that has been without sins. For if He did, all of us would find ourselves too bankrupt to pay. He does not ask just for those who have ten talents, for if He did, too few of us would be recipients of His wonderful blessings. All that He asks for is your life the way it is today regardless of your past, in spite of your lack of talents. "Give Me your life," He says, "and I will give you the treasures of heaven."

Do not miss the blessing because you think you do not have enough to give. You do not, and the Master knows it. Take him at His word and believe that He will make up for what you lack and because of His great love will restore you to fellowship with Him.

The cost of discipleship is a life dedicated to Him. It is the best investment one can make.

TABLE TALK: *Is there anyone of your acquaintance you could talk to and tell him about this life investment?*

APRIL 21

In the Center of God's Love

If any man have an hundred sheep, and one of them be gone astray, doth he not leave the ninety and nine, and go unto the mountains, and seek that which goeth astray? Matthew 18:12.

One day a father and his son were hiking in the mountains. They went from one summit to another. From one of these, the view was especially beautiful and they could see for long distances on either side. They stood there for some time just enjoying the beauty which had come from the hand of the Great Almighty.

Finally, the father began to speak and he said, "Son, how far do you think it is from the north to the south?" "That is too far to measure," said the boy. Then said the father, "How far do you think it is from the east to the west?" "That can't be measured either," said the boy. Then the father drew this lesson: "Son," he said, "so great and measureless is the love of God." The boy stood for a moment looking in all directions as he gazed at the far beyond. "Dad," he said, "you and I are right in the center of God's love, aren't we?"

The life that is lived with a song in the heart is the one that has faith to believe that we rest and remain in the center of God's love. He constantly reminds us that if He had but one-hundred sheep and one was lost, He would leave the ninety and nine as He sought to save the one. He tells us that, if He were the possessor of coins and only one was lost, He would try diligently to recover it. If He were the father of two boys and one had gone to the far-off country, He would follow him there and lovingly and penitently seek his return, and when he did come home, He would greet him with open arms, throw the robe around him, put sandals on his feet, and prepare the homecoming. So great is the love of God, and we, His children, are in the center of it.

TABLE TALK: *Mention instances of the willingness of earthly parents to receive back their children when they are penitent for doing wrong. And show how God's love is even greater than that.*

APRIL 22

In Partnership with God

Both riches and honor come of thee, and thou rulest over all; and in thy hand is power and might; and in thine hand it is to make great, and to give strength unto all. 1 Chronicles 29:12.

Early one morning I had one of those glorious experiences that brings us closer to the Creator. I was driving on the North Shore, going south from Grand Marais, when through the clouds the early morning sun began to rise over the majestic Lake Superior. Painted on the tapestry of the sky were colors that only the Master Artist could create. As my soul was thrilled, I wished that I had a thousand tongues to sing my great Redeemer's praise.

Life cannot always be that beautiful. Sometimes it must rain, sometimes it will snow. The winds may blow and the clouds may hide the sun, but there was a song in my heart this morning as I remembered that in the spiritual kingdom, regardless of circumstance and in spite of storm or hardship, the Sun of Righteousness in all of its beauty rises in my soul.

There is always God. Storm clouds, snow, or rain cannot hide us from Him. The only reason that life ever seems impossible is that we fail to take advantage of the opportunity at hand.

One day a small boy was trying to lift a very heavy stone, but he could not quite budge it. His father passed by and stopped to watch his efforts. Finally, he said to his son, "Are you using all your strength?" The boy replied, "Yes, I am." The father's answer was significant, "No, you aren't, my lad," he replied. "So far you haven't asked me to help you."

Too often in life we give up when the task seems beyond our limited capacity. But ability is not measured properly until the unlimited resources at our disposal are included. God is always willing to give us the assurance that His is the power that will carry us through the difficulties that we cannot master alone. In His vocabulary the word "defeat" is not found. With Him as my divine partner the ultimate end must be victory.

TABLE TALK: *Discuss instances of how two people in partnership are capable of accomplishing greater things together than as individuals.*

113

APRIL 23

Special Things Do Happen

O thou of little faith, wherefore didst thou doubt?
Matthew 14:31.

One day a man who doubted whether God really lived looked up into the sky and said, "God, if you are really there, then make something special happen so that I can be sure." Then the man sat down to wait.

While he sat there the sun began to rise over a distant hill. And it colored everything in a scarlet robe. Then a tiny bird came and perched itself on a near-by tree and sang a beautiful song. Far down in the valley a farmer was harvesting a beautiful crop of wheat and on the road close by children were singing and playing as they walked to school.

The day passed on and the brilliant sun faded in the west and the stars came out. But still the man waited and nothing special seemed to happen. "There is no God," he said, "just a space called time, and a sun, and a field of wheat, and children that laugh and play. That is all that it is." The man started back toward his home. But suddenly he stopped. "I asked God for something special to happen. The sunrise, that little bird that sang, the wheat in the field, and the children playing—God gave all these to me. Not only this day but every day. He has shown me something special every day if only I would have looked."

Yes, God has showered His blessings on everyone. All about you, you can see the master work of His hand. And in the heart that knows Him you see the masterpiece of His love.

How can you doubt his blessings when you view all the special things that do happen every day through his love? Have no doubts about God. He is right beside you willing to be of help and consolation. He asks only your devotion and love in return. The more you rely on Him the closer He becomes to you. Do not forget each day to count your blessings.

TABLE TALK: *Have you ever encountered anyone who did not believe in God? It is difficult to make such a one see. How would you go about it?*

APRIL 24

Always Listening

Be ye therefore imitators of God, as beloved children: and walk in love, even as Christ also loved us, and gave himself for us, an offering and a sacrifice to God for an odor of a sweet smell.

Ephesians 5:1-2.

Do you really know what it means to be a child of the heavenly King? Just think of the great love God must have for each one of us. We are a part of His great family. He has told us that we can pray to God, saying, "Our Father." Think of what wonderful things He will do for us because we are His very own. His everlasting arms surround us with gentleness, and yet with a strength that none can overcome. He speaks to us and He listens to us as we tell Him about our problems and share our joys with Him. He reaches out His hand so that we can clasp it and walk side by side with Him every place we go. This is our own heavenly Father who has invited us to speak to Him whenever we desire to do so.

But we must pray often, not only at the certain times when we fold our hands and lift our eyes to heaven. We should talk to Him as we walk, as we work, and as we play.

The great scientist Louis Pasteur was busy one evening in his laboratory. As his head was bent low over the microscope, one of his students came into the room. Not seeing the microscope and the laboratory equipment, but only noticing that Pasteur's head was bowed low, the student started to leave. Just then the scientist looked up and saw the young man. "Excuse me, Mr. Pasteur," the lad apologized, "I thought you were praying." The great man smiled, and quietly answered, "I was."

Have you captured the power of walking and talking with Christ hour by hour every day? God is with you wherever you go and hears every word you speak. You probably set aside times of the day when you meditate upon God. But take time to let Him come into your heart whatever you are doing and wherever you are, any time.

TABLE TALK: *Have you often thought of praying to God, but put it off, saying "I'm too busy, later on, perhaps"? Discuss when you can pray—all the times and places where you can pray.*

APRIL 25

God Needs You Today

But abide thou in the things which thou hast learned and hast been assured of, knowing of whom thou hast learned them.
2 Timothy 3:14.

Charles Steinmetz was one of the greatest scientists the world has ever known. For many years he devoted his life to the study of electricity and light. He owned many patents and he wrote a number of textbooks which are still being used.

But aside from his untiring devotion to science, he had a deep knowledge of things eternal. At one time in his life he wrote, "Some day people will learn that material things do not bring happiness. Then the scientists will turn their laboratories over to the study of God and to prayer and to spiritual forces. When this day comes, the world will see more advancement in one generation than it has seen in the many passed."

Does it not seem strange that for many years many have worked feverishly in their laboratories trying to uncover the deepest mysteries of life and yet they have overlooked the profoundest truths of real living which lie within their own hearts? Is it not stranger that those who know that the answer is found in practicing Christian living, still fail to use that solution? We need not wait for the men of the laboratories to give us the answer: Christ has told us the way to save the world.

Not only must we pray that the better day shall come, but all of us who live on the everyday streets of life must resolve to devote ourselves more fully to the goodness of God. The winning of the world for Christ must begin with you and me. We are the ones who must plant the seeds that will grow into a wonderful harvest of understanding and love.

The whole world can be a better place just because of one person. That one person can be you. It can be better because of your thoughtfulness, your work, your prayers, and your faith in God. You are privileged to be a tool in the Master's hand. Do not put off working for Him. He needs you today.

TABLE TALK: *Discuss the relative importance of science and religion in the world. Which can win the peace, the atom bomb or the way of Christ?*

116

APRIL 26

When Anything Becomes Possible

And if I go and prepare a place for you, I come again, and will receive you unto myself; that where I am, there ye may be also.

John 14:3.

Because of faith, miracles happen every day. In my lifetime I have seen a small and devoted group of people, worshiping in an old postoffice building, grow, by the power of God, into a congregation of thousands, which worships now in a beautiful cathedral. It all happened because they dared to believe in the promise of God that anything with Him is possible.

I often think of that little boy who was lost in the woods. A man was passing by and heard a voice repeating the letters of the alphabet—A-B-C-D-E-F-G—all the way through to the end. The man, following the voice, suddenly came upon this little boy and asked him, "My lad, what are you doing?" The boy replied, "I am praying." "Praying?" said the man. "You are just saying the letters of the alphabet." The little boy answered, "Well, I am lost and I am praying to God that He might send me someone to show me the way home, and I am just giving Him all the letters of the alphabet because I feel that He can put them together better than I can. And it is true because now you found me and will show me the way I should go."

Too often in our prayer life we limit God because we have not the faith to believe that with Him anything is possible. Think of His promise that whatsoever you want you can ask of Him and He will give it to you, that He might be glorified through His Son. Now that statement is unqualified, and yet some of us worry so much about the future that we seem to live as though God never existed. We worry about security. We worry about what the next day is going to bring. We worry about death. Worry is one of the worst cancers in the lives of people and keeps them from happiness. Worry and faith just cannot live together. So if you worry you do not believe in God, because, if you believe in God, you just cannot worry.

TABLE TALK: *Discuss some of your personal and family worries. When you stop to analyze them do they seem petty beside the overpowering faith in God?*

APRIL 27

Be Helpful to Others

In love of the brethren be tenderly affectioned one to another; in honor preferring one another; in diligence not slothful; fervent in spirit; serving the Lord. Romans 12:10-11.

One day some years ago a little girl went out with her father for a visit in a near-by city. While she was there she saw people living in tumble-down houses, with almost nothing to eat and with few clothes to wear. She was so touched by the great needs of these people that she made herself a promise. When she came home she told her father, "When I grow up I want to live near poor people so that I can help them.

When Jane Addams grew to womanhood she kept the promise which she had made. She established one of the most famous mansions of help and understanding in our nation, Hull House, in the heart of Chicago.

The need of our world is great today. There are so many people that have much less than we and so much more to complain about. It is not difficult to find people who need our help, but often we excuse ourselves and just stand around at the edge and look at the trouble instead of trying to solve it.

Service to your community, to your country, and to your God is much more than just being sympathetic about the needs of other people. It is a conviction to help, an ambition to accomplish something, and a willingness to work. There must be a driving spirit that comes from your heart, a burning desire to bring real happiness to the lives of others who do not know the peace and the mercy of the Master.

Somewhere today you will find unhappiness and trouble. Why not try to uproot it and plant in its place the flowers of love? Somebody is almost ready to give up his dream of victory and you can be the one who brings him new light of hope.

Today will never be here again. So give yourself to God now, promising to help others find wealth, the wealth of a heart that shares God's richest blessings!

TABLE TALK: *Discuss what you can do for someone today. Then do it!*

APRIL 28

A Plan for Real Living

And Jesus, crying with a loud voice, said, Father, into thy hands I commend my spirit: and having said this, He gave up the ghost. Luke 23:46.

An eleven-year-old boy attended the National School Patrol convention some time ago in Washington. He came back to his Wisconsin home sporting a black eye. Before the mother could say a word the boy explained, "At the hotel where we stayed I met a kid from Georgia who didn't know that the Civil War was over."

History records the end of the Civil War, that took place some ninety years ago, and yet there is another war that continues to exist and that will never end until the last day. It is a warring of two natures which causes such incidents as that just mentioned. It is the battle between the old man and the new man, between the flesh and the Spirit, and between God and sin.

A poet has said, "Within my earthly temple there is a crowd." There are conflicting voices. One tries to rise above the other to tell us the way we should think and the words we should speak. Out of this conflict, we must decide what to do. Each day we face the battle within us, but each day also we can be assured of victory if we live closely enough to God so that His power becomes our strength.

Begin the day by turning to Him in prayer. Let His presence fill your consciousness. Resolve to let Him direct you through the course of the day and then keep speaking to Him often when you are tempted to turn to Him to receive the strength necessary to withstand.

During the day, take time to commune with God, seeking His guidance resting on His everlasting arms.

When night comes and the day's occupation is ended, be honest with God as you recount the record of the day's happenings. Do not be too fearful or too proud to confess all your sins. Then pray, "Father, into Thy hand I commend my spirit."

TABLE TALK: *Too often our prayers are limited to one or two set times. Discuss how each of you could talk to God frequently during the day.*

119

APRIL 29

Who Is Your Architect?

According to the grace of God which was given unto me, as a wise masterbuilder I laid a foundation; and another buildeth thereon. But let every man take heed how he buildeth thereupon. 1 Corinthians 3:10.

In the northern part of one of our great states, tons of rich iron ore are taken out of the earth almost every day. It is then shipped to the giant furnaces of the east where it is refined into steel and molded into countless products that we use every day. The powerful steel girders of the skyscrapers still possess all the qualities of the iron which was dug from the hillside. It has just acquired a new form and character. It has been tempered and shaped into a useful product.

The qualities which God has given each one of us cannot be changed but they can be refined and made into something strong and useful. Out of a lost soul a powerful Christian can be created. The great Physician is able to make well a wounded heart and He gives it new life and hope.

God is the great Architect of life. You are His builders. He has given you a library of plans and blue prints, sixty-six books on how to build lives that will last forever. He has provided you with all the tools that you need and also with the ground on which you are right now. By your manner of living you are to prove to the world that you are choosing the materials which will make your building eternal. If there is any doubt about the direction which you should take, the great Architect is always present, ready to answer your questions, to explain His building plan, and to give you His help.

God loves each one of us very much and He proves it to us daily. If you, in turn, really love Him, then you must prove it, too. Perhaps yours is the voice that could call to some discouraged soul who might have lost hope. Perhaps you might be able to teach him how to rebuild his life by leading him to the Master. You can assure him of God's forgiveness and thus enable him to begin again.

TABLE TALK: *Suppose you were to summarize the Divine Architect's plan for a perfect life. What would you say?*

APRIL 30

The Lord Is Our Helper

And they came to him, and awoke him, saying, Save, Lord; we perish. Matthew 8:25.

The ice was beginning to break on the great Lake Superior. In one of the docks the *Eugene S. Buffington* was getting ready to be the very first boat to start the shipping season. The people from the city were all excited because their men would be back to work on the lakes. When the first boats begin to move, it is a sign that spring has arrived.

There I saw a most interesting sight, and one that really amazed me. Two little tug boats, which did not look any larger than rowboats compared to the long barge, were pulling the big ship through the ice and out into the lake. That those two little tug boats could have more power than the freighter was hard to understand.

No one in this world is so big that he does not need help. None of us is self-sufficient. We may have the strength to sail along in smooth waters, but when the seas become rough we must ultimately turn to someone and say, "Help us, or we perish."

As children we ought to be grateful that we have parents who are always willing to help us in time of need and who will guide us along the pathway that we should go. But there come times when even those who love us very much cannot supply the strength that is so desperately needed. Even as the disciples needed the help of the Master long ago, we too, as we get older, need him to help us in the storms of life. How fortunate we all are to be able at any point to turn to God and say, "Lord, You help us, or we perish."

We have a Saviour who is always ready to help us out of the dark places into the glorious liberty of the wide, wide ocean. His strength is always sufficient.

TABLE TALK: *Discuss instances when problems were so great that it seemed impossible that you could conquer them. Tell how God was able to lead you out of them into victory.*

MAY 1

Always an Open Window

In the Lord do I take refuge: how say ye to my soul, Flee as a bird to your mountain? Psalm 11:1.

A gardener one day set out to plant a row of tiny pine trees. He would care for them and watch them grow until some day they would be tall and stately spires pointing heavenward. As he planted them, he noticed that a few were crooked and bent. But he did not throw them aside to be burned. Rather he took special care to set them deep in the ground and gently tried to straighten the branches. When he had finished planting all the tiny trees he looked them over and said, "I won't have to spend much time with those straight young pines, but those others will take a lot of tending. Maybe I can make beautiful trees out of the crooked ones, too."

As God looks down upon His children He sees those who try to follow His laws and commandments, but His eye is also upon those who despise and forsake Him. Like the careful and kind gardener He hopes that even those who travel the roads of sin will some day reach their hands heavenward asking for the Master's grace. Our heavenly Father does not cast aside those with crooked and sinful lives. They need not be forever lost. Rather, our heavenly Father continues to show His love and mercy and when finally we grow stately and straight toward the things that are eternal, He rejoices that another soul has accepted the salvation of His Son. God's love and understanding are meant for all.

Sometime or other perhaps you have seen a bird that has flown into a building through an open window, and it cannot find its way out again. It flies back and forth from wall to wall, imprisoned. Yet that same open window through which it came is still there. All it needs to do is find it and fly out to freedom.

You need never be walled in. God's love has provided for you an open window through which you may gain freedom for all eternity.

TABLE TALK: *Have you ever felt as though life were closing in on you on all sides, as if there were no possible way of escape? What is the solution to such a situation?*

MAY 2

You Can Be Sure of God

The Lord hath been mindful of us; he will bless us; he will bless the house of Israel; he will bless the house of Aaron.
Psalm 115:12.

A news story reported concerning a crewless bombing plane that killed a man and two children when it crashed into a house. Three others were hurt. The B-25 crew, which had been struggling to free a jammed landing gear while circling for four hours, parachuted to safety. The plane was reported to have been put under control of an automatic pilot to divert it from the metropolitan area. There was no immediate explanation why it crashed in a housing development. Among those who were dead because of the crash were two little girls, one seven years and the other two months.

How frequently from the spiritual point of view great damage is done to ourselves and to others because our lives are without a pilot! We think that we can live automatically without the direction and guidance of Almighty God to lead us on. But such thinking on our part spells nothing but disaster. We not only place our own lives in jeopardy but those of our fellow men as well.

How different it is when God is in control! A little boy was accompanying his father as he led a group of mountain climbers to an Alpine peak. Down below the travelers saw some flowers which they desired to have and they offered the boy a sum of money if he would be willing to descend to the depths below in order to get the flowers for them.

The young lad looking at the deep ravine turned to the travelers and said, "I will go down and get them for you if my father will hold the other end of the rope." The young lad felt secure knowing that his father was in partnership with him, for he trusted and loved him. Children of the heavenly Father, you can be sure of God!

TABLE TALK: *Discuss incidents in your life when you felt secure because of your mother's or father's presence. Who do you always have with you?*

MAY 3

The Importance of Littles

The ants are a people not strong, yet they provide their food in the summer. Proverbs 30:25.

You do not have to be much of a naturalist to become fascinated by the way ants live. They are almost like human beings. Sometimes they use even better judgment, especially in their thought for the future. Have you ever observed them carrying particles of food even much larger than themselves and taking them to a storeroom for future use?

Perhaps one day you took a seldom-used path, and walked along leisurely, looking down as you went your way. And then you noticed many piles of fresh-looking sand, with little holes in the center. Maybe at first you could not understand what had made such a number of identical mounds. But stopping to examine, you discovered that the sandpiles were alive with little ants, all in a mighty hurry to be doing the task at hand. Each one had a little grain of sand, which he had taken from down in the earth, and which he was carrying up to the outer regions.

If you watched long those busy little bodies, scurrying to and fro, you probably marvelled at how much work they got done. Compared to the ant, how much do we accomplish? Are we as industrious and untiring? Do we tackle a big job with as much enthusiasm? Do we utilize all of our energies to the completion of a task?

There is much to be done in the work of the Lord! Though our efforts may seem small in comparison to the magnitude of the work to be done, if we are working together, realizing the importance of littles, the work will get done. After all, we are mightier than the ants. There is much that we can do.

Summer vacations are coming, but there is never a vacation in His work. We must prepare for the future even in the summer.

TABLE TALK: *Enumerate the little things that you do that could be very harmful and then the little things which can do good. Resolve to build those little deeds of love into mighty acts of power for good.*

The Change Is from Within

Verily I say unto you, Except ye be converted, and become as little children, ye shall not enter into the kingdom of heaven.

Matthew 18:3.

Once there was a man who wanting his watch repaired took only the hands of his watch to the jeweler. The jeweler told him he would have to bring the entire mechanism before he could be of any help. The man replied, "The only thing wrong with my watch is that the hands won't go to the right numbers at the right time." "But there must be something wrong with the mechanism," said the jeweler, "for it controls the hands and determines how fast or slow they move." In great disgust the man replied, "All you jewelers want is to make a lot of money off us poor people."

We may think the man mighty foolish, but many of us make the same tragic mistake. We attempt to make our hands move in the right direction without doing anything about the power within us that must motivate such action. A life will not give itself to Christian service and act according to the principles of Jesus unless there is a power within that will make it do so.

It is not reasonable to assume a world can be won for God by individuals who have not themselves been saved.

What causes one to live a life of unselfish service? What convinces us that we should lift the fallen, share with the poor, be the Good Samaritan along life's way? It is the life of the Master that constrains us. Our heart has been given to Him and to be consistent we must reflect the spirit which He showed as He went about doing good. When the miracle takes place in the soul, the mechanism has been repaired and life keeps time according to the correct pattern as established by the Master Himself. The heart determines the way that the hands will move, and to attempt to control them without the regeneration of the soul is as foolish as it is to try to fix a watch without making sure that the springs have the power to make it run.

TABLE TALK: *Discuss the effect that insincerity on the part of a Christian, mere surface acting without any inner change, would have on a nonbeliever or on smaller children.*

MAY 5

A Lesson from Nature

Put on therefore, as God is elected, holy and beloved, a heart of compassion, kindness, meekness, longsuffering.
                                                    Colossians 3:12.

There is a little creek outside my office window. It winds its way through the grass and under picturesque flagstone bridges. It flows past many lovely homes where little children play and come out to sail their toy boats.

One morning I learned some lessons, not from books, but from this brook running by our churchyard. It spoke to me about humility. You see, this is not a very large stream where it passes us here at the church, but it sings along its way because it is giving itself to something much bigger farther down the line. It is on its way to join the great Mississippi, and finally it will flow into the mighty ocean. It has a great dream, you see. But it is content to do the humble tasks today in order to help this great dream come true. This little brook tells us today that our great happiness comes in doing our share, whether it be great or small, in building the great kingdom of God.

It teaches us about patience, too. There are seasons when the waters in the brook flow as thin as thread. But the creek bed knows that spring and the rains will come again and fill it to overflowing. It is always waiting to be filled and then it goes on its way to give itself to others.

This little brook looks up and takes its color from the sky. It reflects the heavens above. Just think if each one of us would keep our souls looking up to the hills and the heavens, and then would reflect the goodness and the glory of God in our daily living here upon the earth. Then we really would go about as the Master did, doing good wherever we went and making evident His love toward our fellow men.

Humility, patience, sharing—these are lessons from nature.

TABLE TALK: *Point out the importance of the seemingly insignificant things of life—how little deeds of kindness can have great consequence.*

126

MAY 6

Miracles Still Happen

Verily, verily, I say unto you, If ye shall ask anything of the Father, he will give it you in my name. John 16:23.

One Sunday night a man wandered into a church seeking a pastor. He had heard a radio program originating from that church and it had led him to seek this minister's advice. For three days he had been away from home. He was ashamed to go back. He was near desperation but willing to receive help.

The pastor went with him to his home, where they were greeted with a radiant smile by the man's wife, a helpless cripple. "Why, Pastor," she said, "this is the strangest thing that has happened to me. After listening to your broadcast this morning I wrote you a letter, which I have not yet mailed. You will see what I mean when you receive it tomorrow."

The next day the letter came, and this is what it said: "Dear Pastor, as I listened to your service over the radio this morning and heard your choir sing so beautifully the anthem 'Beautiful Saviour,' once again I became a little girl in a church in a small town listening to that same anthem by the same composer. Wonderful, wonderful memories! Then in memory I became the young mother who five years before had been stricken with polio. I was in an iron lung and a young doctor came into my room and sang for me that same anthem I heard today because he knew I loved it so well."

"And it is a beautiful May day. I am a helpless cripple but I have so much for which to be thankful. I see my two little children playing out in the yard, and I can breathe God's air once more. But I have a heartache. My husband couldn't stand adversity. We are praying that by some miracle you may be able to help him."

To this letter the crippled mother had added this postscript before mailing: "This is the letter I wrote right after the broadcast and yet some people say they don't believe in miracles. I can't tell you how my heart sings and how grateful I am for what you are doing."

TABLE TALK: *Recall instances when prayer has given you an answer. Can you stand alone?*

127

MAY 7

Forever the Same

Thou art nigh, O Lord; and all thy commandments are truth.
Psalm 119:151.

All of us are very familiar with spring house cleaning. You take down the storm windows and put up the screens. The curtains are washed and put up clean and like new. You spend some time taking up to the attic things that are of no use anymore. Perhaps Jimmy needs a new baseball glove because the old one is too small this year. And sister has some dresses she has outgrown.

Lots of things about our lives get outdated and out of style. Constantly we have to look for something new to keep up with the times. But the really important things in our everyday living never change. The values of honesty, kindness, and understanding are forever the same. God's love is just the same today as it was yesterday. It will be unchanged tomorrow for it does not depend on the weather or the calendar.

God's love includes the whole world. He wants everyone to be His own no matter who he is or where he lives. He wants to be our friend and He wants us to talk with Him and get from Him directions for living. He is not attracted by fancy language and high-sounding sentences, but He does listen to the voice of a penitent heart crying for understanding and help.

God is always near. You do not have to kneel at a costly altar to find Him. He lives in your house and works in your office. He is so close to you that He knows your every thought and sees your every action. You cannot hide from Him and He will never hide from you. God's love includes the whole world and yet he is always near to you. Each day take time to pray. Take time to know God better. You will see more clearly what it means to be really living. You will be assured that God's love is forever the same.

TABLE TALK: *Perhaps you need to do a little spring cleaning in your lives. What needs to be done? Discuss.*

MAY 8

The Master Is Interested

And he dreamed; and, behold, a ladder set up on the earth, and the top of it reached to heaven; and, behold, the angels of God ascending and descending on it. Genesis 28:12.

An artist has recently painted a very interesting picture of Christ. He is in a garden with little children. One boy has brought his favorite model airplane to show Him. A little girl is sitting in His lap talking to Him, and she wants to know what those marks are on His friendly hands.

That is the way Christ is. He is interested in the things you enjoy and He talks simply in the language you can understand and appreciate. He is the kind of a friend who wants you to sit down and talk with Him about the things that are on your mind. He tells you how much He loves you and what a thrill it is for Him when you say you love Him, too.

A young lad was telling his father about the things he had learned in church school. It was the story about Jacob's dream, how Jacob had seen the angels climbing the ladder to heaven. The father asked the boy why the angels were climbing up and down the ladder. The little lad stopped to think for a moment and then replied, "Well, I guess maybe they were putting up screens on the windows of heaven."

Maybe the lad had not caught the true meaning of the story, but, nevertheless, his interpretation indicated that his faith was very real. Jesus can be real to you, too. He will come to you each day offering forgiveness, hope, and new courage for living. He is at your side this very moment. His arms are wide open to receive the humble sinner who comes with a heart needing and seeking kindness and compassion. Will you not build your life on this great Rock of Ages?

We need to become as little children, simply trusting and loving God with all our hearts. He is not so much interested in what earthly possessions we may have, but He does want us to give Him our hearts.

TABLE TALK: *Describe some of your favorite Bible pictures. Do you have any on the walls of your home? Maybe you will want to buy one as a special gift for a friend.*

129

MAY 9

Learn to Love Life

And God saw everything that he had made, and, behold, it was very good. Genesis 1:31.

This is the time of the year when the dandelion takes the throne as king. The blossoms are rolled out like a yellow carpet along the pathways of our streets. They twinkle from the lawns and illumine pastures with their brightness.

The dandelion is a sort of "Jekyll and Hyde" of the weed kingdom. Children love it for its blossoms. How frequently a little lad will go from lawn to lawn to pick a bouquet, to bring to Mother as a token of his love for her. And in her heart the value of the gift is greater than if she had received the most beautiful flowers in creation.

Yet the dandelion is an enemy of every good lawn and we do not blame the householder for warring on it with all of his vigor. But the more he tries to conquer, the more overwhelming his job seems to become. Once there was a man who had tried every conceivable method to eliminate the dandelion from his lawn. Then in desperation, and as a last resort, he decided to write the Department of Agriculture and ask their advice. He told them of his problems and asked for suggestions as to what he ought to do. The letter he received in return was brief and simple: "Dear Sir, the only advice we can give is that you learn to love them."

If the dandelion were a rare flower to be pampered in greenhouses and purchased by coin perhaps we would better appreciate its virtues. The trouble with the dandelion is that it is much too common.

Often in life there are things that become too ordinary in your estimation because of their very abundance. How frequently we fail to appreciate the blessings of Almighty God. Each day we receive so much that we are in danger of missing the beauty and the wonder contained in each gift that comes from His hand.

TABLE TALK: *Why is it that things hard to attain are so intriguing? What did Jesus say a believer must do? Is that easy?*

MAY 10

You Reap What You Sow

But grow in the grace and knowledge of our Lord and Saviour Jesus Christ. To him be the glory both now and for ever. Amen.
2 Peter 3:18.

A certain church school teacher, who was trying to show her three-year-old children the greatness of God, used as an illustration how God creates and sustains life.

One Sunday she began to show them how God causes life to grow from a little dried-up brown seed. First she helped the class plant radish seeds in a window box. Then she told them that the very next Sunday they could expect to see the little green shoots beginning to come up out of the soil. She had chosen radishes because she knew how quickly they would grow.

Eagerly the children returned the next Sunday and, sure enough, the plants were already a good inch and a half high. The children exclaimed delightedly over what they had seen. Still, they reasoned, it would take several weeks before there would be any radishes under the plants.

It is an old story, but nevertheless true, that lives are like plants. Sometimes we are in very much of a hurry. We want the fastest results. But lives lived on that principle are not very interesting and sure. They become like radishes, which add a little flavor and interest to a salad, but which have no food value. Other things, of the kind that make the body strong, take much longer to grow.

When we think of the acorn, which takes so many years to mature and become an oak tree, we will become more patient and more willing to abide by the disciplines in living. For even as the acorn we will some day grow into a great tree. Substantial living takes time. So will our lives be substantial if we follow the Master and day by day grow in His grace. Waiting will be worth the while.

"Grow in grace and in the knowledge of our Lord and Saviour Jesus Christ."

TABLE TALK: *Have you ever been impatient for something to take place? What have you learned from the experience?*

131

MAY 11

Let God Be Your Architect

And I will raise me up a faithful priest, that shall do according to that which is in my heart and in my mind: and I will build him a sure house; and he shall walk before mine anointed forever. 1 Samuel 2:35.

An enterprising young man wanted to build a house. Since he had observed many houses under construction, he decided that he would be his own architect. And save money, too!

He proceeded to draw up the plans and when they were all completed, he called in a contractor and told him to proceed to build a house according to the plans. The contractor was carefully instructed not to change the plans in any way. The building was to contain only those things that were specified.

The contractor began to build, and after months had passed, the house was completed. The man came over to see it. He first went through the basement and very proudly looked at the results of what his own mind had created. Then he climbed to the first floor level, and again he was greatly pleased as to the results. He was about to go to the second floor, when he suddenly discovered that he could not find any stairs. "Where is it, John?" he inquired of his contractor friend. "There wasn't any stairway in your plans to the second floor," contractor John answered, "and so I didn't put any in."

Many people make that same tragic mistake as they build their lives. They are so self-sufficient that they think that they can plan their own lives without any help from God. They know how to live an honest and good life without Him and His church. And furthermore, it will save them some cost if they do not have to be obligated to Him as the architect of their life.

But a rude awakening will always come. Some time or other, we will need a stairway to the upper floor, and then we will discover that we are bound to the things of earth.

TABLE TALK: *Recall times when you have said, "I'm old enough to take care of myself. I don't need anyone to run my life for me." We are never able to build our houses of life alone. We must always consult the divine architect who supplies the perfect blueprint.*

MAY 12

A Heritage of Love

Honor thy father and thy mother, that thy days may be long in the land which the Lord thy God giveth thee. Exodus 20:12.

"Children obey your parents, for this is right." St. Paul writes these words in his letter to the Ephesians. It is appropriate that we think about them especially this month when we celebrate both National Family Week and Mother's Day.

We have something for which to thank God, if we have parents who are God-fearing. Those of us who are older look back gratefully to mothers and fathers who gave us the greatest thing in the world when they set our feet on the pathway that leads to God. Perhaps they are not able to leave us much of a material heritage, but greater than all things of the world is the faith which they have taught us, which enables us to live with a song in our hearts today.

In one of his letters to Timothy, St. Paul calls attention to the fact that both Timothy's mother, whose name was Eunice, and his grandmother, whose name was Lois, were women of great faith. They did much to account for the wonderful faith which Timothy had as a grown man. The seeds planted in early life are more important than we can ever determine.

A wonderful sentiment appears on a sundial in the Ulriksdahl Castle grounds in Sweden. Translated into English the inscription reads: "The sun leads me, and I lead you." I think that is a wonderful statement of the relationship of Christian parents to their children. The Lord leads our parents, and they in turn lead us. That is what gives meaning to Paul's words: "Children obey your parents, for this is right." It is important to both parents and children for it means first of all that parents must be obedient to God, and that if directed by His wisdom, they are capable of guiding the lives of their children until they are grown into higher wisdom and deeper understanding and are able to make decisions concerning themselves and God.

TABLE TALK: *What responsibility do the parents have in seeking the obedience of their children?*

MAY 13

Picture Windows

Blessed are the pure in heart: for they shall see God.
Matthew 5:8.

Picture windows have always fascinated me. Especially when they look out upon some view the like of which only the Master Architect could create. How tragic it is that so many people shut themselves off from the beauty which surrounds them!

I think in particular of a picture window found in a chapel in northern Minnesota. In fact the whole front of this place of worship is of glass and looks out over a beautiful lake to a wooded hill on the other side. No combination of stained glass in all the world could compare with the natural beauty which you see here.

Some homes have windows which frame unique and interesting sights. And then, quite often, I go into houses that seem all boxed in and I say to myself, "How different the atmosphere would be if only they had put a picture window into this house to let the beauty of God shine in." Everyone of us can have in our soul a picture window that looks up to God. No matter how complex or troublesome life may become, the soul can still be at peace and quiet, if nothing is allowed to block the soul's vision of God.

Sometimes picture windows get dirty, and the beauty of the view is marred if they are not constantly kept clean. Scripture reminds us concerning the picture window of the soul: "Blessed are the pure in heart: for they shall see God." Each day we should turn to God in penitence and seek the forgiveness of our sins. When we honestly admit our shortcomings and the impossibility of living without being in partnership with Him, we will receive His loving forgiveness, and will find help to keep clean the picture window of the soul which looks to Him and constantly rediscovers in Him a God who so loved us that He gave His only begotten Son to save us.

TABLE TALK: *What inspiration is there in a beautiful sight from a window in your home? Discuss what you could do to make a spot at your home even more picturesque. Could you, for example, plant a spring flower garden?*

MAY 14

Live and Let Live

For ye, brethren, were called for freedom; only use not your freedom for an occasion to the flesh, but through love be servants one to another. Galatians 5:13.

One day I observed the delightful action of some little English sparrows. These birds, you know, are not always among the most beloved, for they can become quite quarrelsome at times. But I had a good example of what can happen in sparrow life.

One little bird had found himself a prize in a piece of bread almost one-fourth his own size. He was trying to get away from his fellow birds so that he could enjoy his feast alone. However, there were two other birds questioning his right to such enjoyment. One of them flew at him sharply and tried to get the piece away from him. The other hopped around quietly on the ground watching what was going on and very obviously wanting to join in the fun. Finally the sparrow with the crust drove off his sparring partner. Then the action which delighted me took place. He took his crust and went over to the shy little bird who had been watching and the two of them together really had a feast. Soon there was not even a crumb to mark the spot.

This bird action teaches us quite a lesson. When someone comes at you trying to get something from you by force it makes you feel like running so far away that you will never have to share it, but when someone comes quietly with an appeal in his eye not forcing you to share but indicating a need, it is much more enjoyable to go to him and say, "I want you to have some with me."

Let us never assume the attitude that the world owes us a living and that we will fight for it to get it. Our lives will be more richly blessed and we will receive far greater rewards if we are satisfied with what we have and if we seek to share with others and serve them, rather than just having others serve us.

TABLE TALK: *What do we as a family owe the world? What makes a "big bully" fight for what he wants?*

135

MAY 15

We Are All on a Journey

For we are strangers before thee, and sojourners, as all our fathers were: our days on the earth are as a shadow, and there is no abiding. 1 Chronicles 29:15.

Jesus came that our joy might be made full, and apart from Him there can be no joyful living. How thrilling are the experiences of those who have discovered what the Master is able to do for a life. It leads them to spend their days in a non-ending hymn of praise for all that has been given to them.

For example, how grateful we should be to live in the assurance that there is no death! How fearful are those who do not share this faith with us. They live in constant worry as they anticipate the inevitable. So often even Christians begin to doubt and wonder when they fail to take God at His Word.

A minister tells of a boyhood memory. He says, "When I was a young lad I was brought up in a Christian home, went to Sunday school and church regularly, and believed the things I was taught. One day my father died, and I will never forget my experience at the funeral service. The minister preached a very beautiful sermon about heaven as our true home. He said that we could always live joyfully and would never have to be afraid because at death we simply took the hand of Jesus and went to our heavenly home. I could not understand why as he continued, all the people were crying. I felt good inside knowing that my father had been a Christian man, that he loved God, and that now he had received his reward. When it came my time to go up to the casket I actually smiled and I suppose people thought I was peculiar. But what I saw there was not my father at all. It was simply the house in which he had lived. For even as a boy my father was to me that dear soul who loved me and did so much for me, and now he was living with God in heaven."

Day by day we need to remind ourselves that through the course of this life we are merely on a journey, and the closer we live to God the less we have to fear.

TABLE TALK: *Mention times when you have been away from home for a long while, and then came the day when you were going to return. How did you feel?*

MAY 16

All Are Precious to God

And why beholdest thou the mote that is in thy brother's eye, but considerest not the beam that is in thine own eye.

Matthew 7:3.

One day I had become especially discouraged because of our human weaknesses. All I had heard was arguing and dissension among people because of the difference of opinion among them. Some seemed to claim that their viewpoint was the only way and if a person did not believe exactly that way there was no hope for them.

As I was reviewing the day's happenings the time was getting toward sunset and the birds seemed to be especially songful that night. Soon I became quiet enough within myself to listen to what they were trying to tell me. All at once I realized that there were many different notes in that medley of song. But in spite of all the differences a rhythm was so noticeable that you would have thought the director of the birds' chorus had set up a metronome for them to follow. That rhythm at this moment was the voice of God talking to me, "Now I have made all kinds of birds. No two of them are alike. Yet each one of them has a place in the world. At times they sing together and make perfect harmony of rhythm. At other times they each go their own way. But I have created them all."

It is the same with human beings. We may belong to different churches, we may have differences of opinion, the color of our skin may not be the same, but we are all created in the image of Almighty God and belong to Him.

This would be a much better world if each one of us could see God at the center and Christ as our Saviour. That is the central harmony and enough to unite us, in spite of our individual differences. Let us respect another's opinion without compromising the convictions which we have in our own heart. Let us persuade by love and by living rather than by heated words and argument. And when men differ with us let us remember that each one has the right to follow his own conscience.

TABLE TALK: *Looking back at some argument in which you took part, can you see how each side was right?*

137

MAY 17

Do You Use What You Have?

Only fear the Lord, and serve him in truth with all your heart; for consider how great things he hath done for you.
1 Samuel 12:24.

It seems that some people have so little and yet do so much for God. Others have so many talents and abilities and yet they seem to be of such insignificant help in the kingdom work. What a great inspiration they are who spend long hours working for the church and in helping others in some way or other, always doing it with such a willing and cheerful spirit. We should remember that no matter how few or how many talents God has given us there is always something for each one of us to do.

No doubt you have heard that great pianist Alex Templeton. He plays the most difficult and beautiful compositions. And yet he can not see the notes on the musical score or the keys on the piano. One of his favorite numbers is a composition by Beethoven, and it is quite amazing to realize that this blind pianist is playing a sonata written by a deaf composer.

We should think about instances like this when we are tempted to excuse ourselves from some task at hand. There is so much you can do if you only set your strength and willingness to do it. Perhaps there are handicaps or difficulties which stand in the way, but if you lose yourself in the service of the Master you will be amazed at the wonderful things you can accomplish.

Sometimes we are so concerned about whether or not God still performs physical miracles today, like healing the blind and making the lame walk. Of more importance is the fact that He continues to perform miracles of the soul. He takes a weary and discouraged heart and gives it new spirit and strength; and He saves a wandering prodigal from the destruction of a sinful world. These are the greatest victories of all, the saving of lives for all eternity. God can give you that power to conquer. There is no better way than to live first for the Master.

TABLE TALK: *Are you using all your talents for the Master? Discuss what more you can do.*

The Water of Life

But whosoever drinketh of the water that I shall give him shall never thirst; but the water that I shall give him shall be in him a well of water springing up into everlasting life. John 4:14.

Someone has told the story about his own boyhood days on the farm. Every day he and his father went out into the fields to work. Many times the days were hard and long, especially in the hot sun. But they always knew that in the corner of the field was a clear cold spring where they could get a refreshing drink of water.

Some years later the young man went back to his old farm home, where another family was then living. They still planted and harvested the same fields but they always carried a jug of water with them. When they became thirsty they had to be satisfied with the warm water from the jug. They did not know that very close at hand was a spring still filled with clear cold water.

The fountain of living waters still flows from the love of God. But so many people just pass it by. The promise which Christ made as He spoke to the Samaritan woman at Jacob's well still holds today. "Whosoever drinketh of the water that I shall give him shall never thirst, but the water I shall give him shall be in him a well springing up into everlasting life."

The shouting of the world is loud. It sets before you a table of apparent success and fame. The choice is yours. You can choose the road of defeat or you can travel side by side with the Master and be led to eternal victory. Christ withstood the temptations and became triumphant. With His strength, so can you.

Do not let the things of the world crowd out God's Spirit, which can supply all your needs and give nourishment through the deserts of despair and the valleys of tribulation. Drink of the spiritual water and you will receive eternal nourishment.

TABLE TALK: *Discuss and name the temptations of the world which try to coax you away from the spiritual realm.*

MAY 19

You Can Make a Difference

Make a joyful noise unto God, all the earth: sing forth the glory of his name: make his praise glorious. Psalm 66:1-2.

Have you ever heard a choir engaged in part rehearsals in various rooms of a building? The sopranos are located in one place, the altos in another, and the basses and tenors somewhere separated from each other. You hear the vocalizing coming from all these several places. That goes on for some time. Then, later in the evening, perhaps all the singers assemble in one large room to make the choir. Each section has its own part to sing, but now it is sung in harmony, in company with all the other parts.

Life is like this kind of choral rendering. Each of us is endowed with some gifts or talents. Fortunately for this world, there is a wonderful variety in what people are capable of doing. It is another one of the master strokes of the divine Creator that He should make us different from one another. What a world of monotony it would be if we should all have to sing the same part and the same note! Nor can we all be soloists. Most of us are placed in a setting where our parts do not stand out particularly. It is our best service to lose ourselves in the whole program of Christ, always conscious of the fact that we are contributing to the total song. If we sing off pitch, even though our part seems trivial, it is going to make a difference. It may be the influence that causes someone next to us to get off pitch, too. And the whole anthem may be done in an inferior way because we have not done the very best we could in our place.

Each of us has a part to play in the world and in the church. We may sing our roles in obscure places. But God knows how important it is for each soul to do his part with a sense of responsibility.

TABLE TALK: *Have you ever said to yourself, "Why should I bother? My little bit won't matter"? Have you heard of battles won or lost because of the courage or treachery of one man? What lesson does this teach?*

140

MAY 20

The Song of the Lark

Therefore by their fruits ye shall know them. Matthew 7:20.

Perhaps at some time or another you have seen that famous painting by Jules Breton called "The Song of the Lark." The amazing thing about the picture is that as you ponder over it for a moment you discover that a lark is not even in the painting. There is a peasant girl walking to the field for a hard day's work. And suddenly she hears the song of a bird. The artist has captured this young girl's expression as for a moment everything is glorified by the song of the lark which she hears.

If you stop to hear the voices that surround you, you find that many people and places are shouting for you to listen to the story which they have to tell. The voice of the world speaks about the great success that can be yours if you will only serve the gods of wealth and fame. The voice of power tells you how strong you can become by wielding the sword of discipline and command. But high above all of these, God speaks in kind and gentle words telling you of the victorious soul and the peaceful heart which can be yours if you will only follow Him and share His conquering love.

You must make the choice. Think for just a moment about those two young men who traveled the busy highways together many years ago. One was called Judas, the other Jesus. They both set out in life with a great purpose and each of them died a horrible death. One took his own life, the other was killed by a thoughtless crowd. One failed, the other was triumphant.

Sometime or other Judas must have shown real promise or Christ would not have chosen him to be one of the disciples. But somewhere along the line he listened to the voices of the world. He traded a faithful heart for worldly gain. When he discovered his mistake he threw away his thirty pieces of silver. "Whatsoever a man soweth that will he also reap."

TABLE TALK: *Think of figures in history who have heard a heavenly voice and others who have answered the worldly call. What effect did they have on others, that is, what did they reap?*

141

MAY 21

Concentrate on the Positive

To the end that my glory may sing praise to thee, and not be silent, O Lord my God, I will give thanks unto thee for ever.
Psalm 30:12.

One day the telephone rang and I was informed that a young lady in my congregation was again a patient in one of our city hospitals. Whenever you feel like complaining about how hard life has been for you, I wish you would think of this young girl. This was her thirty-fifth visit to the hospital and this time she was to stay there for a period of seven weeks.

As I ministered to this valiant soul through the days that followed I spoke to her frequently about her Christian faith. I wondered how she could maintain her spiritual glow in the midst of all of her physical difficulties I talked to her about her philosophy of life and this is what she told me: "I forget my sickness as soon as it is over and I remember only the times that I am well."

How much more happy all of us would be if we would only learn the secret of forgetting our troubles as soon as they have passed and remember only the happy and joyful moments in life! So often people ruin their lives because they constantly call to remembrance something bad that has happened to them. As a result their every day is clouded. They have not learned with Paul to forget the things that are behind.

Said this young girl in the hospital, "I have so much for which to be thankful. Just think, I can turn to God and pray and know that He will always hear me. If it hadn't been for His everlasting arms surrounding me always, I know that I could never have made it this far. And really there isn't anything to worry about, is there, Pastor? For at the end of the trail God will still be with me."

I remember hearing a visitor whisper as she left that hospital room: "If that is what Christ does to a person I want to be a Christian, too!"

TABLE TALK: *Take a mental inventory of all your blessings and then compare them with the little discomforts in life. Do not your blessings far outweigh your hardships?*

MAY 22

Keep Growing

For sin shall not have dominion over you: for ye are not·under the law, but under grace. Romans 6:14.

This is the time of the year when you go out into the garden and begin to plant the summer flowers. All winter the tiny seeds have been lifeless, but when you put them in the ground, the sun and rain quicken them and they start to grow. In a few weeks, they will burst out into beautiful blossoms.

Once there was a little boy who begged his father to let him plant his own garden in the back yard. His dad gave him some seeds and allowed him to plant them in his own little plot. In a few days the lad was back in his garden digging up the seeds to find out how they were growing. And much to his discouragement, they had not grown at all.

There are many people who seem to feel the same way about their Christian living. At some moment they discover the presence of God in their lives and they expect the whole process of sanctification to take place in the flashing of a moment.

Just as it will take time for those tiny seeds to sprout and to flower, so it takes time to grow into close fellowship with God. Even the most devoted soul continues to grow in understanding and love of God as long as he lives.

As you and the Master begin working and planning together, you will soon discover that your life grows richer every day. As His spirit fills your heart and soul, and as God continues to shower His love and to fulfill His promises, living becomes more glorious.

Life is to be found in the things you trust and believe in, the values you have and the goals you set. Make them worth while!

Once you have set your goal, strive for it patiently, working diligently to attain full growth. The process may seem slow, and the efforts tedious, but the result will be worth it all. Keep planning, keep growing!

TABLE TALK: *What are some of your earthly goals? What are your plans for obtaining them?*

143

MAY 23

The Spirit of Real Giving

For I have given you an example, that ye also should do as I have done to you. John 13:15.

Real giving is not the motion of handing over material things from one person to another. You do not really give unless something of your inner being, something of your very life, accompanies the material gift. A part of yourself in the form of love must go with it or it is meaningless.

True generosity is something of the spirit. Here is a person who buys lavish gifts for her family and friends on special days. In fact, the recipients are rather embarrassed to accept so much from her. Some of them are in no position to show their appreciation in any comparable way. But in spite of all this apparent generosity, this woman is ruthless in her treatment of people in everyday affairs. She is the first to criticize and cares not how much she might hurt some individual by her unbridled tongue. Apparently she has never cultivated an appreciation of the deeper needs of her friends and associates.

Here is another woman, living in modest circumstances. She and her husband have a family of four fine young children. This mother does her Christmas shopping months in advance of holiday time because she must take advantage of every sale and bargain in order to make ends meet. The material giving on the part of this woman is meager. Yet she is one of the most generous souls God ever created. She sits down at the telephone in the middle of her busy days and dials the number of someone whom she knows has had a disappointment, or someone who is lonely, or someone who needs some encouragement. She has a beautiful and rare richness of soul, able to sense what people really need in their innermost living, and they love her. The secret of it all, of course, is that she is well acquainted with the One who first gave His life for her. Because He walks with her each day, her life is a constant demonstration of real giving.

Christ asks the eternal question: "This have I done for thee; what will thou do for Me?"

TABLE TALK: *We must continually seek to do more for others. Discuss what you each can do for someone you know.*

MAY 24

Doing What You Can

For God is not unrighteous to forget your work and the love which ye showed toward his name, in that ye ministered unto the saints. Hebrew 6:10.

Being a Christian is not like harvesting a crop from a field and then letting it lie uncultivated and wasted. We must plant new seeds and nurture the ground so that it will produce even better crops in the future. Our Christian lives must not become stagnant or wasted. We must continue to grow in the knowledge of Christ and His great works. We must read the Bible with understanding minds and hearts seeking to discover more of God's will. We must become witnesses for Christ in all that we do and say. Not only will our spiritual growth bring our hearts greater peace and harmony but also our lives will shine more brightly and others will be influenced by our devotion to Christ.

A man once advertised in a newspaper for a gardener. He received a letter that read like this: "John Smith is an excellent gardener. He can manage flowers and shrubs to perfection and make the slightest patch of green appear glorious to look at. He has a thorough knowledge of plants and trees and can make them grow under the most severe conditions. He can arrange flowers into beautiful bouquets and can suggest many new ways of successful gardening." These qualifications seemed to please the potential employer. When he turned the letter over he found these concluding words: "But he won't."

There is much that each one of us can do by the grace of God to help win others to the way of Christ and to make this a more beautiful world. But we must do more than think about it and write about it. We have the possibilities, but we must put them to work. There is so much to be done if we will only let the vision of the need lead us on. The command is to begin today, for the night may come when no man can work.

God will bless the worker who will do what he can.

TABLE TALK: *Do you recall knowing persons who had extraordinary talents, but refused to share them? Discuss how you would convince John Smith to use his abilities in God's kingdom.*

145

A Life Is Like a Garden

In the beginning God created the heavens and the earth.
Genesis 1:1.

Our souls are often likened to gardens. We know how quickly weeds make their way in among the flowers and vegetables. We have to be out with pruning hoe and fork to pull them out before they crowd out the plants we want to keep. In the garden of our souls, weeds such as dishonesty, unkindness, and meanness make even faster headway unless each day we pull them out by the roots. Gardens within us require work, too. We must learn the right methods by listening to the Master as He speaks to us through His Word. He is the companion willing to help us. With His power we seek to make our lives more beautiful.

We could not have a garden with greenery and color without watering it. We gain new life for our souls as we speak to God in prayer and as we go to His church to learn more about Him. What would be the use of having a garden if we did not walk in it and enjoy it? You remember how, in the Garden of Eden, Adam and Eve heard the voice of God while walking in the cool of the day. Even He enjoyed walking in the garden. In our soul gardens, we need to take time to commune with our Lord and Master. What joy and refreshment that can bring!

When you go into a beautiful garden, does not a sense of wonder come into your soul? How marvelous it is to have a God who could create all this beauty! Of course, we have had the privilege of helping Him to cultivate it, but without Him we could have done nothing.

If we walk in the garden of our soul, we cannot help but experience an even greater wonder. How thrilling it is to have a God who cares enough to save us from our sins through Jesus Christ our Lord. The greatest wonder of all is that we may be His and that He is ours forever.

Our life is like a garden. We must take care of it.

TABLE TALK: *Some of the weeds in our soul's garden are dishonesty, unkindness, meanness. How can we be rid of them?*

The Victor's Crown

We are ambassadors therefore on behalf of Christ, as though God were entreating by us: we beseech you on behalf of Christ, be ye reconciled to God. 2 Corinthians 5:20.

It is not enough merely to keep the lamp of your own life lighted. You must take that spirit of godliness and touch the spirit of others around you.

Many years ago Christ chose twelve men as special ambassadors of God's Word. They went out into the streets telling the people of their time the glorious news of salvation. They moved from one soul to another pointing to each the way of victorious living and winning both young and old into the Master's flock.

The old legends tell us how hundreds of years ago the young men of Rome would meet together to test their strength and skill. Each year they would have a race across many miles of the countryside. Every runner was given a torch to carry. The winner not only had to cross the finishing line first but also his torch had to be burning.

It is not enough just to run the race of life and to cross the finishing line. The torch of your soul must still be burning. God gives you a period of years to live upon this earth and yours is the task to see that that life is filled with good deeds. This will require that you live close to Him, with a heart of undying devotion.

Remember that for the Christian the victor's crown is greater than all the silver and gold in the world. The winner's reward is an eternity spent in God's house meeting the Master face to face and living in the riches of God's love.

Many who have lived before testify to the faith we can have in our God. They have left their mark behind them. At every turn of the road we see a light that has been set aglow by consecrated Christian soldiers of the past. From such eternal flames we take the courage for our own lives and with the light from above we carry on with the hope that our footsteps will mark a better way for those who follow after us.

TABLE TALK: *If your light is set aglow, you will want to be a present-day ambassador. What can you do?*

MAY 27

A Child of the King

That, being justified by his grace, we might be made heirs according to the hope of eternal life. Titus 3:7.

Any earthly king has a magnificent palace in which to live. He is usually surrounded by royalty. Common people do not have a chance to see him very often, perhaps never to entertain him in their homes.

How different with the King of kings! You cannot excuse yourself for not having Him as guest by saying that your house is not adequate to entertain Him. For He seeks not the splendor of a building made with hands. His throne is the human heart. Each soul is valuable in His sight. No matter how humble a person may be, it can be an adequate place for Him to make His abode.

The story is told of a woman who at one time had great wealth, but also a tremendous faith. She lost her money, but fortunately she kept those riches which are not perishable. In fact, this woman became so poor that she spent the last days of her life at a charity home not far from where she had once lived in great splendor.

Her pastor would frequently come to visit her for she was an inspiration in his ministry. Then one day when she sensed that her earthly journey would soon be coming to an end, she turned to him and said, "Pastor, I have one request to make. When I am gone I would like to have you conduct the memorial service and I want you to be sure to have this song as a part of the service: "I Am a Child of the King."

When she had entered into the great beyond, her pastor carried out her wishes. He says he can never forget the inspiration of that moment, when in a most simple setting, a plain box casket was the earthly resting place of this queenly Christian woman. A rich contralto voice sang, "My father is rich in houses and lands; He holds the wealth of the world in His hands. I am the child of a King."

You, too, have the privilege of becoming a joint heir of God!

TABLE TALK: *Discuss the pomp and ceremony attending earthly kings. What have they often failed to realize?*

MAY 28

God Is Still Creating

And I will walk among you, and will be your God, and ye shall be my people. Leviticus 26:12.

One day there came to my office a young woman who appeared to be very intelligent. To her credit it must be said she was a seeker. She had some kind of faith in God, but she could not come to the conviction that He was in the world today. She believed that He had stood at the beginning of time possibly to wind it up as a clock and then let it run its own course.

I turned to her and said, "Do you mean to tell me that God is not creating today? Think of the severe winter that we had, and now it is spring with green grass once more, and buds upon the trees, and flowers that bloom. Who is causing this to happen? Man? Or is it the power of God creating today even as He created the world centuries ago?"

A certain man awakened in the morning to express his exuberance over the coming of spring. As he looked out of the window he exclaimed in delight, "Lois, it looks as if it had been raining green paint during the night." Miraculously, spring had come.

I am sure that we have all thrilled to see the world take on its summer colors again. The grass is such a vivid green, and the buds on the trees just cannot wait to burst into bloom. The heavenly Painter, who mixed all the colors of the rainbow, busily dips His brushes to give another beautiful summer world in which we may live.

The miracle of spring comes in such regularity that we often forget to recognize the hand of the Almighty which causes it. No, creation did not end at the beginning of what we call this world. It is a process which continues under the loving hand of God. For ours is a heavenly Father who is just as present with us now as He was in the beginning when He called man into being and made him after His own likeness.

TABLE TALK: *Talk about various miracles in nature that take place about us every day, but which we so often fail to recognize.*

MAY 29

Making the Most Out of Life

Joseph is a fruitful bough, a fruitful bough by a fountain; his branches run over the wall. Genesis 49:22.

In this very interesting verse we find a magnificent character analysis of man. Joseph was fruitful. He was producing that for which his life was intended. He was drawing his strength from a fountain. That is a significant factor in the effectiveness of his life. His branches ran over the wall, which indicates that they extended beyond what could have been their limited confine.

Now in the springtime we see many fruit trees at the height of their glory, so full of blossoms that each one looks as if it were a mammoth bouquet. We think forward to harvest time in August and September. Will all these promises of fruit grow into their intended ripeness? If there should not be enough moisture, if drought should come, has the tree anything to depend on for sustenance? Joseph's life had resources. He drew nourishment from a fountain which had deep wells. Therefore, even if the seasonal rains were meager, he still had a source of strength. For it was God who was this power in Joseph's life. When difficult circumstances came, he still had the promise of God that He would never forsake him.

How about your life? Youth holds so many promises. It is springtime with blossoms giving off rich fragrance. There is an enthusiasm and a rich potential in the talents which God has planted in each person.

All do not have the same gift, just as all trees do not bear the same kind of fruit. But each of us has something to do and we will find our greatest joy in living if we catch the impormost of them. The secret of doing so is to dedicate our gifts to the highest purpose. That is to secure the future. God will bless and give strength to those who tap His resources of power in their lives.

TABLE TALK: *Think of various members of the church. Point out how they use their talents to the glory of God.*

Those Who Know the Secret

When they saw the star, they rejoiced with exceeding great joy. Matthew 2:10.

A father was once attempting to teach his boy how to plow a straight furrow. Finally he turned to him and said, "Son, if you want to plow a straight line you must not rivet your attention on the ground where you are working. Pick out some object across the field, something that is immovable like a tree or a big rock. Keep watching that goal, and plow right toward it."

There are too many "ground gazers" in the world today. With their eyes focused on the things of the earth they never know what abundant living really is. They miss the beauty which is all about them because they never look up. Too attached do they become to the things of the world. And eventually their lives become crooked and warped, without meaning or purpose.

There are others whom we might call "pleasure pursuers." They are not interested in the narrow way with all of its restrictions. They forget that to attain great living that is the only way they can follow, so they become attracted by the forces about them. They are influenced and persuaded to commit one sin after another, and finally they discover they are empty handed. They have accumulated no real values. And the pleasures which they thought they possessed have vanished. There is only one thing left now, a deep heart hunger and a vacuum of the soul which cannot be filled by anything except the righteousness of God.

Then there are those who know the secret. We might call them the "star gazers." They are not just idle dreamers, but fix their vision upon something that is constant. They build toward an immovable object. They choose the way of the cross. For great as its disciplines are, greater still is the joy of the journey and the heaven which is ahead. And even though the night should become dark, a light shines through the gloom, and that light keeps leading them on.

TABLE TALK: *What would you say to the "ground gazers" and the "pleasure pursuers" in order to make them "star-gazers"?*

MAY 31

Strength from Living Waters

And he shall be like a tree planted by the streams of water, that bringeth forth its fruit in its season; whose leaf also shall not wither; and whatsoever he doeth shall prosper. Psalm 1:3.

Have you ever noticed the trees in all of their spring-green finery arching overhead as you drive down a beautiful avenue? The branches on one side of the street meet those from the opposite side. At that place they form a pointed arch. That sight suggests cathedral windows. The street is the base suggesting the window sills. What a beautiful visual reminder it is of the glory of God which is all about us.

Of all the trees that line the avenue, the tall, stately elm seems to make the most graceful arch. As we admire the beauty and strength of this tree we pause to consider what is their source. We arrive at one major conclusion. The secret of the elm is that it sinks its roots deep into the earth.

One of the obvious benefits is that it reaches into the hidden reservoirs far below the surface of the ground. Even if drought comes it can sustain itself and grow while other vegetation which has only surface rooting will shrivel and die. In seeking a constant source of nourishment, this tree has sunk its roots deep into the soil. Therefore it grows both tall and strong. With its roots deep, it is able to brace itself and has a firm anchorage when the strong winds descend upon it.

The story of the tree is very obviously a parable of our human lives. Some people are satisfied to live only on the surface. They are easily disturbed when the conditions of life become severe. Their roots are not sunk deep, and they are therefore weak in the face of trouble. But there are also human souls who have probed deep into God's Word and have learned to keep looking upward to the heavens to gain the true perspective of things. God helps us to draw strength from living waters. With our roots sunk deep, we have firm anchorage against the storms.

TABLE TALK: *Compare the lives of people you know who are fearful, anxious, and insecure with those who are radiantly happy, and confident. Which would you say have surface roots, and which have hidden reservoirs in God?*

JUNE 1

Our Horizons Can Widen

I will not fail thee, nor forsake thee. Be strong and of a good courage. Joshua 1:5-6.

June is commencement time when speakers all over the country give advice to the young graduates as they are about to step out into a new role in life.

A newspaper columnist, sitting at his typewriter preparing his annual commencement address, was confronted by a graduate of an earlier year, who said to him, "Why don't you give some good advice to graduates who have been out six months or a year? No one ever thinks of them and their troubles, such as the problems of adjusting their ideals to the conditions of the market place." The newspaper philosopher pondered for a few moments on what he had just heard. Then he put a new sheet of paper into his typewriter and proceeded to write some mighty good advice to the graduate of yesteryear.

Among other things he pointed out that perhaps the world does not hold the rosy hue it did when we left school. Probably our job seems small and unimportant. Maybe we yearn for a larger role. Then he shares with us this bit of truth: "Remember you are still in the shake-down crews. An attorney isn't usually elevated to the United States Supreme Court twelve months after he leaves law school nor does the Navy turn over its battleships to Annapolis graduates of the year before. Getting ahead in life is still a matter of painfully climbing steps, in a series of high jumps. It takes a lot of years and bruises to translate the dreams you had in school years into reality."

This is a day when too many of our dreams have been shattered. Too many of us have given up hope. Too few of us have dared to keep on dreaming. But only when we lose faith in God need we give up in despair. If we believe and trust in Him, every day can be one of victory. For He can take an apparent defeat and make of it an opportunity for even greater service. Living with Him, we are forever widening our horizons.

TABLE TALK: *Perhaps you can think of advice which would be helpful to a student starting school, or beginning a job, which could be a "motto" of life for him. All make suggestions.*

JUNE 2

Light for the Way

Thy word is a lamp unto my feet, and light unto my path.
Psalm 119:105.

In a small rural community there lived a lad who was not able
to see as well as those with whom he played. As he started to
go to school, he kept along with his grades because his class-
mates would help him with his studies. A few weeks before he
was to graduate from high school, he suddenly became totally
blind. He was brought to the best eye doctors in the nearby
city and was told that he would never be able to see again. He
went back to school, took his examinations orally, and ranked
as one of the highest in the class.

Quite dramatic was commencement night when some forty
seniors entered the auditorium, marching in single file to the
strains of a familiar processional. The last two seniors came
in together. One was wearing dark glasses. He was the blind
boy being led by a classmate. He took his place upon the plat-
form and listened to the commencement address. When his turn
came to receive his diploma, a tremendous ovation greeted him.
It was a community tribute to the courageous spirit which had
been his, and which had enabled him to complete his high school
education in spite of his handicap.

A visiting clergyman went up to him after the exercises and
shook his hand, hardly knowing what to say. The blind boy
seemed to sense his predicament and said, "You don't have to
worry about me. I have enough faith in God to know that He
has some work for me to do in life. I am not complaining about
my fate for I know that God will answer my prayer that I may
continue to have strength for the tasks He leads me to."

So often we complain because of very insignificant happenings.
Whenever you are tempted to go forth into any day feeling
sorry for yourself, think of the blind boy who was led by God
each day into more expanding horizons.

TABLE TALK: *Stop and think how many times you have
grumbled or complained over trifles. Think how fortunate you
are compared to others. Resolve to make the most of the gifts
God has given you.*

JUNE 3

Divine Transformation

For in him we live, and move, and have our being; as certain even of your own poets have said, For we are also his offspring.
Acts 17:28.

Some people were looking, one day, at a summer camp that was all overgrown with weeds. It had not been used for several years and in some places, as they attempted to walk through the grounds, they found the weeds shoulder high. The place was on a beautiful inland lake in the glorious North of our country. These people were interested in the location, but they stood there wondering whether it could possibly be transformed into anything of beauty. It was so ugly now as it stood there untended. But suddenly one of the party caught a vision of what it could become. He went to the owner and paid the price.

That was just the beginning. Not by some miracle was the transformation to take place. There was hard work to do. The weeds were all cut down. The grass was mowed. The cabins were painted. One would never have known that it was the same place. Everything about it seemed to have taken on new beauty.

Oftentimes when we have allowed the weeds of sin and defeat to grow in our lives, we wonder whether there is any chance that our lives can ever become beautiful again. It is then we should remember that there is One who has paid the purchase price in our behalf. But in a sense that is just the beginning. The Atonement has made possible our personal salvation. If we choose to accept the new life in Christ a long process follows that requires sacrifice indeed, but that also gives glorious returns. The closer we live to Christ and the more earnestly we seek after holiness, the more glorious will our life become. We should add something, by the grace of God, to our life each day. Life becomes increasingly glorious the longer it continues, if it is lived in partnership with Him!

TABLE TALK: *Discuss how you appreciate something which you have worked on and improved. Think how you can daily improve your living, too.*

JUNE 4

On Being a Friend to Man

A friend loveth at all times; and a brother is born for adversity.
Proverbs 17:17.

No doubt you have often heard this suggestion: "If you want to have friends, be one." Apparently God does not intend that all of us shall be rich or powerful or great, but it is His intention that we shall all have friends.

So often we get lonesome and downhearted, but the smile of a single friend can change the complexion of the whole world for us. One great author has said that it is friendship that makes the flowers seem so beautiful and makes the sunshine so bright even on a cloudy day. It would be difficult to go through even a day without a friendly "hello" or a neighborly chat. Those are the little gems that brighten up the hours and help make life rich and meaningful.

Perhaps today you will have the chance to make a new friend. And if you do, you will add another bit of happiness to life. There is a lot of glory in lending a helping hand or in passing along a kind smile. But the real joy of friendship is in knowing that someone believes in you and is willing to share his happiness as well as his problems.

The greatest friend of all stands at the door of your heart anxiously waiting for you to welcome Him. He is willing to share the precious things of His kingdom with you, and you just cannot afford to pass them by. The Master can supply you with riches and contentment and prosperity, the riches of undying love, the contentment of a faithful heart, and the prosperity of a soul that will live on forever. Those are the things that cannot be bought in a store or discovered at even the most exclusive shop. There is no price tag on this kind of happiness. All you have to do is to take the friendship that Christ offers you. God's love can be sunshine today. You never have to be alone or friendless as long as you can be sure of His presence. Let the stars at night assure you that God's friendship is eternal.

TABLE TALK: *How long has it been since you have made friends with someone? Are there new members in your church you could befriend? Make plans to do this.*

JUNE 5

It Can Happen to You

Prepare to meet thy God, O Israel. Amos 4:12.

It was a cold, wintry evening. A minister was busy in his study. The telephone rang and on the other end was the voice of a prominent businessman in town. They talked for a few moments, and then the man said, "What I really called about, Pastor, was to ask you where in the Bible are the words: 'Prepare to meet thy God.' I heard someone preach a sermon on that text about forty years ago and I was just sitting here thinking about it know."

As each day you answer the call to serve God, never forget the influence you may have. It may take many years to show itself in the lives of others. But inevitably it will be known.

There was once a young woman who had what everyone called a radiant personality. She was always happy and congenial and had a kind word for everyone she met. Someone explained her secret of life in this way, "She heard about a beautiful castle that was built on a high hill. All the people who lived near by could tell what was going on there by the number of lights which were burning. When an important guest was being entertained, the castle was all aglow with brilliant lamps which lighted the countryside all around. I think this young woman's personality is so radiant because she is always entertaining the Master as a royal guest."

Sunshine and happiness is what life can become if Christ is always the unseen Guest in the temple of your heart. Then there will be no darkness for you but what a new radiance will come into your being! Christ can change your life from defeat into victory. This is no idle dream. It has happened to countless souls through many centuries and it can happen to you.

TABLE TALK: *Can you think of a sermon, or even an illustration in a sermon, which has had an influence in your life? Tell about it.*

JUNE 6

Now Is the Hour

Today if ye shall hear his voice, harden not your hearts, as in the provocation. Hebrews 3:15.

I once observed a group of children who were playing and seemingly having the time of their lives. It was around the noon hour. They seemed utterly oblivious to what was going on around about them. All of a sudden above the chatter came the clear shrill sound of a whistle. Most of the children went right on playing, but Dickie, a sturdy little fellow around five years old, stopped his activity. He recognized his mother's signal that it was time for lunch. He called to his brother Timmy, a little fellow of three years, and told him it was time to go home for lunch.

Here is where the struggle really began. Timmy just did not want to leave and paid no attention to Dickie's pleas to go with him. In fact, Dickie was becoming so upset by his failure to get Timmy to come that he was almost in tears. You could tell that Mother was quite strict about obedience to the whistle and that she held Dickie responsible for his younger brother. I never did know how the struggle came out because I had to go on my way down the street.

But my smile over Dickie's predicament was fading. I was realizing how very much like those two children are followers of Christ when it comes to obeying the signals given by our heavenly Father. Some of us do hear these calls and we try to get others to listen and to follow them, too. And we become very unhappy when they will not. But there are others who hear the voice pleading with them to come home to the heavenly Father, but they say: "I will play for just a minute longer before I go." Sometimes the minute is gone and still they have not come to Him. When we hear God call, let us never forget to answer.

"Jesus is tenderly calling today." Will you answer His call?

TABLE TALK: *Sometimes we forget to witness for Christ. Discuss whether there is anyone in the neighborhood you could bring to Christ. How would you go about it?*

158

JUNE 7

Honesty Is the Only Policy

Now we pray to God that ye do no evil; not that we may appear approved, but that ye may do that which is honorable, though we be as reprobates. 2 Corinthians 13:7.

One day a popular newspaper columnist took issue with the old and time-honored maxim, "Honesty is the best policy." This has been a revered precept ever since Cervantes set it down in *Don Quixote*. The columnist declared it fallacious, immoral, misleading, and deceitful. Her point is well taken. Honesty is not the best policy. It is the only policy. And the sooner more of us realize this fact the better our country will become.

The writer went on to tell how, when she was a little girl in third grade, the teacher would quote certain truisms and would make the pupils write them a hundred times as a practice in penmanship. One night her father happened to glance over her shoulder and saw that she was writing for the eighty-ninth time, "Honesty is the best policy." Her father insisted that she write, "Honesty is the only policy." She then tells how a private war began between the third grade teacher and her father. One day he marched into school and confronted the teacher. His arguments went something like this: "If you say that honesty is the best policy, it implies that there are other policies, and that there is an element of choice in the matter. But there is no choice. Either you are honest or you are not. You cannot be a little bit honest without being a little dishonest at the same time."

It would be well if this father's conviction that honesty is the only policy could sweep our whole country and become a part of the philosophy of everyone in public office and of every individual citizen. If this truth is basic in your thinking and conscience guides you by this principle, then you are going God's way. For there is not room for deceit or hypocrisy where He is found.

TABLE TALK: *Have you ever been caught in a half-lie or little white lie? Did you come to the conclusion that honesty is the only policy? Discuss.*

For God or Against Him?

Yea, verily, and I count all things to be but loss for the excellency of the knowledge of Christ Jesus my Lord.

Philippians 3:8.

It is always a thrill to be on the winning side. You have seen youngsters sad and downhearted because their team lost the ball game though they promised themselves that next time would be different. No matter how good the spirit, if the team keeps losing one game after another, the players soon lose their enthusiasm and begin to give up.

In this game of life you have to take sides. You are either for God or you are against Him. You have to make the choice. You can pick the winning team or you can give your allegiance to one who is sure to lose. God has already chosen you. He wants you on His side, but you have to be willing to accept His invitation.

Maybe you have heard the saying, "It isn't whether you won or lost, but how you played the game." There is a lot of truth in that sentence, but, as far as the game called life is concerned, it is not quite right. If you are on God's side and you know that He is on your side, you cannot possibly lose. For the Christian knows that there will never be an end to the life of the soul. Every penitent sinner has a promise that some day he will wear the victor's crown.

Take time during the course of each day to reassure yourself of this wonderful promise, "The Lord is on my side. I will not fear." Stop to think what that means. A peace will come into your soul, a new joy will fill your life, and you will have added courage to meet each day with faith and hope. All this can be yours because God has chosen you to be one of His own. And in His love and unselfishness He willingly offers you His victory. Then the defeats of the world will lose their sting as your heart will sing a new song and everyone about you will know that you are a child of the ever living, ever loving King.

TABLE TALK: *Discuss why everyone seems to want to win.*

Getting Back What You Give

Whosoever hateth his brother is a murderer: and ye know that no murderer hath eternal life abiding in him. 1 John 3:15.

A prominent medical professor recently warned that anger is extremely unhealthy. He told about a patient who once was the happiest man that he had ever seen. He said the man got into a court fight with his daughter, lost his temper, and in no time at all was in poor health. He died soon after of just plain anger.

Anger and hatred go hand in hand. They are almost always inseparable. Each of them causes death. Scripture warns, "Whosoever hateth his brother is a murderer: and ye know that no murderer hath eternal life abiding in him."

But not only do anger and hatred cause future suffering. They ruin life in the present. The story is told of a boy who became very upset because his mother did not allow him to do something he desperately wanted to do. He went out to the edge of a big ravine and shouted at the top of his voice, "I hate you! I hate you! I hate you!" And then as he stood there, much to his surprise, he heard a voice cry back, "I hate you! I hate you! I hate you!" He became very frightened and ran back to his home and said, "Mother, there is a bad man in the hill across the valley who shouted at me, "I hate you!"

This was an opportunity for Mother to teach her little boy a lesson. "Now, my son," she said, "go back to the same place and call out, 'I love you!' " The boy did as he was told and the voice from across the valley called back, "I love you!"

It is well for us to learn that in life we get back just about what we are willing to give. If hatred and anger are found in our own hearts we will no doubt find them in the hearts of others, but if love is in our hearts, love will also come back to us.

We get in this life according to what we give.

TABLE TALK: *Discuss what things make you angry and cause you to lose your temper. How can you overcome this?*

JUNE 10

Speaking of Pretense

What then? only that in every way, whether in pretense, or in truth, Christ is proclaimed; and therein I rejoice, yea, and will rejoice. Philippians 1:18.

If you had walked down a certain street one night you would have seen a sight which perhaps would have reminded you of your own childhood. Here was a little girl, eight years of age, who had decked herself out in Mother's dress and high heels. She was dragging along a young man of five or six years of age, who had his father's hat on almost down to his eyes. In their dream world they were Mother and Father out for a walk calling upon their neighbors. What fun they were having, "just pretending." They were in a world all their own and did not even know that anyone was passing by. If you had been there you would have been amused as the young miss said to her companion, "Now when we come to Sally's house, be sure to straighten out your tie and try to act like a man."

What fun children can have in the land of make-believe! Of course, pretense may be bad and it may be good. Surely we know that we must not go through life pretending to be what we are not. Sooner or later we will be found out and will lose respect. We cannot pretend to like a person and then when that person's back is turned say belittling things about him. We should not pretend to love God if we do not live in everyday life according to the way He has commanded us. God sees through all pretense which makes the soul small and ugly and which ultimately destroys it.

But that is good pretense, too. Take for example the days when you are not feeling up to par. Everything seems to be going wrong. Then it is time for you to pretend you are feeling better. Smile at the other fellow. Cover up your feelings of disgust within. It is amazing how within an hour or two you will find yourself feeling much better. The Master never felt sorry for Himself. He always lived radiantly, silently bearing His crosses, and so should you!

TABLE TALK: *What pretenses have you carried on which were good? What effect did they have on you, and on others?*

JUNE 11

Build Reservoirs of Power

If any man thirst, let him come unto me and drink. John 7:37.

An elderly Christian lady has a very fascinating collection of cactuses. She has so many that when you come into her home you feel overwhelmed by them all. All her friends know about her hobby and when they go on trips and find a new cactus plant somewhere, they buy it and send it to her. They know how happy she is when she receives them.

Often she tells very interesting facts about these plants that she loves. A cactus does not need to be watered very often. The plant is created by God in such a way that whatever water is received by the roots is absorbed into the leaves. The leaves are so finely grained and so hard on the surface that the moisture does not have much of a chance to evaporate.

Oftentimes we read stories of people who are lost in deserts and are unable to find any water. If they should find a desert cactus, they could break off the thick leaves and get as much as half a gallon of water from them. Of course, these people would have to know about this strange reservoir of water or they could lie down right next to the cactus and yet die of thirst.

We Christians should be more like the cactus plant. As we receive the water of life from God we should absorb it into our souls and not just let it evaporate, leaving us nothing to retain. We, too, can build up reservoirs of power and strength that will enable us to withstand and conquer in our time of need. Our help is very close at hand, but if we do not recognize the presence, we may lose the power. How unfortunate it would be for one to lose his soul with the Saviour so near, offering His forgiveness and redeeming love. Right now He is close to you. Why not invite Him in?

TABLE TALK: *Our source of inspiration is our worship service. Discuss the need for attending church regularly.*

JUNE 12

God Wants All of You

Blessed are they that hunger and thirst after righteousness: for they shall be filled. Matthew 5:6.

It may not take a great man to make a Christian but it takes all of him. You do not have to possess a college degree to know God's love but you do have to be constantly devoted to Him.

The Psalmist describes a good man in these words: "He is like a tree planted by the streams of water, that bringeth forth its fruit in its season." In other words, the faithful follower of Christ grows in richness and beauty and never lacks the things that bring happiness and love.

If you have ever traveled across the plains of western United States, you know that you can go for miles and miles and never see anything but barren land, frozen shut in the winter and scorched dry in the summer. Then, suddenly, a lone tree appears not far ahead and it stands as a reminder that somewhere in that desolate land there is life. Chances are you will find a rivulet of water near that tree. Maybe you cannot see it on the surface, but deep down the roots have found nourishment. As long as the stream keeps flowing that tree will continue to grow and become green.

The righteous person has been promised that there will always be strength and food to keep growing. The river of God's abundance will always keep flowing. All the heart needs to do is tap its veins.

The life of the wicked man is so different. Not only does he constantly hunger and thirst but he has no one to direct his way. He is like that bombing plane that had a jammed landing gear. For four hours the crew struggled to set it free. Finally they parachuted to the ground. The plane, now without a pilot, became like a life without God. It was not long before it crashed into a near-by house, killing a man and two innocent children. Without God, there is always death. With Him, life goes on forever.

TABLE TALK: *Think of all the different kinds of people, from many professions, and varied backgrounds who belong to church. Discuss in what way they are all alike.*

Your Faith Must Keep Growing

And he cometh unto his disciples and findeth them sleeping, and saith unto Peter, What, could ye not watch with me one hour? Watch and pray, that ye enter not unto temptation.

Matthew 26:40-41.

One morning a little boy was chided by his mother because during the night he had fallen out of bed. When she asked him why, he said, "Mother, I guess I fell asleep too close to where I got in."

That is the trouble with most of us in everyday living. We fall asleep too close to where we get in. Nothing of any great merit can be accomplished unless we are willing to pay a price. If we fail to make that sacrifice, we cannot expect to receive any reward. In fact, we may have to suffer instead.

Consider the case of Peter. He had lived with the Master for three years. He had heard Him preach. He had listened as He spoke His wonderful parables. He had watched as He performed the great miracles. Peter had promised that though everybody else should forsake Jesus, he would never do so. In spite of all this, the day came when Peter failed utterly to prove that he meant what he said. Three times in the courtyard of the high priest he dishonestly denied that he knew Jesus. How he could deny the Master in such a way we cannot understand until we take an honest look at ourselves and discover that by our living we have done the very same thing. The trouble with Peter was that he "fell asleep too close to where he got in." It was easy for him to promise that he would never forsake the Lord, and yet, when the crucial moment came, it was he who denied Him.

And yet we must not forget the sequel of this story, for it applies to us also. The Master did not condemn or criticize Peter because of his action. Knowing Peter's repentant heart, Jesus looked on him with love even as He looks on us with love. He is willing to forgive all that we have done wrong, if we are sincerely sorry for our mistakes.

TABLE TALK: *How have you grown religiously since the time you accepted Jesus? Have you, like Peter, ever denied Him in words or actions?*

JUNE 14

Morning Glory

Are not two sparrows sold for a penny? And not one of them shall fall on the ground without your Father: but the very hairs of your head are all numbered. Fear not therefore: ye are of more value than many sparrows. Matthew 10:29-31.

So often the tempter comes to us after we have committed some sin and tries to persuade us that God will not receive us back now. We have gone along with the crowd. In wanting to be broadminded we have compromised our faith. The devil tries to convince us that it is too late for us now and that we might as well go his way.

At this point we should listen very carefully to the voice of God. Perhaps you remember how as a little child something happened to you during the course of the day. Probably someone had hurt you. You were sobbing tears as you went to bed at night. Then you heard the tender voice of Mother speaking beside your bed, "Go to sleep now. Everything will be different in the morning."

God is much like a loving mother. When life is weighed down with burdens and we have lost our wings of faith, we need to hear God tell us, "Do not worry, tomorrow will be another day. I will be in it to help you and to give you strength to face your problems. I will carry your burdens, too. I will forgive you for past mistakes and forget them, and tomorrow we will start a new day."

So often people have come to me with tremendous problems. And the first thing that they always say is this, "Pastor, I look at my own resources and I don't see how I am ever going to have the strength to face my problems." That is our trouble. We look inside at our own little talents and capacities. None of us would have enough resources, if that were all that counted. What we fail to realize is that there is still God, concerned and caring for each one of us, ever conscious of all the problems and difficulties in our lives.

TABLE TALK: *Can you think of instances when you have worried about a problem at night, only to find that it looked so different in the light of the morning?*

166

JUNE 15

Save Yourself for Him

Ye therefore shall be perfect, as your heavenly Father is
perfect. Matthew 5:48.

Members of the Boys' Clubs of America, in announcing their
selection of favorite American fathers, said they had decided
that "a dad that won't go fishing or play ball with his son isn't
worth his weight in fatherhood." According to a poll the boys
were overwhelmingly of the opinion that a real dad must share
activities with his boy. "It is not enough," they declared, "to
supply Junior with material comforts."

It was interesting to note the qualifications they desired most
in an ideal father. They wanted firmness—a steady hand to guide
them on the right path. They wanted understanding and appreciation of the fact that boys and adults think differently—
that sometimes a boy would rather play with his friends than do
chores. They wanted a sense of humor—the ability to laugh
when a window was broken by a baseball. They wanted a companionship that would give the boy the feeling that, come what
may, he had a real friend in Dad.

But more important than all of these is that a parent shares
with his children in spiritual things. The greatest inheritance that
can be left them is the memory of a godly life.

A young man who had the privilege of being raised in a fine
Christian home went to Paris to study art. When Saturday nights
came the rest of the boys would pursue the pleasures of the
world. This young man would remain at home writing letters or
reading books. Finally one of the older teachers, having observed
that he never joined in the worldly pleasures of his friends, asked
him the reason why. A gleam came in his eye as he said, "Across
the sea there is a girl whom I love very deeply. I am saving
myself for her."

The young lad trained in the way he should go, will always
remember that there is a God who loves him very deeply.
He will keep himself from the sins of the world in order that he
might please God.

TABLE TALK: *What qualities would you name as being most
important in a father? In a son?*

JUNE 16

The Master Wants You

Blessed are the peacemakers: for they shall be called sons of God. Matthew 5:9.

Some of the top atomic scientists of our nation have come to the conclusion that the hydrogen bomb could easily be made a suicide bomb for the entire world. It would kill slowly by poisoning every living thing by radio-active dust. The dust would be carried around the world by winds.

As we read of things like this we are reminded of an editorial which appeared in a metropolitan newspaper not long ago. It told about an incident which the writer had observed on one of the busy avenues of the city. A little spaniel dog had been run over by an automobile and lay dead in the street. A big shepherd dog seemed to sense what had happened and was just pulling the little body to the side of the street. The writer of this editorial, thinking in terms of the effect of the hydrogen bomb and of man's inhumanity to man, seemed to be asking, "Does a dog have more concern for life than man?"

The real Christians of our day must give answer to that question. We must all let God come into our lives that we might help Him redeem this world in which we live. Only by the total commitment of ourselves to His program can the world possibly be saved. A missionary told of an Indian Chief who had been converted to the cross of Christ. When the call came to bring the gift most acceptable in the sight of the Master, the Indian Chief brought something very precious to him, his favorite blanket. But the missionary turned to him and said, "My friend, the Lord wants more than that from you." He thought for a moment and then understood. Humbly he said, "Indian Chief gives *himself* to God." The Master wants you!

TABLE TALK: *Discuss what you as a family can do to bring more humanity into our world politics. What avenues of expression are available? Resolve to do something, and do not forget to pray about it!*

JUNE 17

Your Living Tells the Story

My little children, let us not love in word, neither with the tongue; but in deed and truth. 1 John 3:18.

Day by day there are many opportunities for each one of us to witness for the Master. We should be careful, however, to use methods that will draw people to Christ rather than drive them away.

A woman stepped off a streetcar one evening. As she walked along she heard footsteps behind her. She glanced back and saw a man following her and looking intently at her. A little frightened, she hurried her pace only to find that he also quickened his. She did not recognize him as a friend, and so began to run. She was now in sight of the doorway to her apartment. The man began to run too, and just as the woman neared the door he caught up with her and thrust something into her hand.

She threw open the door and dashed into her apartment. As she stood there she opened her hand to see what it could be that this pursuer had given her. Imagine her consternation when her eyes fell on a printed folder bearing in boldface type the message, "God is Love." This is, perhaps, an overdrawn picture and such things are not usual occurrences. But an instance like this does point out the fact that people are not always tactful in their witness for God.

A good merchandising house will use only the most respectable advertising methods to bring their products to the attention of the prospective buyer. The business of the Kingdom is the greatest business on earth. In seeking to win disciples for the Master, we should be careful to exercise the best of judgment and allow ourselves always to be directed by His power. Every act of our daily life should help tell the world that we belong to God and that God is love. Such witnessing can be most effective in helping to make His plans come true.

In deed and truth, your living tells the story.

TABLE TALK: *As a Christian everything you do "advertises" for God. With this in mind, discuss what things should be eliminated from your life and what should be added.*

Do You Believe This Way?

But Jesus, not heeding the word spoken, saith unto the ruler of the synagogue, Fear not, only believe. Mark 5:36.

So much of our faith is simply lip expression without any depth of heart conviction. We say we believe something but we really do not. The way we react to certain situations is proof of what we really are.

During the course of a certain week, a family which had been very active in their church, lost one of their little children by death. The very next Sunday each member of the family was back in his accustomed place, the mother singing in the choir, the father teaching his Sunday-school class, and the oldest boy helping with the ushering. Many in the worshiping congregation were much impressed by the great faith of these people who did not waste their time in mourning, but rather had the hope in their hearts that their loved one was safe in the "house of many mansions."

As one family walked home from church that day, the boy turned to his father and said, "Dad, those people certainly believe it, don't they?" "Believe what?" asked the father. "Oh, the promise in the Bible that when we die we go to heaven to live forevermore." "Why, certainly," said the father, "everybody believes that." "Oh," answered the son, "but not *that* way!"

It is fairly easy when the skies are blue to confess with a cheerful heart that you believe in God but how about your faith when the days get dark and the skies get cloudy? Do you have the conviction that there is no defeat for the Christian and that all things do work for good to them that love God? The world will pay little attention to a person who says he believes one thing and then lives contrary to that confession. We will be instruments in the hand of God in winning the world for Him only if we put into practice our confession, thereby letting the world know that we believe it *"that* way."

TABLE TALK: *Discuss the way you, as a believing Christian, should accept sorrow.*

JUNE 19

Living Positively

Rejoice, O young man, in thy youth; and let thy heart cheer thee in the days of thy youth, and walk in the ways of thy heart, and in the sight of thy eyes; but know thou, that for all these things God will bring thee into judgement. Ecclesiastes 11:9.

A noted psychologist has made this very significant and thought-provoking statement: "It is the over-optimist who can best survive trying situations. At concentration camps only those prisoners were convinced that the day of liberation would some day come."

In this world we are each day called upon to face trying situations. We are becoming more and more engaged in a battle of survival. When trouble comes some people blame God. Much better, it would seem, to recognize that it is human sin and not God that is the cause of the misery in the world today. There is hope only when we come to the conviction that His eternal purposes will ultimately work out. Much better it would be for us, if we would steep ourselves in His Word and promises.

For many this world is like a concentration camp where there are those who wait in fear as prisoners. There is the fear of sickness, of material insecurity, of death, and many other fears. Only those will survive who are convinced that because of God the day of liberation will ultimately come.

Not long ago an ad in a newspaper read like this: "Enjoy yourself—it's saner than you think." That all depends. If this refers only to the physical things of life, I am not at all sure that it is true. We have been misguided by a philosophy that maintains that we may as well let ourselves go for tomorrow we will die. If it applies to spiritual things I would positively say "yes." If it means that we should be sure that God is ever present, that we may always rest in His almighty and everlasting arms, it gives us a kind of philosophy that Christ would want us to have. He said, "I came that they may have life, and may have it abundantly."

TABLE TALK· *An optimist is living positively; a pessimist sees the negative side of life. Discuss the effects of a positive approach in your life. What effect has a negative approach?*

171

How Grateful Are You?

Every man shall give as he is able, according to the blessing of the Lord thy God which he hath given thee.

Deuteronomy 16:17.

We would be more satisfied with living if very frequently we would stop to take inventory and to count the many blessings which have come to us from the hand of Almighty God.

A home missionary was working in the southern part of our country among some of the poorer people of that area. He preached the gospel with conviction. Those to whom he ministered had very little from the material point of view, but spiritually they were very rich, for they had come to the knowledge that God had done great things for them through Christ. In return they were always willing to give out of their meager circumstances for the helping of others.

One day the minister announced that the next Sunday an offering would be received to buy milk for some people who were poorer than they. When the service was to begin the minister placed a milk bottle on a table by the door and invited the congregation to leave their gifts as they left the church that morning. Among those present at the service was a young girl whose heart was full of love, but whose life had not known many material blessings such as each day come to us. As she shook hands with the pastor and placed her gift for the poor, she turned to the minister with quizzical eyes and asked, "Would you please tell me what milk looks like?"

Here was a Christian saint who was giving of her little to help those who would now receive benefits greater than she had ever known. She was rich, however, for she had come to learn the blessings which come to those who are willing to give.

Make a mental list of all the things for which you have reason to be thankful. Gratefully acknowledge that they have come to you from God. Then go out and prove your thanksgiving by sharing what you have with others.

TABLE TALK: *What project could you take part in to share your material wealth with others?*

JUNE 21

Music in the Soul

O sing unto the Lord a new song: sing unto the Lord, all the earth. Psalm 96:1.

A young Polish lad came to America. He found it to be a land of great opportunity where he was given the possibility of developing the talent which was in his soul. He was born to be a great musician. After much sacrifice and a willingness to pay the price, he became an outstanding pianist.

A very close friend was an American boy, and they spent much of their time together. When war was declared they joined the service in the same unit. As time went on they became engaged in some fierce fighting with the enemy. On one particular night the battle was extremely dangerous. The young Polish lad was very seriously injured. The American boy who was his friend, sought him out in the hospital that very night and discovered that the doctors were about to amputate his arm. He turned to one of them and said, "You can't do that, for this boy is a great pianist and it will ruin his career." The doctors replied, "If we do not operate, he will lose his life."

They performed the operation. In the morning the American boy had the unpleasant duty of going to the Polish lad and telling him the verdict. He said, "My friend, I am sorry to have to tell you that you will never be able to play again. To save your life, they had to amputate your arm." Through his intense pain the Polish lad turned to his American friend and said, "Though I will never be able to play for the entertainment of others, thank God, I will always have music in my soul."

The Christian can live each day with the calm assurance that though the storms of life might buffet him about, though there might be heavy burdens to carry and temptations to meet, because of God there can still be music in his soul. And remember there is nothing more worth while than that song which is within.

TABLE TALK: *Suppose you had to break bad news to someone. What would your approach be?*

173

JUNE 22

Pray and Work

Even so faith, if it have not works, is dead in itself.

James 2:17.

A little girl was disturbed by the fact that her brothers had set traps to catch some birds. When she was asked what she had done in the matter her answer was, "First, I prayed that the traps might not catch the birds. Then I prayed that God would prevent the birds from getting into the traps. And finally, I went out and kicked the traps all to pieces."

We can learn a lesson from this little girl. She indicated by her actions her belief in the fact that faith without works is dead.

A similar incident is told of two youngsters who were afraid they might be late to school. They were running as fast as they could. Suddenly one of them said, "Let's stop and pray that we will not be late." The other answered, "I think it would be better if we prayed and kept running."

It is not enough just to pray God that certain sins and social vices be eliminated from a community. We must not only pray, but we must be willing to be used of God to help "kick these traps all to pieces." God has promised to give us strength to do all things.

It is well to remember in prayer our neighbor and all of his needs, and the suffering and starving people throughout the world. But along with our prayers we must give and share of our means to help the neighbor, and to provide food for the starving. We should also remember in prayer our missionaries and the heathen people in the darkened corners of the globe. But more than that, we should help God answer our prayers by being willing to give and share our earthly means that this work might be carried on.

"Ye are the light of the world. A city set on a hill cannot be hid." "Let your light shine before men."

TABLE TALK: *Mention instances in your own community where people have not only prayed for certain evils to be done away with but also helped bring about the reform.*

174

JUNE 23

Emphasize the Positive

Is any among you suffering? let him pray. Is any cheerful? let him sing praise. James 5:13.

Modern therapy relieves mentally ill war veterans of their terror dreams by means of the power of suggestion talking through a loud speaker. A veterans administration doctor has described a recorded "suggestion treatment" administered while patients are trying to go to sleep. Repeated over and over again in a monotone all through the night, in the otherwise quiet hospital, are statements like these: "I can rid myself of any symptoms completely and in less than a minute. I am not over dependent on medicine or doctors," and every once in a while the loud speaker repeated these words, "Mind a blank, relaxing more." There is also a shorter daytime broadcast.

Some remarkable results have been attained by this power-of-suggestion therapy. Most patients have reported gratifying results within two to four weeks after admission. Some have stated that they are able to take daytime naps for the first time in their lives. Others say that sleep has become less fitful and more refreshing. Terror dreams are reported as being replaced by more pleasant ones, and dreams of all sorts are being reduced.

All of us need to put into practice in our daily living the principle which has just been stated. Instead of complaining about our aches and pains, instead of constantly reminding ourselves of the heavy burdens we have to bear, we should concentrate upon the moments of health and the blessings which so freely come to us from God who loves us.

One of the secrets of the Master's vibrant personality was that He constantly emphasized the positive. So frequently He prayed, "Father, I thank Thee." He counted His blessings, and learned the secret of forgetting the unpleasant things in life.

No one will ever travel a rougher road than the one that led to His Jerusalem. No one will ever be called upon to suffer as He did. By showing us His ability to conquer He gives us the hope that, through Him we shall be victorious.

TABLE TALK: *Prayer and meditation are the Christian's therapy. Recall the times it has helped you.*

JUNE 24

We Do Not Weave Alone

And be not fashioned according to this world: but be ye transformed by the renewing of your mind, that ye may prove what is the good and acceptable and perfect will of God. Romans 12:2.

There is a small hand-woven rug. Its threads are beautiful shades of blue, red, and gold, with traces of white and purple running through them. It is not clear what the pattern really is, because it is a bit mixed up and confused. The margins are not very even and a few of the threads are broken and misplaced.

Perhaps you are not especially impressed by this little rug until you discover that it was woven by a little blind girl. It was the first time she had tried to make anything. Knowing this, the rug appears different and the colors are more beautiful than before. The pattern takes on new meaning as you overlook the broken threads and uneven margins. You realize that it represents the best efforts of an unfortunate girl who is trying to do a worth-while thing.

With a little help she can do even a better job. The girl asked her mother to help her mend the broken spots, straighten the pattern, and fix the edges. And now it has become a precious thing. It is an accomplishment of patience, hard work, and love.

The lives we weave are sometimes like that. We make mistakes and follow a crooked path. But God looks down upon this life we have made and seeing our good intentions and our never-dying purpose to do the things which are right and honest, He says, "I understand. Just turn your life over to Me the way it is and I will make it more beautiful. I will forgive your sins and straighten the crooked paths."

And so as we give ourselves to God, He mercifully takes our life and makes it worthy of eternity. He erases our errors, gives meaning to our prayers, and strengthens our faith. He is able to change discouragement into new hope, and despair into happiness.

Let God's hand work in your life.

TABLE TALK: *The spiritually blind need your help and guidance. What have you done to help others make their life beautiful?*

A Wisp of Hay

And Jesus said unto them, How many loaves have ye? And they said, "Seven, and a few little fishes. Matthew 15:34.

A king decided that he would build a cathedral and pay the entire cost himself. It was to be a memorial in his honor and glory, that people of all generations might remember his name and his generosity to the community.

The king's intentions were carried out. The cathedral was constructed at a great cost. It was a magnificent building, placed high on a hill where it could be seen from miles around. All who came to view it were thrilled with its beauty.

Finally, on the day of dedication, the king had these words placed upon the cornerstone, "This building has been erected and paid for by the king."

That night he had a dream. He saw the cathedral, but his name was not written on the cornerstone. Rather, he saw there the name of a woman. The next day he dismissed the thought, but the following night he had the same dream and saw this same name. He became very angry and told his servants to search the community to discover who had that name. They found her living just below the hill. The king called for her. "Can you explain," he asked, "why I should see your name on the cornerstone in my dream? Did you do anything at all to help build the cathedral?" "No," she replied, "but I was so happy when I heard that you were building such a beautiful place of worship, I did want to help. All I could do was to feed the horses a wisp of hay as they pulled the wagon loads of bricks up yonder steep hill." The king was so impressed with her action that he had his own name taken off the cornerstone and the name of the woman put on.

Only a wisp of hay, but given to the glory of God, is precious in His sight. You may not have much to contribute, but God can multiply your loaves and fishes so that thousands will be blessed.

TABLE TALK: *Start thinking about the little things you can do to make God and your fellow men happy. Why not resolve right now to do them and each day find more that you can do to make others happy.*

Which World?

And if it seem evil unto you to serve the Lord, choose you this day whom ye will serve . . . but as for me and my house, we will serve the Lord. Joshua 24:15.

God is always giving us choices. There are two ways, the high and the low. There are two masters, and two destinations. Which world will it be for you? And what price are you willing to pay? Today you are determining your future by the way your soul will go. "Whatsoever a man soweth that shall he also reap." And do not forget it. There are those who are selling life at an awfully cheap price But they are going to have to live with themselves in the days that are ahead. And tragic has been the experience for those who have lived so.

The first person created by God compromised his conscience by taking something the great Creator did not want him to have. Because of this he was expelled from the garden. For a mess of pottage Esau sold his birthright, and regretted it to his dying day. Judas sold his Master for thirty pieces of silver. He could not bear the torment of his soul and so he went out and hanged himself. And there are people today who choose material things above real living and who ultimately discover, like the prodigal of old, that they are in a far-off country without anything to satisfy the deep longings of the soul.

Which world, what future do you want to face? You will be creating it by the very way you are living today. If you want to face a future of nothingness, then build with material blocks and stones. If you want to face a future of increasing joy with a crescendo of happiness in your life, then give yourself unselfishly to God and to the things of His kingdom.

Beware of selling your real self for any price. Remember that you have a soul that lives on forever. Which world do you face?

TABLE TALK: *Discuss the choices you must make daily in your business, at home, or at school.*

JUNE 27

The Perfect Engineer

In all thy ways acknowledge him, and he will direct thy paths.
Proverbs 3:6.

One night a crack streamliner was speeding toward its destination. Having been delayed by stormy weather it was running five hours late. Suddenly a freight train loomed up on the tracks just ahead. The engineers quickly tried to avoid the crash, but it was too late, the two trains collided head on. The schedule was interrupted, the signals mixed, and the crash was inevitable.

A certain poet has likened this life of ours to a railroad train. There are hills and tunnels and the race down the tracks as we try to reach our goal. Oftentimes our signals seem to get mixed. The schedule of events seems confused. Switches are turned to lead us down the wrong track and we meet troubles and sorrows head on. In spite of the fact that we try desperately to avoid a collision, tragedy occurs.

So often we ask, "Why do these things happen? Is not God the perfect engineer who does not make a mistake?" That is perfectly true, and the only time real tragedy comes is when we fail to follow His directions. The forces of evil draw us into troubles and disappointments.

Our life is also like a little boat upon a lake. If we do nothing the winds may blow us in many different directions. But if we use the powers and energy that we have to keep rowing, by the grace and strength of God we will reach our destination.

Perhaps we shall encounter difficulties along the way but our journey can be made all the more challenging because of it. We Christians know that ultimately we shall be victorious. For no power is greater than our God. If we go His way, follow His signals, obey His commandments, and listen to His voice, tragedy can be avoided and victory will be assured.

"In all thy ways acknowledge him, and he will direct thy paths."

TABLE TALK: *Can you recall a time when you consciously violated your father's or mother's command, and a calamity resulted?*

JUNE 28

God Is Counting on You

What doth it profit, my brethren, if a man say he hath faith, but have not works? can that faith save him? James 2:14.

If you have indicated that you desire to follow in the way of the Master, you have volunteered to become one of His missionaries. Then Christ is counting on you to preach the gospel wherever you go and to teach others concerning His love as you minister for Him wherever you may live in the modern world. As you meet your associates in the busy market place, or your friends on the street, at home, in school, or at play, you should remember that you are one of His disciples. He is counting on you as a devoted follower to carry His Word to people in every dark nation far across the oceans, to all those who have never heard about the loving Saviour.

This mission task and obligation is yours today. If you fail, some one will still be living on the road of despair which leads away from God. If you accept the challenge, some soul will discover the high road of victory which knows no end.

A man had a dream. In it he saw the angels come to God one day to ask Him what plans He had for carrying out His work upon the earth. "I sent My Son to die for the salvation of men," God replied, "and then I told some of His disciples that they should tell the story to others and that these should tell it to still others, until all people would know of the saving message of the cross. I am counting on those faithful people who love Me and are willing to serve Me to be missionaries of the gospel." "But suppose they fail? What other plans have you made?" asked the angels. "I have made no other plans," said God, "for I am counting on them."

The growth of the Christian church, the winning of souls for the Master, the victory of eternal peace and love for His kingdom, these rest in your hands. Your willingness to work, together with His never ending help, assures you that you cannot fail.

TABLE TALK: *There are many ways of being a missionary at home. What are some of the home mission programs of the church?*

JULY 1

A Light That Never Goes Out

Jesus therefore said unto them, Yet a little while is the light among you. Walk while ye have the light, that darkness overtake you not: and he that walketh in darkness knoweth not whither he goeth. John 12:35.

One learns many lessons by traveling the highways that stretch across our countryside. To reach our destination safely, we must stay on the right side of the road. If we get into somebody else's territory, we are in danger of a head-on collision and the result will be tragedy, perhaps even death. It teaches us that we have not only our own life to live but that others have the right to live also.

There are also bridges to cross. Someone has built them for us. Were it not for them, there would be no way in which we could cross the ravines and the rivers. Great sacrifices have been made by those who have lived before us in order that traveling might be made easier for us today.

If the night becomes dark, we have headlights to show us the way to go. They point out the narrow road which leads us to our destination. They warn us of the curves in the highway, which we must take with care if we are to reach our goal safely.

One night a man was driving alone at a rapid speed. The night was dark. Clouds were hiding the moon, which sought to give light to lead the weary traveler below. Suddenly the lights on the car went out and all was darkness before him. Fortunately he was able to come to a stop safely. This experience impressed him with the truth that without the Master life is a perilous journey with no light to lead us.

It at this moment darkness enshrouds you and you do not know the way that you should go, turn to Him who says, "I am the light of life." He has the power and the strength and the capacity to lead you safely to your destination. His light is unfailing. It will never go out. If you obey His command and seek to discover His will, you will be led along the highway to the land of eternal light.

TABLE TALK: *Using the analogy of traveling on the highway, what other lessons can you learn?*

God Always Answers You

Answer me when I call, O God of my righteousness: thou hast set me at large when I was in distress: have mercy upon me, and hear my prayer. Psalm 4:1.

Within the poetry of the Psalms there are thoughts that will never be outdated. Here we see the diary of men who lived many years ago. But they solved their problems by a help that we can have also today.

Even the most God-fearing men of all time were not immune from the troubles of life. David, for example, raised countless questions which he could not answer himself, but He knew where the answers could be found. He was well acquainted with the fact that prayer is power, and often he pleaded with God to listen and help him. The very first words of the Fourth Psalm are these: "Hear me when I call, O God." His only hope when the people turned against him and when it seemed that wickedness was going to overrun godliness, was to turn to God.

All of us remember that old story about the shepherd who was tending his sheep. Many times he called for help just for the fun of seeing the men come running. But when the wolf actually did steal into the flock no one came running when he called. They thought it was just another prank. Each one of us has often prayed without meaning. What we were saying was just so many words. When God listened to us He saw a thoughtless heart that was wandering away. But whenever we come in humility and sincerity asking to know His will, God always answers. He will never forget the things we need and pray for.

"Ye have not, because ye ask not." That is what James tells us. But he is not talking about money, or position, or fame. He is talking about the power that makes a sick soul well again.

Prayer is living in the same house as the Master, working on the job together with Him, and being His hand to help others. Walk and talk with God all through the day. You will discover that your day with Him is well spent.

TABLE TALK: *Stop and consider your family table prayer or your personal evening prayer. Do you find that sometimes you say them mechanically? How can you overcome this?*

JULY 5

Tomorrow Begins Today

For now we live, if ye stand fast in the Lord.

1 Thessalonians 3:8.

It is easy to put off today what can be done tomorrow. And each day of delay makes the task harder. Unless we become partners with God early in life, we may never get around to it. Our living should become like that of the old Scotchman who was on his death bed. A friend of his asked, "Is there anything I can do for you now?" The dying man replied, "No, I thatched my roof before the storm came."

If we live our life with God and allow Him to mend and repair the structure as it is damaged by fear, worry, anxiety, and sin, we can face anything victoriously. And that opportunity is given each one of us now.

The devil is most happy when he can cause people to delay their quest of the secret of power. Once, legend says, he called the evil angels together and asked, "Which of you can figure out the best plan for wrecking humankind?" One evil angel said, "I will go down to earth and dwell among the people. Then I will tell them that there isn't any heaven." The devil replied, "No, you can't go; they will never believe that."

The second evil angel said, "I will go down to earth and dwell among the people. Then I will tell them that there isn't any hell." The devil replied, "No, you can't go; they will never believe that."

The third evil angel said, "I will go down to earth and dwell among the people, and I will tell them that there isn't any hurry about loving and serving God." That evil angel has dwelt among us ever since. And this is what he constantly keeps telling us: "There isn't any hurry about loving and serving God. There isn't any hurry about establishing the family altar in your home. There isn't any hurry about taking time to pray. There will always be a tomorrow."

Today, if you hear His voice, harden not your hearts. Today belongs to you. Who knows about tomorrow?

TABLE TALK: *Have you ever put off a task or an obligation? Was it not more difficult to do each day you waited?*

Keep Looking at the Master

Therefore leaving the doctrine of the first principles of Christ, let us press on unto perfection; not laying again a foundation of repentance from dead works, and of faith toward God.

Hebrews 6:1.

It is a progressive age in which we live. There does not seem to be any place for people who drag their feet or hinder the program. The watchwords of our modern day seem to be: "Keep Learning," "Keep Discovering," and "Keep Inventing." And why not? We are expected to grow and look ahead.

But we must not forget the great gain when we take a moment to look back. We can then see our many mistakes and the countless things for which we have to be sorry. But this backward glance is not worth very much unless it makes us want to do something to correct these wrongs.

Someone has said that when your soul has laid down its faults at the feet of God, it feels as though it had wings. Just being sorry for the sins others commit against us is not nearly enough; true repentance means taking the step toward a new and better life and persevering therein.

As you compare your life with the kindness and sinlessness of Jesus it is easy to see how often you have fallen short of His high standards. It is as though our lives were tiny candles standing beside a powerful beacon light. But God can make something great out of that little candle, if you will only let Him.

A young woman who had lived apart from the church and all that it stood for, said she changed her way of life when she caught sight of Jesus. She took her life, which had been greedy and proud, and placed it beside the Master's. It was then that she saw how far from real goodness and love she had been living.

When you are truly sorry for your past sins, your whole outlook on life will change. You will see God's way instead of your own. There will be greater peace in your heart, for you will know that the Master is with you leading you along His pathway of light and love.

TABLE TALK: *Discuss the value of having a measuring stick to gauge your degree of perfection.*

JULY 7

God in Every Day

Blessed is he whose transgression is forgiven, whose sin is covered. Psalm 32:1.

It is always a thrill to hear a masterful organist play upon a great organ. Some of the most famous organs have as many as 2,000 pipes. Some of these pipes are twenty feet long, while others are no larger than an ordinary lead pencil. Each one is tuned to a single note. It has a particular part in the beauty of the great instrument. When a talented musician plays upon the keys, the notes are blended into a glorious harmony, which thrills everyone who listens.

God is the master musician, and if we will only let Him show us His skill, He will weave our life into a glorious composition. The condition is that we obey the touch of His hand. Then we will also do our part in helping redeem the community of which we are a part. Perhaps we shall be able to do a great deal for Him. Or maybe our task will seem very small. But with God's help we all become an important note in His symphony.

Herbert Smith once said, "The religion which is found at the altar on Sunday may be found at the washtub on Monday." He meant that Christianity was an everyday thing and not just a "dress up and go to church" proposition. This statement indicates that one's spiritual life is very closely connected with one's everyday task. If you work for God and His kingdom, there is no job that is just ordinary. Everything you do and say in behalf of Him fills a part that would have gone undone if you had overlooked it.

As you spend each day may you so live that you can honestly, from the depth of your heart, turn to your heavenly Father and say, "God, I have done my very best to be of help to You in Your kingdom work. Forgive me my failures. But thank You, God, for the joy with which You have enriched my life."

You are an important musician in God's symphony of believers. He wants to hear you play your part every day.

TABLE TALK: *God needs all ages in his symphony of believers. Discuss the importance of bringing a child to God at an early age.*

JULY 8

Keep Climbing

And they rose up early in the morning, and gat them up to the top of the mountain, saying, Lo, we are here, and will go up unto the place which the Lord hath promised: for we have sinned. Numbers 14:40.

In a valley of the famous Swiss Alps lies the peaceful village of Zermott. In many ways it is quite like other mountain villages of Switzerland but it has one distinction all its own. Towering above it is the Matterhorn, one of the most beautiful mountains in all the world. It is as treacherous as it is beautiful, for its rock walls rise straight up the sky. For many years after all the high peaks of the world had been conquered, the Matterhorn still kept any man from reaching its top. Finally, four brave and skilled English mountaineers, along with three Swiss guides, fought their way to the very peak of the mountain and there they beheld a sight which was almost unbelievably entrancing. They could see most of the peaks of the Alps, the ice-capped glaciers, and the fertile valleys of Switzerland below. In the distance were the rich plains of Italy. The spectacle far surpassed anything they had imagined. As they stood there beholding all this beauty, they thanked one another, for they realized that without the help of one another they would never have reached the top.

Spiritually, too, we are climbing. Each day we attempt to reach a higher mountaintop in our Christian living. We try to achieve the very highest point of faith and trust in God. Traveling alone we shall meet defeat. We shall never reach our destination. We need the presence of the Master who has traveled the way before. We also need the help and encouragement of friends, for we must remember that we are not climbing alone. Likewise, we should realize our obligation to help others reach the mountaintop of Christian living. If we know this wonderful experience ourselves, we will want to tell the whole world about it. We must speak words of trust and wisdom which will lead more closely to God. We should be witnessing Christians.

TABLE TALK: *Teamwork is necessary in a church. Discuss its importance.*

JULY 9

God Is Always with You

But by the grace of God I am what I am: and his grace which was bestowed upon me was not found vain. 1 Corinthians 15:10.

There was once a young soldier who had both his legs and both his arms amputated. In the hospital there was one nurse who became his very special friend. She was not particularly beautiful to look at, but one day this young lad said to her, "You know, I think you are the most wonderful nurse in the entire hospital." She smiled as she replied, "Oh, there are a lot of wonderful girls serving here." "Oh," he replied, "but you are my favorite because you have such a shining face." The nurse kidded the boy by saying, "Well, then I better go and put on a little powder." His answer was, "No, I don't mean that. Your face shines from the inside." Tears started down her cheeks as she turned to the lad she had so faithfully served and said, "That is the most wonderful thing that has ever been said about me. If it is so, let me tell you why. It is because God lives within me."

How many of us really understand what that power can do? Here is a young widow who wrote me not long ago. Her husband had just passed into the great beyond and she was left to care for three small children. This is what she said in her letter: "As I looked out of my window last night, I saw the moon shining in the heavens and I thought about it shining on my husband's grave, and for a moment I was lonesome. But then I thought: 'No, he isn't there.' The next day my little six-year-old boy came home from school. He fairly burst into the house excited because of what he had to tell me. He said, 'Mother, just think, Daddy has seen Jesus now.'" And then this woman added, "I thought to myself, 'Yes, Son, how true! And he has seen Peter, and Paul, and Martin Luther, and John the Baptist.'"

Such faith can be born only out of the assurance that God is within you.

TABLE TALK: *The face of a person often reveals the state of mind of the individual. Think of those in your community. Can you put a smile on someone's face today by something you say or do?*

JULY 10

This Is the Way

And thou shalt love the Lord thy God with all thy heart, and with all thy soul, and with all thy mind, and with all thy strength: this is the first commandment. Mark 12:30. (A.V.).

So often we give evidence of the fact that we fail to understand what Christianity can do for a life. It was never meant to be a religion of sorrow and gloom. In fact, it was to bring joy into living. Christian faith is reflected in happy, joyful faces, not in countenances of gloom and sorrow. God seldom speaks in negative terms, saying, "Do not do this and do not do that." More often He gives positive commands. "This is the way. Walk ye in it." "Ye are my friends, if ye do the things which I command you."

A man by the name of Hugh Brown put it this way. "Christ is not extra weight but added wings. He is not subtraction but addition." That is why living with the Master makes it possible to do wonderful things. Instead of taking away our power, He adds His all.

We are important in the sight of God. It does make a difference whether or not we follow Him. Up in the mountains of Switzerland there is a small church quite a distance up the trail from a village. There are no lights or lamps in this church and when it is time for an evening service you can see the villagers winding their way up the mountainside each carrying his own light. When the first arrives, there is only a tiny glimmer in the darkness. But when everyone has come for the service, the little church is all aglow because of the many lanterns. If there are some missing there is less light and more darkness.

One Christian life may not seem like very much, but if everybody will just shine a little for the Lord, each drawing radiance from the great light of God, we would discover that the darkness is soon driven away. The symbol of Christ is not the blackness of the last hours on Calvary, but, rather, it is the sunshine of Easter morning. Let its light shine through you.

TABLE TALK: *State each of the Ten Commandments positively. These were the Old Law. What did Jesus say was the First Commandment?*

JULY 11

Over the Fence Is Out

And he answering said, Thou shalt love the Lord thy God
with all thy heart, and with all thy soul, and with all thy
strength, and with all thy mind; and thy neighbor as thyself.
Luke 10:27.

A man recalled how as a little boy he used to love to play
ball. Large groups of children in the neighborhood would
gather each day after school on the corner lot. Spirited rivalry
developed as each team made its attempt to win.

Living next door to the ball field was a woman who saw very
little sunshine in life. It irritated her very much when the ball
was hit into her yard. A fence separated her place from the field
and the corner lot, but when the ball went over it, she would
be out to hide it before the boys could come and retrieve it.
One day the inevitable happened. Someone hit a ball so far
that it broke one of her windows and fell inside. This time the
youngsters could not redeem it until they had earned sufficient
money to pay for the damage they had done. But afterwards,
they followed the rule, "Over the fence is out."

That is a mighty good rule to follow in living, too. We not
only have our own life to live, but we have neighbors to consider. They have the right to live also. Truly, "no man liveth
unto himself." When we criticize our neighbor because his religion is different from ours we are hitting the ball over the
fence and are out, as far as any good we might do on the
democracy team for more hopeful living. When we condemn or
belittle others because of the color of their skin, or because they
have a different political philosophy, or when we speak about
other races in derogatory terms we are hitting the ball over the
fence. Repeated actions such as these by large groups of people
could easily bring about the end of the "ball game."

There is but one way to win. That is to go about living in the
spirit of the Master, giving all men equal opportunity regardless
of their race, color, or national origin.

TABLE TALK: *Analyze your opinion critically. Are you
prejudiced against any race, religion, or political thought? What
can you do to overcome these prejudices?*

JULY 12

A Road That Leads to God

Blessed are they that have not seen, and yet have believed.
John 20:29.

In one of the deep valleys of Switzerland there is a place that is called "The End of the World." A giant mountain stands at the end of the road blocking the way for the traveler who wants to go farther. At the foot of this mountain there is a small hotel where you can stop and rest before you make the journey back again. If you search hard enough in the valley of "The End of the World," you will discover behind the hotel a tiny zigzag path. If you follow it, you will find that it leads to the very top.

There is a narrow road that enables you to keep climbing higher and higher. It leads to the most wonderful victories you can achieve in life. It is the Christ road that leads home to God. Finding that path, should make you eager to share the experience with others.

A story is told of a young man who played a French horn in a Salvation Army band. He was supposed to play the bass notes and keep time for the rest of the players. But he always played much too loudly. The leader of the band hesitated to say anything to the young fellow, but finally in the interest of better music he mentioned it to him. "Well, Sir," answered the French horn player, "When I think of what the Lord has done for me, I just can't play any horn softly."

Probably that young man was a better Christian than he was a musician. He knew that God had changed his life and he was so happy about it that he wanted others to know Him, too. It is true that when the Master really comes into your living you cannot possibly hide it. Too many fail to catch the spirit of spreading the Word. They do not find the tiny zigzag path and reach the very heights of Christian experience, which leads to the joyful sharing of the wonderful message. You have to tell the world what a wonderful experience it is. God expects it. He is counting on you to be one of His missionaries.

TABLE TALK: *What verbal testimony have you made of your Christian faith in the past week?*

194

On the Air

Let us therefore give diligence to enter into that rest, that no man fall after the same example of disobedience. Hebrew 4:11.

If you have ever sat in a radio studio to make a broadcast you have seen the sign on the wall: "On the Air." You wait until the proper time when the green light flashes within this sign. Then the broadcast is ready to begin.

"On the Air," that is really the situation of every Christian for we are told, "Ye shall be witnesses unto me both in Jerusalem, and in all Judaea, and in Samaria and unto the uttermost part of the earth." We do not live unto ourselves. There is always an audience about us listening to the good or evil which is broadcast by our lives. This should not be a situation to fear; rather, it is an opportunity that each one of us should grasp. It should keep us alert and alive. It should challenge us to produce our best. It calls for our full attention.

When one speaks before a microphone in a radio studio, he never knows who might be tuning in to listen to the broadcast. That is true in daily living, too. The things we say are often carried farther than we dream at the time we express them. That goes for fine and noble speaking as well as the spreading of something unkind about another person.

Perhaps someone today is looking to you for an interpretation of what it is to be a Christian. If that person should hear you use profane language, severely criticize your fellow men, or very subtly infer unjust things about someone, he could become very much disillusioned about the Christian way. But if you today begin and continue with the prayer that God would give you grace to spend your waking hours as His true representative, then you will become a helpful influence to the souls who hunger for the way of peace.

People are listening. You are "On the Air."

TABLE TALK: *Have you said anything in the past few days which would be a real testimony to your faith? Have you said anything detrimental? Discuss.*

JULY 14

God Is Our Helper

Trust in the Lord with all thy heart: and lean not upon thine own understanding. Proverbs 3:5.

How often in our living we leave untapped the great reservoirs God has provided for us. We think we can find the resources we need in our human strength but we learn, painfully sometimes, that life would be much simpler were we to call upon Him.

Once there was an old man who had no relatives or family but had some friends with whom he lived. He had known these people for many years and they had received him unto their home, only because of Christian kindness. The old gentleman was exceedingly grateful for all their goodness to him and it weighed on his heart that he could do so little for them.

He was loved for his genuine humility, his devotion to duty, and his trusting faith in God. He had one habit however which was a bit disturbing, though it was finally accepted as just a part of his makeup. He wanted to be self-sufficient. He did not want to cause any more inconvenience than was absolutely necessary. Where this characteristic especially showed itself was at the dinner table. Someone would ask him, "May I pass you the butter?" or "May I pass you the rolls?" Immediately the old man would say, "No, thank you, I can reach." Then he would bend over the table and stretch his arms as best he could to the particular plate which he wanted at the moment. Many times a minor catastrophe would happen during this procedure, a spilled glass of water, or the cover brushed off the sugar bowl. His friends would have been glad to pass the food and thus avert these embarassing incidents.

We smile at the old man, but there is something in his behavior that can be found in most of us. God is near at hand to give us help. He wants to do just that. But we go on our clumsy way, never consulting Him or laying our requests for what we need in His hands. If we make known our requests unto God, He is not only able but willing to answer them.

TABLE TALK: *Think carefully of the earthly goals you have set for yourself. Have you sought the help of God for their attainment?*

JULY 15

The Homesick Angel in the Soul

Great is the Lord, and greatly to be praised, in the city of our God, in his holy mountain. Psalm 48:1.

One day a lady was telling about an experience she once had as she stood on the balcony of a beautiful hotel in Southern Germany. The whole setting was like something snatched out of a dream. This dazzling hotel was situated high on a hillside that was landscaped with trees in every green tone that seemed possible. Accenting it all were borders and beds of flowers in a riot of color. Down below, for miles to the east and many miles to the west, stretched magnificent Lake Constance in queenly blue. White sailboats and large excursion steamers were plying the glistening water. Billowy white clouds drifted across the sky like some sort of heavenly barks with sails full blown.

The traveler reveled in the glory of it all. Something caused her to look longingly to the south. There she could see the shoreline of another country: Switzerland, that fantastic land of majestic mountains. Ever since she could remember she had listened with wide-eyed delight to descriptions of that beautiful country of chalets, white peaks, and spotless towns. Much as she sensed and appreciated all the beauty which surrounded her right where she was, it could not still the deep longing in her heart for the sight of Switzerland, the country which lay on the other shore.

God has meant for us to live abundantly in the here and now, and to enjoy the beauties and opportunities for service. But He also wants us to keep in mind the there and then. He wants us to see the vision of a beautiful far-off country, a land of unbelievable loveliness and happiness. As someone has so beautifully said, God has put a "homesick angel" in our souls and we shall never be really satisfied, nor shall we really understand, until we have reached the other shore. Though we live each day to the fullest in the here and now, we look with longing for that glorious day when we shall live forever in our heavenly home.

TABLE TALK: *Have you ever been thrilled by a beautiful sight? Discuss the meaning it held for you.*

Somebody Needs You

He doth execute justice for the fatherless and widow, and loveth the sojourner, in giving him food and raiment.

Deuteronomy 10:18.

The newly established state of Israel has these last few years been receiving immigrants from all over the world. A number of the people who have come to this little country have gone through the persecutions of Europe. Many of the children are orphans and are being taken care of by the state.

Israel today is not a land of plenty. Much of it is sand and barren and only by irrigation and hard and persistent work can crops be grown. A strict rationing supplies nothing but the bare necessities to those who live there. And yet the people are thankful because they have a place they can call their own.

Never will I forget an experience I had while visiting this country. Less than a year before, it had been accepted into the United Nations. I had just come from the town of Nazareth where Jesus had spent His boyhood years. There I relived in memory the story of how He grew in wisdom and in favor with God and man, until the time came when He should begin His public ministry. He went about doing good, sharing with those who were in need and always lending a helping hand to those who were in trouble.

We travelled along the highway that led from the town of Nazareth to the Sea of Galilee. We stopped at Tiberias, right on the lake, where some little boys were swimming. Through our interpreter we were able to converse with them. One freckle-faced lad especially attracted my attention. He learned that I was from America, which he had heard of as being the "land of plenty." Never will I forget the pleading voice of this little orphan as he looked up at me and said, "Please, Sir! Please, Sir, take me back with you to America!"

Each one of us can help answer the pleadings of that little lad and others like him by showing ourselves a Christian America in providing help and good will to those less fortunate than we.

TABLE TALK: *How long has it been since you sent a CARE package? Do you care? Discuss sending one today.*

JULY 17

Clouds Will Turn to Sunshine

And we know that to them that love God all things work together for good even to them that are called according to his purpose. Romans 8:28.

Some years ago during the Second World War, a little girl attended summer Bible school. During the course of instruction she learned a song which she loved very much. The lines of it went like this: "Clouds will turn to sunshine, night will turn to day, if you just remember, He's not far away." She would often sing this melody with its comforting thought and it seemed so fitting an expression of the radiant little personality that God meant her to be.

After Bible school was over she moved with her family to California, where her father was stationed as an officer in the United States Navy. The little girl became seriously ill. She had been stricken with typhoid fever, the first case reported in California for many years. For eight weeks she was unconscious, hovering between life and death. During several of these weeks her temperature exceeded 105 degrees. Then one day when her family was at her bedside and some of the doctors and nurses were in attendance, she came back to consciousness and the first words she uttered were the words of the song that she had learned to love: "Clouds will turn to sunshine, night will turn to day, if you just remember, He's not far away."

What a beautiful philosophy for living! What a challenging thought to keep in mind when the burdens of life weigh heavily upon you! Beyond the clouds the sun still shines. You are in living relationship with One who is able to lead you through the darkness into the light. Beneath the snow there is still the power of the rose. Perhaps one will have to have the patience to wait until the proper season comes, but when that virtue is cultivated one is certain that ultimately "all things work together for good to them that love God." He then dares to live in confidence.

TABLE TALK: *Discuss together times when life has looked discouraging, when things have looked so dark there seemed no way out, and then how miraculously everything came out all right.*

JULY 18

A Living Commentary

Let no man despise thy youth; but be thou an ensample to them that believe, in word, in manner of life, in love, in faith, in purity. 1 Timothy 4:12.

Whether you want to be or not, today you are going to be an example for someone. There will be those who look at your life and say, "I am glad I don't have to live it that way," or better still, if you follow Christ, "I wish I had that wonderful spirit and that happy smile."

Perhaps you will try to tell somebody what it means to live close to Christ's friendship. But no one will know what you mean when you say, "God is love," unless you act it as well.

Thousands of people over the centuries have written commentaries about the Bible. You will, no doubt, agree that the best evidence of what it can do for you is a good example. As you write upon this page of life called "Today," be sure to place something there that will inspire another soul to love God. Watch your own living for the pitfalls which may cause others to stumble. Do not pass by on the other side, but offer a helping hand to make their journey a bit brighter.

If you hope to make of your life something worth while, you cannot just rely on ordinary life or on a second-rate plan. You will need the unerring guidance of the Master. Some years ago a ship was wrecked upon the high seas. As the sailors were making their escape in small boats one of them suddenly jumped overboard and began swimming back to the sinking ship. After anxious moments he appeared again swimming toward the rescue boats and holding something high above the waves. It was the compass which they had forgotten. And that sailor knew that, if they did not have it, there would be little chance of finding the way to safety again.

Do not attempt to live without a compass. Let your prayer be: "Jesus, Saviour, pilot me."

TABLE TALK: *Point out the things you can do that will be a creditable commentary on the Christian faith.*

JULY 19

God Proved His Love

For there is one God, one mediator also between God and men, himself man, Christ Jesus, who gave himself a ransom for all; the testimony to be borne in its own time. 1 Timothy 2:5-6.

Tourists in the Swiss Alpine country see much of the edelweiss flower in all of the souvenir and jewelry shops and in the picture galleries of that country. This flower is painted on wooden plates, pins, necklaces, and bracelets. It is engraved on spoons, and it is painted on postcards.

The traveler is curious to know more about this flower because he does not see it actually growing anywhere as he travels in that country; at least very few people ever see it except in a dried and pressed form in the shops. Therefore, it is not because of its prolific growth that it is given such attention.

If you would ask a shopkeeper you would learn the tradition surrounding this simple blossom that has endeared itself to the Swiss. The old story is this: Before a young woman would pick a suitor she wanted proof of his real devotion to her. The evidence of his love which the young woman asked of her sweetheart was that he be willing to climb to one of the mountain crags where the edelweiss grows. Search and search he would until he found the rare blossom for her. Then he would pick it, and bring it down the mountainside to her. It all involved danger, sacrifice, and hardship. But if the suitor really loved the woman he was willing to pay the price to show how genuine were his feelings toward her.

Now this is just an old tradition yet an appealing story to the Alpine country and to those who travel there. God, too, has proved over and over again how much He loves us. But the greatest thing He ever did was when He, too, in the person of Jesus, climbed a rocky hill. It was not the Swiss Alps, to be sure, for this mountain was called Calvary. He faced the bitter cold of friends who forsook Him. He felt the sting of swirling storm clouds about Him. But He climbed that hill for us.

TABLE TALK: *God does not often demand us to risk danger to show our love for Him. How are we, as Christians, to prove our devotion to God?*

JULY 20

Use What You Have

But thanks be to God, who giveth us the victory through our Lord Jesus Christ. 1 Corinthians 15:57.

In this day and age speed and methods of transportation seem most important. Newspapers come out with reports of some new jet plane which goes so fast you can hardly see it as it streaks across the sky. Even little children are caught up in this whirl of speed psychology.

One day as I was walking along I noticed two boys about four and eight years old respectively having a race. The four-year-old was riding a tricycle and the eight-year-old a bicycle. They were coming down the sidewalk in a fashion dangerous to any pedestrian in their pathway. But they were so intent on the race that they seemed to be oblivious of the fact that there might be any people in the way. For a while the bicycler was thoughtful enough to slow down to give the boy on the tricycle the feeling that he was going to win the race. But after a while he could not resist the urge to really put on the speed. The little tricycler was left far behind. He was pedaling as fast as his little legs would go and using all the breath he had, but finally he saw that he could not keep up with his older rival. He stopped and cried his lungs out as he sobbed out his failure to the whole world.

The race of life is just as uneven as the one between these boys and often we make the same fatal mistake as the little lad. When we do not have as much as our neighbor next door, we become bitter. We are jealous of the more talented businessman in the office across the hall, and as a result we do not improve in our own work, spending our time instead in thinking about others who get all the breaks. Each one of us has some talent. God only expects that we make the best possible use of that which we have. Then, even if we appear to lose, we will win!

TABLE TALK: *Tell of some incident when your seeming inability to "keep up" made you feel a failure. What did you do to adjust to the situation?*

JULY 21

A Light to Lead Us On

Then shall the righteous shine forth as the sun in the kingdom of their Father. He that hath ears, let him hear. Matthew 13:43.

Christianity is not merely an attempt to abide by a book of rules; it is a striving to achieve a life that has meaning. The Commandments of God are guideposts to help us reach that destination. When one has a heart that has stored up the riches of God, the real glory comes in sharing and in using them to help win the world for something worthwhile and lasting. When one begins to invest his life in this way, he begins to discover that He is not losing his riches, because the dividends which he gains become greater than all that he has been able to give. The glory of the wealth of the spirit is that it can never be taken from us.

A missionary from China told a story about what it really means to be Christian. One day as he visited an inland Chinese city he came upon a church which had been ravaged by the enemy. He noticed that the bulletin board had been torn down and crosses destroyed; even the name of the church had been chiseled out of the foundation stone. All the signs of Christianity had been erased on the outside, but when he stepped inside the church he found a handful of people kneeling in prayer.

Here in the midst of destruction were a people who had the spirit of Christianity deep down in their hearts. That was the treasure that nobody could take from them.

For those who remain faithful there is a promise that even the clouds will disappear. When days are dark, the Light of the world will still lead us on, giving the assurance that some day the sun will shine in all of its glory and each one will be rewarded according to the way that he has lived. Foolish indeed is the man who spends his time pursuing worldly pleasures that can be taken from him. Wise is he who seeks the spiritual riches which come from following God and which offer a treasure which can never be taken away.

TABLE TALK: *Discuss and compare what it requires to live as a Christian in the United States and in Russia or any of the Soviet-occupied countries.*

JULY 22

It Is Worth the Struggle

And the Lord shall guide thee continually, and satisfy thy soul in dry places, and make strong thy bones; and thou shalt be like a watered garden, and like a spring of water, whose waters fail not. Isaiah 58:11.

A family had been out fishing one late afternoon. Suddenly a great wind came up and a storm seemed to have originated from nowhere. The father hurriedly drew in the fish lines, put out the oars, and rowed in a very determined way toward the nearest point along the shore. This was an alarming experience for the children. It began to frighten them. Finally one of them burst forth, "Daddy, quit rowing, you're stirring up the whole lake."

Obviously the child's mind was not grasping the entire situation. It was the wind, the gathering storm that was responsible for this state of fury in the waters and not the father's oars as he wielded them to bring the family to safety.

Perhaps some of this childish thinking stays with us in adulthood. Are there not times in life when we are in the midst of a storm of confusion and instead of recognizing the hand of God as He tries to steer us away from the terrors of the storm we complain that He is of no help? We pray and there does not appear to be any answer. Difficulties still come and there are apparently no solutions to our problems. Actually, all the while God's hands are on the oars, unless we become so determined in our own stubborn, unseeing ways that we choose to leap headlong alone into the angry waters. If we decide to drown ourselves in a life of impenitent sinning, that is a matter of our own choice. There is a point at which God's hand cannot reach us to help; it is when He hears our resisting "No" to His pleading invitation, "Come unto Me."

The Christian way is the best way, but it does not always appear to be the easiest one to take. A Christian cannot drift with the winds and expect to reach home. But no matter how hard the struggle, the reward is worth it.

TABLE TALK: *Discuss why the Christian life is worth the struggle it entails.*

JULY 23

On Keeping Your Promise

So therefore whosoever he be of you that renounceth not all that he hath, he cannot be my disciple. Luke 14:33.

Some years ago a group of young students met at a camp on the shores of Lake Champlain in Vermont. One evening they gathered around the campfire for a candlelight communion service. Each one was given a candle to light from a flaming birch log. When the service was finished, the pastor told them to carry the lighted candle back to the cabins and then to put out the flame. He suggested that they take the candle home with them, too, and each month they were to light it again and look into its burning flame. With that light they could rekindle the fellowship and self-dedication of that communion service and they could remember with a renewing devotion the one who is the Light of the world.

"You are modern disciples of Christ," said the pastor. "Here at this hour it is easy to think high thoughts and resolve to do more, to work hard for the kingdom of God. Do not let your resolution die with this flame."

Sometimes we make bold promises to God and tell Him how much He means to us. So often it is easy to forget and to put our own desires before His. We might even go to church each Sunday to worship Him, to confess our many sins, and to affirm our faith in His almighty power. But then, during the week, we often drift away from our commitment and try to go the way alone. Our Master wants our full-time service, but we also desperately need Him every moment of life, if we are to make it useful and happy.

Within your heart there must be a cathedral where you can go during the busy day to find peace and comfort. Here you and God can be alone to talk about the task that lies ahead or the troubles that you must face. Then no matter how high the raging seas of despair, you will have the eternal light of love and hope.

TABLE TALK: *Have you ever been to a Luther League rally or some similar gathering? What inspiration did you receive? Did you later lose enthusiasm?*

The Faith of a Little Child

See that ye despise not one of these little ones: for I say unto you, that in heaven their angels do always behold the face of my Father who is in heaven. Matthew 18:10.

A little girl was being prepared for a very serious operation. She had been a very good child, faithful in Sunday school and the church. She loved her Lord with a childlike faith that never wavered. She trusted solely in His protecting care.

But now, momentarily,she was frightened as the nurses came into her room to prepare her for her operation. They put her on the litter and spoke kindly as they gave her the anesthetic, yet fear again crept into her little heart. But the doctor said, "You don't have to be afraid. It is just like going to sleep." She smiled and answered, "Well then, I better say my prayers first." She folded her hands and with childlike faith prayed:

> "Now I lay me down to sleep,
> I pray Thee, Lord, my soul to keep.
> If I should die before I wake,
> I pray Thee, Lord, my soul to take.
> If I should live for other days,
> I pray Thee, Lord, to guide my ways."

It seemed as if there was a presence in that room, and peace had come to this little heart. No longer was she afraid and quite willingly she accepted the anesthetic. The operation was a success; but more than that, she had preached an unforgettable sermon to those about her.

Except you have the faith of a little child, you cannot know the blessings of God as you should. How confident are these little ones in Him whom they have learned to love! They trust Him because they really believe Him. They take Him at His Word. Their faith is one of perfect and complete trust in the Master. How wonderful if all could have that kind of faith! How foolish we are when we allow ourselves to grow away from that simple trust which enables us to face anything victoriously! Each day of living should be faced with a faith like that.

TABLE TALK: *If you had to have an operation, what spiritual preparation would you make?*

JULY 25

What Makes Us Really Free?

And Nathanael said unto him, Can any good thing come out of Nazareth? Philip saith unto him, Come and see. John 1:46.

Perhaps you have visited some of the famous historical places in our country. There are those that are very beautiful and others that are plain and simple. But all of them are symbols of our democracy.

At Mount Vernon, high on the banks of the Potomac River, is the home of George Washington, the Father of His Country. Your visits may have taken you to Richmond, Virginia, and to the quiet old church where Patrick Henry spoke the famous words, "Give me liberty or give me death." If you have been in Philadelphia, you no doubt have visited Independence Hall, and on a busy street corner you may have looked through the iron pickets at a stone carved with the name of Benjamin Franklin. At Springfield, Illinois, you may have visited the great memorial to one known as a liberator of men, Abraham Lincoln.

Wherever we go, we understand that the places have been made important because of great men and women who have lived, worked, spoken, and died. Often their theme was one and the same, freedom. Notice how such words as slavery, liberty, independence, are woven into the pattern of these men's lives. Everything they said and did was aimed at setting a nation free.

In spite of gallant and courageous men throughout the centuries, none of us would ever have been freed from our own sin and guilt had it not been for a man called Jesus who died upon the cross on a little low hill called Calvary. In memory we need to visit that humble place each day we live, for it reminds us of the victory which can come to us by faith. Here we are told of God's great love and mercy, which cleanses us from all sin. Here we discover that we are redeemed from the bondage which has imprisoned us. Here indeed is the truth which sets men free.

TABLE TALK: *Name some gallant men of the church who spent their life for the Christian cause; for example, Luther, Calvin, Wesley. Who are some of our contemporary courageous men?*

207

JULY 26

Help Wanted

But be ye strong, and let not your hands be slack; for your work shall be rewarded. 2 Chronicles 15:7.

If you walk down the business streets of any city today you will probably see signs advertising "Help Wanted" and "Positions Open." However many people are now employed, business concerns are still looking for more workers. But we are warned that someday jobs will be hard to find and many people will be walking the streets looking for a chance to make a living.

In God's kingdom there will never be any unemployed. There will always be work to do, like winning others to His side, or helping His followers to grow wiser and stronger in the ways of Christian living. Someone once called the Apostle Paul the first "relief administrator." He raised money in the churches to help the poor and the sick and wherever he went he looked for a chance to lend a helping hand. He understood that the whole world was his mission field. At every turn of the road he found some hungry soul that desperately needed spiritual nourishment.

Some years ago there was a meeting of farmers from a large area. College professors and scientists had given long speeches about the best way to till the soil. Finally one man stood up and said, "I am just a plain dirt farmer and I can prove it by my hands. I appreciate all these suggestions, but I have myself learned an awful lot by just getting out and plowing the fields."

It is good and well, and also necessary to tell how the world must be won for Christ. But it is more important that we invest hours of toil which give proof of our enthusiasm and spirit. God wants the enlistment of people who are willing to give themselves totally to His kingdom work.

A job is open for you today. Find the sign "Help Wanted" wherever it might be. For the Master is counting on you to answer His call.

TABLE TALK: *Suppose you were answering the "Help Wanted" ad. Discuss what abilities and talents each of you could offer for His service.*

JULY 27

How Are You Building?

Except the Lord build the house, they labor in vain that build it: except the Lord keep the city, the watchman waketh but in vain. Psalm 127:1.

Building a life is like building a house. First a good foundation has to be constructed. The Bible tells about two men who built houses, the one upon the sand, and the other upon the rock. When the winds and the rains descended, the house upon the sand collapsed. There are also storms that beset our lives. Sometimes they appear suddenly, and strike severely, but if our lives are built securely on Christ, the Rock of Ages, we have nothing to fear.

After the foundation, we must construct the framework; that is, the vertical and horizontal pieces that hold the roof. In a spiritual building, the framework can be likened unto character. Framed by His principles, a life is well on its way toward the goal of successful living.

But the house must also have a roof to protect it from the elements. So life needs courage to give it strength to meet all manner of adversity. Stephen was stoned to death, and willingly he gave his life for the cause. In so doing, he was strengthened by a power beyond his own.

And yet the house is not complete—at least, not if we really want abundant living. There must be wallpaper, furnishings, and electric lights. These are the things that create the personality, and that help make the walls and the roof a home. Even so, life must have appreciation for the spiritual qualities, such as music and art and good literature. Only in developing the spiritual, as well as the material side of our life, can we hope for the integrated personality, that knows peace within.

The building of a life is like the building of a house. Some lives are beautiful, some may seem insignificant, but all can be important in the sight of God, if within them are found the elements of faith and love.

TABLE TALK: *If you were remodeling your house, you probably would make a few changes. Are there any changes you would make in your life in a similar remodeling?*

JULY 28

Every Step More Worth While

For as many as are led by the Spirit of God, these are sons of God. Romans 8:14.

Some years ago a group of men spent a few weeks in a famous resort in the Canadian Rockies. One day they thought they would climb one of the foothills so as to gain a better view of the highest peaks and the beautiful scenery that surrounded the whole mountain range. It was a bit more of a climb than they had anticipated. And as they were about half way up the hillside they met another party of vacationers coming down. In passing one of the men simply said, "Is the climb worth while?" Without the slightest hesitation the answer came from one of the other party, "Yes, sir! Everything above this level is worth while."

People who are willing to climb above the many earthly troubles and temptations will find a life filled with strength and power greater than anyone could ever imagine. But you must venture to the mountaintops of Christian living. You must make a commitment to Christ to follow Him every step of the way. Otherwise you will be led down the crooked pathways of life which bring worry and dissatisfaction.

Did you ever see a river which flowed in a straight line? Probably not, because rivers from their very source wind back and forth as they travel across the countryside through the niches in the earth and through the valleys surrounded by hills. The river becomes crooked because it always takes the easiest way. And it will flow many extra miles in its journey to the sea just to take the path of least resistance.

Your life will wind through the valleys of temptation and defeat if you always choose to take the easiest way. But the road that Christ leads you upon, though difficult at times to travel, will bring you to victory, for you will have a true friend at your side who will go with you. And never forget that the climb is worth while!

TABLE TALK: *Suppose you were going on a trip. What should your prayer be before the journey? Upon the return?*

JULY 29

Making Life More Radiant

Ye have not chosen me, but I have chosen you, and ordained you, that ye should go and bring forth fruit, and that your fruit should remain. John 15:16.

A man who lived in an apartment building went out shopping one day and bought a beautiful vase. He brought it home and put it on the shelf. But it seemed out of place there. It was much too beautiful compared to the surroundings. He had not noticed how ugly some of the other things in his apartment were until he saw them in relationship to this beautiful vase. First, he noticed that some stuffing was coming out of the davenport. The wallpaper was torn. The carpeting was frayed.

He had the choice of doing one of two things. Either he could take the vase out of the apartment and leave the setting just as it was, or he could leave the vase in the apartment and change the setting. He chose the latter course. He had the davenport fixed, the rooms repapered, and new carpeting installed. When all the work was done the entire apartment had become transformed. Everything had come into the right relationship with the vase.

In a similar way the miracle happens when Jesus comes into a person's life. Each one of us has two choices. We can either change the setting of our living to make Him feel at home, or we have to get rid of Him because He does not seem to fit in with the other things which clutter up our place of abode.

The cost of keeping Christ in our lives should certainly not be a deterrent. No merit or worthiness is necessary on our part. We come as trusting children to one to whom we will always be debtors. We ask Him to come into our lives and to make the setting worthy of His presence. Our lives are made new again, the ugly marks of sin are erased, and we begin to know radiant living.

TABLE TALK: *Can you think of any life that has been changed materially as well as spiritually by Jesus' presence. Imagine and discuss the changes that could be wrought by taking Christ's examples of radiant living into a slum or poor section of your town.*

JULY 30

To What Are You Listening?

And he said, Who hath ears to hear, let him hear. Mark 4:9.

A friend told us how as a youngster she lived on a busy street corner where there was traffic all night long. She was used to going to sleep with the sound of cars passing by. One summer when she was about twelve years old she was invited to stay several weeks at a home in the apple orchard country. She just could not sleep nights there because it was so quiet. The little noises of the chirping crickets, the croaking of the frogs, and the drone of the irrigation pump were disturbing to her sleep.

This incident can teach us a lesson. We hear what we want to hear, what we are accustomed to hear. In the city, where we become used to certain noises, we become so accustomed to them that we can sleep in spite of them. If we remained long enough out in the country, we would get used to the sounds of a night there and learn to enjoy them, too.

But we hear the voices we want to hear! A mother will hear her baby cry even though she can sleep through much louder disturbances. The minute the young one cries her ears are tuned to his call. A doctor will hear his phone, because he is listening for the call of the sick.

There is a blind piano tuner who will work and work until middle "C" is in correct pitch and then he will tune the rest of the notes accordingly. He will work at his tones long after we might think they are correct, for his ear still hears the discordant sound.

In this busy world there are so many sounds which can attract our ears. We have to learn to listen to some and shut out others. But there is one call to which we must be tuned at all times and that is the call of Christ. If His note is sounded in our hearts all the rest of life can be tuned by it.

"He that hath ears to hear, let him hear."

TABLE TALK: *Each person has a different voice. What voices do you think are especially pleasant? Try to develop a cheerful pleasant sounding voice.*

JULY 31

God's Strength Is Sufficient

They that trust in the Lord are as mount Zion, which cannot be moved, but abideth for ever. As the mountains are round about Jerusalem, so the Lord is round about his people from this time forth and for evermore. Psalm 125:1-2.

An adventurous young lad once set out in a small boat to travel down a long and treacherous river. With a great deal of skill and strength he managed very well until, one day, he came toward dangerous rapids. Though he pulled with all of his strength on his oars, the current was stronger than he, and it seemed certain that the small boat would be dashed upon the rocks. A farmer near by spotted the boy. Realizing his danger, he ran quickly to the river bank and threw a long rope into the water farther up stream, hoping that it would be carried to where the boy was. Then he began to shout, "Drop your oars, take hold of the rope, and I will pull you in." The boy's hope was not in trying to row his small boat against the treacherous current with his own strength, but rather in grabbing hold of the rope which the man on shore held securely.

Victory is not in our own strength or wisdom, but in the almighty power and understanding of God. We are God's own masterpiece, but only because He lives within us and gives of His great love. Man possesses great God-given powers, a knowledge that allows him to probe into the very center of existence and the scientific laws that govern our daily living.

But more than all this, God has given us a soul that can become greater than all the discoveries and achievements of mankind. In living close to the Master, one discovers the peace which the world with all of its inventions cannot give.

What are you making of your life? Is it something that glitters just for a moment? Something that is helpless against rowing the rapids you encounter? Or is it a life that is confident and sure because you have taken hold of a Saviour who will pull you out of the rapids of life to firm ground and will direct you as you build upon true foundation stones a life that will endure.

TABLE TALK: *Has there been a time when you were alone and not able to stand? Who helped you?*

213

AUGUST 1

There Is Sufficient Power

For the joy of the Lord is your strength. Nehemiah 8:10.

One day she walked into my office with a radiant smile. She was a young woman whose husband had gone through a very serious operation. Just the night before he was to go into the operating room he had been notified by telegram that the company by whom he was employed had gone out of business. There was serious doubt on the part of the doctor as to the success of the operation. The young woman was told that the verdict might not be known for several months. So this was the situation the young woman faced, a husband who was unable to provide, a family to support, no money coming in, and bills coming due.

"You don't know how grateful I am, Pastor," she said, "because things have worked out as well as they have. I don't know what door is going to open for me but I have faith to believe that, if I try to do everything in my power to help, God will see me through. I have a wonderful feeling of peace within."

There were two choices that presented themselves to her and that present themselves to each one of us who is faced with similar trouble. She could give up, thereby rendering ineffective any possible solution of her problem. Or confidently she could face the future with God, knowing that if, in reliance upon His power, she used her own best judgment, there would come some solution for her.

She took the latter road and this was the result. She is now employed. Doctors even suggest that there is a possibility of her husband becoming well, and through some adjustments in their living they are managing to pay their bills.

With God as a partner one always has the power that will conquer. If we face our cross, whatever it might be, He stands beside us to help us through. "For the joy of the Lord is your strength."

TABLE TALK: *Have you ever been faced with two choices, despair or hope? Which did you choose?*

AUGUST 2

Deliver Us from Evil

For this cause I also, when I could no longer forbear, sent that I might know your faith, lest by any means the tempter had tempted you, and our labor should be in vain.

1 Thessalonians 3:5.

A good friend of mine used to tell of an imaginary conversation between the cornstalk and the morning-glory. He stood in a field one day and this is what he thought he heard: In a very inviting voice the morning-glory said, "Mr. Cornstalk, won't you please let me lean upon you?" The cornstalk replied, "No, because it is my ambition to grow up to be the tallest and most stately cornstalk, in the entire field." "But," replied the morning-glory, "if you let me lean upon you I will make you the most beautiful cornstalk, so that people will admire you and think more highly of you." Finally the morning-glory overcame the vanity of the cornstalk and was allowed to lean upon it.

As time passed on they both began to grow. Without the cornstalk knowing it, the morning-glory kept winding and winding itself around it. One day the cornstalk said, "I want you to leave me, because you are choking me to death." But the morning-glory paid no attention to what it said. Finally one day the cornstalk fell to the ground lifeless. The morning-glory had ensnared and strangled it with its cruel beauty.

This is a parable of life. So often the tempter comes and encourages us to commit some sin. "If you do this," he says, "I will make you the most popular person in your whole group. It really won't hurt you any. Just try it once and see for yourself the pleasure it will give you." Whenever we give way to such temptations, tragedy always results. We awaken in the morning with an unhappy feeling because we have done wrong. Many times, we continue in this sin until all spiritual life is choked out.

The man is wise indeed who uses the strength of God, which is available to all, as he faces the tempter and refuses to go his way.

TABLE TALK: *Have you ever been faced with a temptation to do something questionable that would make you "popular"? How did you react?*

AUGUST 3

Are You Going Anywhere?

And thine ears shall hear a word behind thee, saying, This is the way, walk ye in it.   Isaiah 30:21.

Two friends were driving fast to reach their destination. They had been vacationing in the South and were on their way home. At one point of the journey they became careless about consulting the road map. Finally, wondering where they were, they stopped and asked a filling station attendant if they were on the right way to St. Louis. "St. Louis?" the man replied, "Why, you are on your way to Memphis." They had missed a turn in the road because of their failure to follow the map, and the result was that they had gone many miles in the wrong direction. Now they had a choice: They could either continue in the direction they were going and get farther away from home, or they could retrace their course, though the process seemed long and tedious, and find again the right road to their destination. Only by such a course could they find the happiness which they desired.

God has provided a map for us in His Word and, if we follow it, it will lead us safely to our destination. Only when we neglect reading the Bible and following its instructions do we lose our way and find ourselves in some far-off country. If we go His way, we do not need to travel alone nor journey in our own strength, for He gives us the power to go on.

A man walked down the tracks to find a Pullman coach. The porter suggested he get into a certain car. "Will it be all right if I get into this one?" asked the passenger. "Well, it is all right with me," was the answer, "but it isn't hooked to anything that is going anywhere."

Each day we should take careful inventory of our lives to make sure that we are taking time to hear God and to let Him lead us to our proper destination. He is ever willing to supply us with all that we need for abundant living. Only when we fail to follow His instructions, do we become lost in a lonesome world. His way is the only one that leads home.

TABLE TALK: *Have you ever taken the wrong road? Discuss what caused the mistake. What does it suggest for life's journey?*

AUGUST 4

Knowing Where Home Is

Come unto me, all ye that labor and are heavy laden, and I will give you rest. Matthew 11:28.

A woman was once visiting in the cottage of a shepherd girl in the mountains of Norway. The setting of this humble home was as beautiful as one could find. There were green mountain slopes with rushing streams tumbling down so fast and stark white against the green grass and gray boulders. Olga, the shepherd girl, told the visiting friend that she grazed and milked eight cows. "And how many sheep do you tend?" she was asked. Olga really did not know how many there were in her flock. "Then how do you know how many to look for when you go out in the evening to bring them home?" she was asked. "Oh, I don't have to do that. They always return home in the evening, coming right down the slope that descends to my cottage," Olga replied. "They know where home is."

These sheep know where home is. They have their bearings and know where their security is to be found. They start out early in the morning to graze on the slopes. Perhaps the day is good for them. They find lush green grasses wherever they go, and streams from which they drink refreshing waters. Or the day may not be of such a sort. The grass is sparse and the streams inaccessible because of large boulders in the way. There may be thistles with which they have to contend. But they know at end of day where home is.

Do you see the parallel in our lives? There is a loving heavenly Father who waits for us at the close of each day. His invitation is always the same: "Come unto me, all ye that labor and are heavy laden, and I will give you rest." Whether the day has been good or bad there is no greater happiness for us than to know where our true home is, and to be assured that underneath are the everlasting arms of God.

TABLE TALK: *What are some of the reassuring comforts of home that you do not find in the business world, the schools, or the stores? What benefits would there be if comforts such as "love" and "peace" were carried out of the home?*

217

AUGUST 5

A Power Beyond

For thou hast delivered my soul from death: hast thou not delivered my feet from falling, that I may walk before God in the light of the living? Psalm 56:13.

There is a small Austrian town which lies in a beautiful valley surrounded by high hills. On one hillside stands a large grove of trees which reaches toward the peak of a slope. That village has a law which places a serious penalty upon any person who cuts down one of these trees. Although it sounds like a peculiar law there is good reason for it. These militant soldiers of nature form a natural barrier on the hillside protecting the village below from heavy landslides which might bury the small houses and stores.

There are many things in this life which threaten to crush us beneath our own selfishness and pride. And we need a strong barrier to protect us. Many people believe that money or prestige can be that wall, but we need something infinitely stronger than anything we can find in this world. Since actually it is the things of the world that threaten us, we lift up our eyes unto the hills and find that our help comes from God, whose strength and wisdom tower above even the most valuable of earthly goods. He is like a strong barrier of trees that keeps us from being destroyed by the avalanche of sin. Apart from His protecting care we can expect temptation to fall upon us, surround us on every side, and smother us to eternal death.

Have you ever had the feeling that somehow you are walking the road of life alone? Even though friends and loved ones surround you, there can come a sense of loneliness and despair. There is one real friend who can give you courage and hope. It is Christ the Master. When such loneliness comes, think of it as a call from God to walk closely by His side and to feel His loving arms about us. Remember the gracious invitation of the Master, "Come unto me, and I will give you rest."

TABLE TALK: *Christ is the towering strength in which you can lose your weakness. Heed His call and He will give you power to throw off sin and live an abundant, happy life.*

Are You Ashamed of God?

Jesus answered, If I glorify myself, my glory is nothing: it is my Father that glorifieth me; of whom ye say, that he is your God. John 8:54.

The tables were close together in a crowded hotel room, so close that you could eavesdrop on your neighbor's conversation without even wanting to do so. At the next table were a young man, his wife, their four year old daughter, and the young man's mother. From what they were saying it was a rare experience for them to be at a restaurant. They were thoroughly enjoying dining out on the occasion of celebrating grandmother's birthday. Just as they were leaving the table the little girl turned around with a radiant smile, and with no introduction or preliminary pointed to her father and said, "That's my Daddy."

The father hearing his daughter's words grinned rather sheepishly, but you could see there was joy in his face over the enthusiasm of her introduction.

It was a thrill to see how proud the little girl was of her father and how much her open expression of love meant to him. Much as we should love our earthly parents, there is a heavenly Father who should mean even more to us. He has been so good to us. Why is it that we fail to introduce Him to our friends and acquaintances who do not know Him? Why is it that we do not invite our friends to His church?

If we are ashamed of our heavenly Father, how can we expect Him not to be ashamed of us? Each day we are so dependent upon Him. We greatly need His love and mercy. But if we are unwilling to admit to others that we belong to Him, we run the risk of separating ourselves from Him, and there can be no happiness or joy apart from a friendship with Jesus.

Each day let us remember that He is present with us. Let us make it one of our objects in life to introduce Him to the many friends we meet, and let them see what He means to us.

TABLE TALK: *Discuss those you know who could be "introduced" to Christ. Is there a business associate, a schoolmate, a neighbor who is not affiliated with a church? Plan a method of approach to each.*

AUGUST 7

Do You Love to Serve?

And that in the good ground these are such as in an honest and good heart, having heard the word, hold it fast, and bring forth fruit with patience. Luke 8:15.

Sometimes the most insignificant deed can have tremendous consequences. We should be careful, therefore, in each act of our daily lives. We may be influencing someone else by the things we do and say.

One morning, a waitress came to the table of a party of people to take their orders. "Are the pancakes really good?" she was asked. "What do you expect me to say?" she snapped, "What do you think the boss would say if I told you they weren't?" Then one of the party turned to her and said, "I just thought perhaps you would put honesty above any other consideration, and that you would tell the truth regardless of the outcome for yourself." The whole attitude of the waitress was vindictive, and when the party left the cafe, they resolved never to return again. The spirit of this one person influenced their thinking the entire day.

But consider another. She could not be helpful enough. She kept the coffee cup filled. She brought extra rolls when the plate was empty and she smiled as she waited on her customers. Finally someone said to her, "I like your spirit as you go about your work." Her face just beamed as she replied, "Oh, I just love to serve people!"

That is the spirit of the Master. How He loved to serve people! As He went about doing good, He never thought about Himself, or the cross to which He was to be led. He was not afraid of losing His life, but stood firmly for the things He knew were right and just, and was willing to pay the price of His convictions.

Never compromise for the sake of safety. "Whosoever saveth his life shall lose it, and whosoever shall lose his life shall save it." Always be honest, regardless of the consequences. If in so doing, you lose your earthly occupation, you will gain eternal employment in the "house of many mansions."

TABLE TALK: *Discuss the various types of service you receive each day from others. What is their attitude and how does it affect your living?*

AUGUST 8

Make Sacrifice Worth While

I can do all things in him that strengtheneth me.
Philippians 4:13.

A little lad wanted to go roller skating with other youngsters on a fine spring day. But his roller skates were locked up in the garage. Finding an open window he started to crawl through. In the struggle to do so he knocked out the prop which held up the window sash and it came crashing down upon him. Unable to free himself, he was strangled to death before help could reach him. The thought of having fun with the other children was enough to make the lad risk climbing through the window, and in the end it cost him his life.

Each and every day, all of us pay high prices for things of little value. Too often we put our faith and trust in material wealth, which will some day rust away. We take the risk of losing our souls when we forget how much greater is the value of the eternal than that of the material.

A group of American soldiers were stationed on a small tropical island in the Pacific. One evening they were attracted by singing coming from a nearby native village. They discovered that a missionary had worked there for three years and this night his converts were gathered together in a service of praise. They could not understand the words which were being sung, but they could easily catch the spirit which filled the heart of each singer. As they stood there they could not help thinking that here were dividends from the investment of a missionary who was willing to make the sacrifice of going to this faraway place and bring the gospel to these people who had never heard of Christ. This missionary had made sacrifices for something of value; the little boy had sacrificed his life for a passing sensation.

A worth-while investment will bring worth-while returns. In this case these natives had helped save many American lives during the course of war, only because they had been taught about Christ the loving Saviour by a missionary who had first sacrificed himself for them.

TABLE TALK: *Name some things in life worth sacrificing for. What are some that are not worth the cost?*

AUGUST 9

Singing Through Life

For he is our God, and we are the people of his pasture, and the sheep of his hand. Psalm 95:7.

An old Chinese philosopher was once asked, "What was the happiest moment in your life?" He replied, "It was the day a little girl walked down the road singing after I had told her the way to go." Just meditate upon that statement for a moment. Ask yourself this question, "Am I helping people to go singing through life because I am showing them the right way to go?"

There are so many people who are still walking the pathways of darkness. In spite of our increased missionary efforts, almost half of the people in our own country are yet unchurched. Almost every other person does not even belong to church, and a great many of those who do belong are not contributing to its work as they should.

A wonderful goal for any soul would be to resolve to help more people to go through life singing. We need more Andrews to find brothers like Peter and to bring them to Christ. Remember, you keep preaching the gospel by the way you live. People are watching you to see whether or not your religion is doing anything for your life and if it is, they too will be attracted by it. Remember to be careful in the words that you speak and in the things that you do. For you are somebody's ideal and you may be persuading him to do the very same things.

As you live day by day remember to take the high road, because someone may be following you. "No man liveth unto himself." We are our brothers' keepers. We will be held responsible not only for our own lives but for the influence which we exert on the lives of others. No greater thrill can come to you than to hear someone singing after they have been told the way!

TABLE TALK: *Have you ever known an ideal person whom you admired and whose example you followed? Were you ever disillusioned by your ideal? If someone admired you, in what ways would you wish to change in order to be a better example. Discuss.*

222

AUGUST 10

He Makes All Things New

Behold I make all things new. And he saith, Write: for these words are faithful and true. Revelation 21:5.

In northern Minnesota there are rich iron mines. For many years various companies have mined the best iron ore, which was found in the surface layers. When they reached the grade called taconite, drilling ceased, since in time past the second grade ore was not thought useable.

Now the people of that area are not so sure that the supply of good iron ore is unlimited. They cannot afford to waste any portion of the ore. And so they are beginning to redeem the taconite. They bring it out of the earth, grind it to dust, and wash out the impure particles. What remains is usually sixty per cent iron ore content. The whole process is involved and costly, but the final product is worth all the inconvenience.

A parallel comes to mind. God's children are like taconite. There is good in them and also bad. We never know our real worth until we are broken by penitence. Then the great Creator separates the good from the bad and remakes our personalities, molding them according to His will so that we may become a blessing unto mankind. Then we can be used, not as steel to erect buildings of material strength, but as instruments in the hand of God to build spiritual fortresses in our own lives and in the lives of others.

Once more the parallel holds. To reclaim the good taconite is a very expensive process. But infinitely more costly has been the redemption of man. For the price was the Son of God, who died at Calvary that new life might come to those who choose Him as their Saviour.

But God has declared that the cost is not too great, if more can be claimed for His kingdom. As we give the broken pieces of our lives to the Master, He takes them and remakes them into something that can become a blessing for this is His promise: "Behold, I make all things new."

TABLE TALK: *A life is redeemed when Christ is brought into it. Can you think of someone in your community who should be told about Christ's redemption?*

AUGUST 11

Practice Makes Perfect

Blessed are the eyes which see the things that ye see: for I say unto you, that many prophets and kings desired to see the things which ye see, and saw them not; and to hear the things which ye hear, and heard them not. Luke 10:23-24.

More of us need to practice our Christian faith. There is much theorizing about Christianity today. But what we need more than anything else, if results are to be gained for His kingdom, is that all of us set our feet upon His path. Paul's instruction to Timothy is this: "Exercise thyself unto godliness."

Have you ever watched somebody use the typewriter? To those of us who have not had that training, it is a fascinating experience. We marvel at how quickly the fingers find the keys. It all looks very simple but let the untrained sit down and attempt to go through the same procedure. He will find himself very awkward and clumsy. His fingers will hit between the keys as often as directly upon them. And to be able to translate a manuscript into typewritten form without looking from the copy to the keys is of course an impossibility.

As we analyze what makes the difference the first observation would obviously be that the typist has had the desire to learn. She has had to study and practice, and all this takes time and patience.

So often we see a life of love and service exemplified in someone else and breathe the deep desire, "Oh, if I could only be like she is!"

If our desire is to do those Christlike things there is someone to whom we can go for help. His invitation is, "Come and learn of me." He will teach us with infinite patience telling us how to use every moment of our life so that life will be joyful and satisfying. His chief textbook is the Bible, but we gain further instruction by talking to Him in prayer. If we enroll in His school we will at the end receive a diploma, as we hear His voice: "Well done, good and faithful servant, enter thou into the rest of the Lord."

TABLE TALK: *We learn of Christ's way each day. Discuss how your conceptions have changed from year to year.*

AUGUST 12

The Power to Overcome

The Lord is nigh unto them that are of a broken heart; and saveth such as are of a contrite spirit. Psalm 34:18.

If today you should feel like complaining because your lot in life has been difficult or your burdens too great, think of a man I know who has shown me how a victorious Christ-given spirit can overcome outward circumstances. I met and heard him one night as he appeared on a program with me.

This is his background. He has been blind from birth. Now in his forties, he has mastered a trade. As an electrician, he can do a complete wiring job in a home. He can measure accurately, knows what materials to order, and is able to take care of the installation and complete the job to such satisfaction that it will pass examination by the most critical of experts.

He has had very little, if any, voice training. When he sang there flowed from his soul a rich mellow voice, as he gave expression to his faith in the words of the Twenty-seventh Psalm: "The Lord is my light and my salvation. Whom then shall I fear? The Lord is the strength of my life. Of whom then shall I be afraid?"

There was not a person who heard him that night who was not a little ashamed of himself for the many times he had complained that life had not gone just right for him. There were many who resolved because of his testimony that they would seek to concentrate more on the many blessings which they possessed, rather than on the little irritations that so easily upset us. Many wonderful sermons have been preached by great men of God, but rarely have I heard one that inspired me as much as that which came from this voice in the wilderness. He was physically living in the darkness of another world, but spiritually singing his way into the hearts of men and making glad his homeward way.

TABLE TALK: *Discuss someone you know who has had a similar hardship. Were they able to conquer it in this manner?*

AUGUST 13

You Never Walk Alone

For he will give his angels charge over thee, to keep thee in all thy ways. Psalm 91:11.

A pastor had been calling upon one of his parishioners and he tried as best he could to convince her not only of the love of God, but also of His presence. But each time he came to her hospital room she would only complain about her sickness and her terrible pain. And she couldn't understand why God had allowed her to suffer so much affliction. At night she couldn't sleep.

Finally one day the minister turned to the passage of Scripture which reads like this: "He shall give His angels charge concerning thee and they will guide thee in all thy way." Quietly he told her that God was in the struggle with her and that if she would just open her heart to Him she would discover His presence and would find one who is able to soothe and quiet her and grant the peace beyond all human knowledge.

When he returned the next day, he saw her radiant smile as she greeted him with these words, "Pastor, the angels were here last night to take care of me." Then she proceeded to tell him of how she had had her first good night of sleep in many a week and of how grateful she was that God had revealed His presence to her, enabling her now to withstand any difficulty that she would have to encounter.

As a man was about to leave the shop of an old Christian tailor he heard this salutation: "Peace be unto you two." Surprised, he turned around to inquire, "To me and to whom else?" Radiantly the tailor replied, "The angel looking over your shoulder."

We never do have to walk alone. Each day we can remind ourselves of the assurance as children of the heavenly Father that He is with us always even unto the end of the world. "For he shall give his angels charge over thee, to keep thee in all thy ways."

TABLE TALK: *What changes would you have made in your life today if you had remembered an angel was walking beside you?*

For What Are You Searching?

Canst thou by searching find out God? Canst thou find out the Almighty unto perfection? Job 11:7.

Each one of us is searching for something every day we live. The question is whether we understand what really is of value. Too often we lose sight of that for which we so diligently search.

Henry W. Grady found the answer to his searching. He was a well-known newspaper editor and had attained a great deal of success in his job. But as time went on he seemed to lose the spark and ambition of life that had made him so popular. He became ill and decided that a vacation trip was what he needed. So he spent a few restful months at the seashore. Upon returning to work he still seemed to lack the spirit which he had to have for the fast moving newspaper business. And so he consulted the best doctors available to see if they could effect a cure. Each time as they thought he was ready to begin anew, he would sink back into mental and physical despair.

Then he returned to his home and relived with his mother the days of his early childhood when he had learned of Jesus. In his search for health and contentment he made this great discovery. He learned not only in words, but in actual fact, that God is the most wonderful Physician of all. In His eagerness to find earthly security and happiness he found the treasure of faith and trust in Christ.

A family left Europe many years ago to find a land of freedom and prosperity. They landed in America and set out across the country to find a new home. When they reached a promising bit of land they cleared away the trees and bushes from a small patch of ground and there built a house. When it was finished the mother seemed to be unhappy. Very concerned, the husband asked, "What is it you don't like?" "We are so surrounded by trees and forests that I can't even see out of the windows." "That is true," he said, "you can't see out, but you can always see up."

In discovering that secret, you will have found lasting joy.

TABLE TALK: *Do you know someone who is searching for happiness, health, and success? What can you do to help him find real happiness?*

AUGUST 15

A Cathedral in Candlelight

And one of them, when he saw that he was healed, turned back, with a loud voice glorifying God, and he fell down upon his face at his feet, giving him thanks: and he was a Samaritan.

Luke 17:15-16.

A group of high-school boys had spent several weeks at one of the church camps located in the midst of God's great out-of-door glory. They had been much inspired, not only by the spoken messages, but also by the countless number of sermons God had preached to them in the beauties of nature.

They wanted to do something to show their gratitude to God. One day they were conspicuous by their absence from most of the camp activity. No one knew what they were doing, but they asked the camp dean, their minister, to join them in their evening devotions.

It was a night he will never forget. As he approached their cabin that evening, he heard boys' voices singing, "Thank you, Lord, for saving my soul; Thank you, Lord, for making me whole; Thank you, Lord, for giving to me, Thy great salvation so rich and free." The pastor walked into the cabin, and found a small cathedral in candlelight. The boys had spent the day building a cabin altar. The backdrop was painted white. Upon the altar table stood two birch candle holders, and a birch log was on the floor to be used as a kneeler. The pastor was asked to dedicate this altar to the glory of God, and after the simple, impromptu, but impressive service had taken place, each of the lads walked up to the altar, read a verse from the Bible and then knelt and said a word of prayer. The evening rendezvous with God ended as the group together prayed the Benediction.

What a different world this would be if all of us would have that same devotion to the God who loves us and gives so freely of His abundance! Why not build Him an altar in your heart?

TABLE TALK: *Discuss instances in which you have desperately needed help and have prayed to God. Afterward, when all was well, did you thank God? Do you ever just in the course of a day stop to talk to God, to tell Him how happy you are and to thank Him for being so good to you?*

AUGUST 16

God Is Our Refuge

God is our refuge and strength, a very present help in trouble.
Psalm 46:1.

Driving along the city streets, you have no doubt often passed a fire station. You may not have paid much attention to it except to glance at the shiny red engine standing inside. But if suddenly you should discover a fire in your home, you would quickly call the fire department and it would be only a matter of minutes before help would arrive to help put out the flames. When there was no danger you did not give much thought to that engine in the fire station, but when flames threaten your security you are very glad someone is on the job waiting to help in time of need.

So it is with God. He keeps eternal vigilance even when you think you can get along without His guidance and help. He is still there, willing and waiting to answer whenever you call. God's power, wisdom, and love will never end, and become ours to share just for the asking.

God walks beside us day by day asking us to follow Him. But before He can show us the way which leads into the beauty of His love, we must first open our hearts and let Him come in and take control. When He does, we can battle the fiercest storms, walk through the deepest forests, and put out the most flaming fires of life. It is His will that we shall be led safely home.

In good times or bad, if you but listen, you can hear the voice of heaven speaking the promise which gives strength and courage to meet each new day with a smile and a feeling of victory. "Though the earth do change, and the mountains be shaken into the heart of the seas," the foundation of God stands fast. He is waiting to show us the way. He promises never to leave us nor forsake us. The symbol of the great victory, which ultimately will mean the resurrection experience for everyone of us, is the Cross.

TABLE TALK: *Name some other organizations which stand ready to help someone, such as the Red Cross, Big Brothers, etc. Discuss the motive behind each of these.*

AUGUST 17

Truth Can Make You Free

Jesus therefore said to those Jews that had believed him, If ye abide in my word, then are ye truly my disciples; and ye shall know the truth, and the truth shall make you free.

John 8:31-32.

Jesus once said, "If you abide in my word, then are ye truly my disciples and ye shall know the truth, and the truth shall make you free." Some of the people listening to Him on this particular occasion could not understand what He was saying. They were thinking of themselves. "We have never been slaves. How can you then suggest that we shall be free?" Then Jesus went on to explain that everyone who commits sin is a slave. He is hemmed in and restricted. He follows the dictates of evil desire. His conscience condemns him. He simply is not living the full life that God has intended for him.

A young American woman went to New Guinea as a doctor. She had the privilege to be the first white woman to go into the interior of this particular settlement. She was invited by some army personnel to fly to an inland point to make some preliminary studies that would enable them to introduce sanitation and other health measures in this interior region. On this trip Dr. Agnes took with her a phonograph. Of course, the party had many things with them which the natives had never seen. For example, they were much intrigued by a mirror. One of the men struck a match and that was nothing short of magic to the natives. These white visitors began to appear as God. But what was most interesting of all to Dr. Agnes was the reaction of the natives to her playing of the phonograph. As she played a record one of them rushed up to her and exclaimed, with decisive gestures punctuating what he was saying, "Let the man out of the box!"

Dr. Agnes could never forget that exclamation. It came to be a kind of a definition of her purpose on that lonely isle. She was there to release people who were imprisoned because of sin.

TABLE TALK: *In many countries freedom and truth have been suppressed. How has this affected the gospel of Christ? What is your responsibility in these circumstances?*

230

AUGUST 18

Lest Thou Forget

Beware lest thou forget the Lord thy God, in not keeping his commandments, and his ordinances, and his statutes, which I command thee this day. Deuteronomy 8:11.

At the Cathedral of the Pines Camp in northern Minnesota are many boys and girls who spend their summer days learning to know God better. They also enjoy themselves by becoming better acquainted with each other. One eleven-year-old boy was having such a good time that he forgot all about writing letters home to his mother and father. His parents went to the mailbox every day as they anxiously waited for some word from their son. Finally, they were so certain that something was wrong with their boy they called him by long distance telephone. When the pastor asked the boy why he had not written home to his parents his answer was, "I just forgot."

How often God's heart must be saddened by the fact that we, His children, who claim to love Him so much, so often "just forget" to talk to Him in prayer! We are too busy having fun, going places with our friends, watching television, and attending school, to speak to Him as "good friends should and do." He is anxious to have us come to Him often and at any time.

So many things happen each day. For example, there are so many joys. At these times why not go to the heavenly Father and tell Him how happy you are to be alive? There are moments of temptation when the evil one would seek to be the victor. Remember your God is sufficient and if you will turn to Him, He will give you the strength to withstand. There are problems to face and burdens to bear. If you speak to the Master you will discover that underneath are His everlasting arms—that they are strong enough to give you the help that you need and to lead you to ultimate victory.

Let us remember that God never forgets us. Each day He "daily provides us abundantly with all the necessities of life." Let us not forget Him!

TABLE TALK: *Mention blessings that occur in the everyday life for which many people forget to thank God.*

God Believes in You

I beseech you therefore, brethren, by the mercies of God, to present your bodies a living sacrifice, holy, acceptable to God, which is your spiritual service. Romans 12:1.

When doctors really get to understand the chemistry of the body they may add another twenty years to the average life span. This is the opinion of one of the officers of the medical association. "But what will the added years mean?" he asked as he addressed a recent convention. "Longer life should mean a better and happier life," he said, "but we are uncertain of our abilities to achieve it."

No matter where you turn these days you find fear abounding on every hand. It is an enemy and the Christian should be well aware of it. Faith is the only antidote to fear.

Some time ago the bank in a small town was about to fail. The news spread from one person to another. It was not long before the folks of the village were rushing to the bank wanting to withdraw their money. Realizing the seriousness of this situation, the banker called in one of the town's most respected businessmen and said, "If this continues, we are certain to fail. But if the people will only leave their money where it is, we ought to be able to keep our promise that we will pay every dime we owe them."

"I want to help," said the businessman. So he went back home and gathered together $300. He returned to the bank and spoke these words to the anxious crowd: "You know that I have lived in this town for many years. And you are all good friends of mine and believe and trust in me. I have faith in this bank and, to prove it, I am not going to withdraw any money, but rather, I am going to deposit the $300 I hold in my hand." It was not long before the entire crowd had disappeared and the bank had been saved from collapse.

When the storms are the darkest, take a look at Calvary and see God giving His Son because He believed life could be saved.

TABLE TALK: *If you knew that you had twenty extra years of life, what extra kindnesses and plans should you include in them?*

A Fortress in the Soul

I will give unto thee the keys of the kingdom of heaven: and whatsoever thou shalt bind on earth shall be bound in heaven; and whatsoever thou shalt loose on earth shall be loosed in heaven. Matthew 16:19.

There is an old pine tree that has withstood the winds and storms for many years. Courageously it has faced the fierce elements and today it stands as straight as ever, undefeated by any outward enemy that has attacked it.

Yet that tree faces almost certain death. And the reason is this: it is being eaten away by an enemy from within. On the outside, it still looks strong but if you would look at it closely you would notice that on the inside it is almost hollow. The day is not far distant when it will fall to the ground, defeated by the enemy from within.

No civilization has ever perished from any outward cause. Any civilization that has spent its day upon the stage of the world's history and has been forgotten is one which has died from causes within, from moral cancer.

And so it is with individual lives. Outside circumstances may be severe. The valley of the shadow of death may leave us lonesome and with a heartache. The storms of persecution and temptation may blow against us. Adversity may cripple us and darkness may enshroud us. But if within us there is a divine fortress, we shall be able to withstand evil.

Each day you either reinforce your life for ultimate victory or you weaken your life for eventual defeat. Each day you have the privilege of living close to God. The more of Him you put into your living, the stronger you will become and the more sure you will be of final victory. The world can never defeat you with the weapons of outward circumstance. But you can be defeated by doubt and fear from within. Trust the promise, "It is my Father's good pleasure to give you the kingdom."

TABLE TALK: *Think of decadent nations. Name some of them and point out the real cause of their fall. What lesson does this hold for the United Nations?*

AUGUST 21

Who Guides You?

For this God is our God for ever and ever: he will be our guide even unto death. Psalm 48:14.

A fifty-five-year-old Long Island motorman was once brought into court to account for a crash that killed twenty-nine of his passengers. There were two trains involved in the accident and an estimated one thousand people were aboard. In addition to the dead, more than one hundred were injured.

To make mistakes is human. We all make them. "All have sinned and fallen short of the glory of God." That is why we cannot direct our lives by our own strength. That is why we cannot answer for our human mistakes standing alone. We always need God as our guide.

Who dares to go into the vast unknown, even into the hours that are ahead this day without the knowledge that God is his guide? With Him as the engineer of your life you do not have to worry about being derailed. You can enjoy your journey through life, as you will travel in complete confidence.

A little boy was riding on a transcontinental train. It was traveling over the steep cliffs and making hairpin curves as it snaked its way through the mountains. The boy was sitting by a window completely unconcerned and certainly evidencing no fear. Finally a woman across the aisle turned to him and said, "Aren't you afraid? Look at the deep ravines. What if the train should go off the tracks?" The boy turned to the lady and replied, "I am not afraid, for you see, my father is the engineer on this train."

As we look into the future, we can have utmost confidence that God will direct our way if we will but allow Him. Though there are steep cliffs and hairpin curves on our life journey, confident that our Father is the engineer, we need never be afraid. He will keep us "on the right track," safe from all accidents.

TABLE TALK: *Perhaps you can retell stories of children who have had implicit faith in their elders. What lesson do they hold for you?*

AUGUST 22

God Goes with You

Sing unto the Lord, all the earth; show forth his salvation from day to day. Declare his glory among the nations; his marvellous works among all the peoples. 1 Chronicles 16:23, 24.

A man who was very indifferent to the church and the ways of Christian living once criticized his neighbor, calling him "an ordinary, everyday Christian." What he thought was a profound complaint, however, was not. For that is exactly what a Christian must be—an ordinary, everyday Christian.

Have you ever noticed a sign in some store of the city in which you live that reads, "Experienced help wanted. Full-time workers only." Perhaps you were reminded of the fact that there should be no such a thing as a part time helper in the Master's work. Ours is full time service, regardless of what our occupation might be. For whatever we are doing, there are opportunities of witnessing in behalf of the Lord we love.

So many of us are poor examples of Christian faith. During the worship service on Sunday we pretend to believe what we confess, but in everyday living we are beset by fears, anxieties, and worry. If our partnership with God is real, this cannot happen, because then we know He is always with us. And if He is, there is nothing to fear.

A young lad once planned to make a visit to a strange part of the city in which he lived. His mother carefully instructed him how to go, but at the last minute he became just a little frightened. "It's a long way and I don't know the road too well," said the boy. "I am not exactly afraid, Mother, but would you go along part of the way with me?" His mother understanding his fears and doubts took his hand in hers and said, "My son, I will go all the way with you."

God stands ready to go all the way with us. He does not ask us to take one step alone. All He asks in return as our part of the partnership is to walk the road of consistent Christian living day by day.

TABLE TALK: *Recall the times when you had to go to some strange place alone. Imagine what it would be like to go through life alone.*

AUGUST 23

Keep Marching On

The Lord is on my side; I will not fear: what can man do unto me? Psalm 118:6.

David once declared that he would not be afraid if there were ten thousand people against him. He was sure he would win the battle because the Lord was on his side. That is real faith, the kind that proves the power of the heavenly Father.

About 450 years ago there lived a young man who was often in danger of losing his life. He was called a traitor by some people, and he was a hero to others. He marched steadily toward the city where he was to meet his enemies face to face. Suddenly a messenger came running to warn him. "Don't enter the city. They are waiting for you, and they will kill you in the twinkling of an eye." The young man turned to the messenger and courageously answered, "Even though there are as many devils in the city as there are tiles upon the housetops, I still will enter." And he marched on.

That man's name was Martin Luther, the Reformer. In him there was no doubt but that God would have His way. There could be no turning back. He was not afraid. He knew the Lord was on his side.

This faith in God really works. It has been proved by courageous souls through the centuries and by faithful Christians today. The Christ that will dwell within you is many times stronger than the forces that are against you.

Remember, if you sail in a boat that follows the tide wherever it happens to go, or drifts wherever the changing winds happen to carry it, you will never reach your destination. Sometimes you have to sail against the tide and against the wind if you want to stay on the course. That means that there must be a willingness on your part to take ridicule, to be laughed at, and to make sacrifices. But it also means having something infinitely great, God's strength and wisdom, which no power can destroy.

TABLE TALK: *Who are some present-day reformers who have had to withstand ridicule and make sacrifices? Discuss the need for such people.*

AUGUST 24

Our King Is Alive!

Thine, O Lord, is the greatness, and the power, and the glory, and the victory, and the majesty: for all that is in the heavens and in the earth is thine; thine is the kingdom, O Lord, and thou art exalted as head above all. 1 Chronicles 29:11.

On a dark dreary day five-hundred years ago, a group of men was gathered in the palace of the French capital. Here were some of the great men of the world, trying to work out the fate of their nation. This time they were gathered together for a more important reason than usual. The young king was desperately ill and these men stood by waiting for the end which seemed inevitable. Some were afraid, others looked anxious; some went to their knees to pray. Then the message came. The monarch had drawn his last breath. Among these great men who had come together was one who knew that they could not battle the future alone. He lifted his eyes upward and offered a simple prayer. Then he turned to the others near by and, in a spirit of understanding and reverence, said, "Gentlemen, the king is dead. That must teach us to live."

We Christians live in the assurance that our King is not dead. He rose again on Resurrection Morn. Faith in His victory is what keeps us looking toward tomorrow with hope. Apparent death does not cause us to give up but rather inspires us to more noble living. The King of our hearts is not dead. He lives that we may have life and faith and assurance.

Faith is the daring of a soul to go farther than it can see. You may not be able to tell what the next hour will bring or what tomorrow has in store for you, but with a trust in the Master you know that it will be something worth living for.

Someone has said that this faith which a Christian has is like a great cathedral filled with beautiful windows. If you stand outside, you see no glory at all. But standing within, every ray of light reveals a harmony of unspeakable splendor. Out of your life together with God you can be a great cathedral that will never be destroyed.

TABLE TALK: *Describe some beautiful churches you have seen. Why is it fitting that a place of worship be beautiful?*

237

AUGUST 25

God Knows

Upright men shall be astonished at this, and the innocent shall stir up himself against the godless. Yet shall the righteous hold on his way, and he that hath clean hands shall wax stronger and stronger. Job 17:8-9.

Six wise dogs with a special air of innocence met up recently with three wise magistrates in a small town in England. The three wise magistrates stared at the six wise dogs and tried to determined which one was the culprit, the one that liked to take an occasional bite at someone passing by. But it so happened that the six wise dogs were six remarkably identical collies. They sat with a calm and satisfied air while their owner told the court that it was impossible for him to know which one of them should be punished. The man who was on the receiving end of the dog's bite said that he did not know either.

The three wise magistrates stared sternly at the six dogs and the canine sextet looked back happily with expressions that would betray no one. The magistrates conferred quietly for a moment and then one announced that a solution had been reached. 'The court," he informed the owner, "has ordered that the dog which caused the trouble must be kept under control, but it is up to you to decide which one it is."

There are many times in life when we have committed wrong and think that we can get by with our sin. We look innocently at the world pretending to be somebody we really are not. But God, the great Judge, is not as easily fooled as were those three wise magistrates. You cannot hide from Him nor cover over any of your misdeeds. He knows those who follow Him, and He knows those who reject Him in their hearts.

You are the steward of your life. You know whether or not you have done wrong. Your conscience is God's voice that tells you. Keep it ever alive so that within your heart you may be your own court of appeals. When you sin, admit it and penitently seek forgiveness.

TABLE TALK: *Have you ever tried to cover up your guilt in a guise of innocence, and maybe with a few lies? How did you feel about it afterwards?*

AUGUST 26

The Greatest Conqueror

Nay, in all these things we are more than conquerors through him that loved us. Romans 8:37.

There is always room in this world for people who live and work squarely and honestly. If your rule book is God's Word and if your pattern is God's way of life, then you can be certain that you will be a winner. As a Christian you must believe that right is stronger than wrong and that life can be a success. The Christian's dictionary may define words like success and victory quite differently than others. But they mean exactly what they say: achieving all the worthwhile things of life and winning the victor's crown for all eternity.

The story is told of a great military general who had an unusual reputation for winning battles. He was strong and fearless and had a magnificent ability for leadership. Whenever his troops went into battle he led the march at the very front of the lines. Never once did he look back to see if his men were following him. He had faith in them and they believed so strongly in him that they moved as one great army.

Christ, the commanding general of our lives, marches before us into the hours that are ahead. If we follow Him, we can be assured of being conquerors. For this general never makes a mistake or loses a battle. Only those who reject Him are losers.

Today is a day of hope. God's love is greater and stronger than hatred and revenge. The Christian believer stands high above the troubles of the world every follower of His is destined to become more than conqueror. Knowing this, there is no need to fear the outcome, but we must dedicate our lives to Him and His Christian world. The world is sorely in need of a conquering force of good over evil, justice over injustice, love over hate. The soldiers of Christ are destined to bear the banner of faith, and they must seek reinforcements by bringing others to know the glory of Christ. When the love of Christ has permeated the world, there will be everlasting peace.

TABLE TALK: *We worry about the international conflicts. They cannot be ignored. When we think about them, what reassurance can God give us?*

AUGUST 27

Are You a Talking Christian?

I am as one that is a laughing-stock to his neighbor, I who called upon God, and he answered: the just, the perfect man is a laughing-stock. Job 12:4.

Have you ever stumbled over a piece of furniture in the dark, or perhaps over a lamp or radio or telephone? When you finally turned on the light and saw the broken pieces scattered about the room, you gathered them together and put them back as best you could. If the inner connections were still good, the radio would play and you could still talk to your friends on the telephone.

Sometimes our lives are broken in the darkness of despair and disappointment, but if the inner connections are right we can still talk with God and our life can still glow with happiness and faith. If we resolve to go about our Father's business nothing can persuade us away from our accepted task, not even the sneers of the crowd and the jesting remarks of a pagan world.

People will respect and admire a talking Christian. Perhaps there will be biting accusations when you speak about Christ in a public place. Maybe there will be a few smiles when you bow your head to say a table prayer at the restaurant. Perhaps your friends will taunt you by asking why your God does not save you from your failures and disasters. But soon your cheerfulness, kindness, and devotion to the greater things will turn others to admiration and respect for your Christian faith and love. They will discover that Christ in your life does not take away from enjoyment and happiness but rather adds to the pleasure and understanding of each day, and that He gives meaning and purpose to living.

There may be some who think you foolish for not fighting back. They may think that you are ridiculous for running an honest but unprofitable business. They may doubt your wisdom when you go hungry so that someone else may be fed. But it is well to remember that it is far greater to serve God than to try to conquer the world without Him.

TABLE TALK: *Have you ever encountered the ridicule of the crowd? What did you do?*

240

AUGUST 28

God Knows You

But even the very hairs of your head are all numbered. Fear not: ye are of more value than many sparrows. Luke 12:7.

There is a man working in a downtown club who has a very unusual job. He is seated at a small desk just inside the entrance. There he watches the hundreds of people who every day go in and out of the door. As each member goes by, this man checks a name off a long list in order that a record may be kept of the persons who are in the building at any certain time. Just a matter of noticing every person as he enters or leaves is quite a job in itself, but the amazing thing is that this man knows each of the hundreds of members by name.

It is even more astonishing to consider that God recognizes not just a few hundred people in a certain place in a single city, but He knows each of His children by name the world over. He knows their life history. Our most secluded thoughts are like an open book to Him. Nothing in our life is a secret in His presence. He not only knows all about us but He is concerned about the most insignificant things that may be troubling us. What a privilege is ours to be able to consider ourselves children of the heavenly Father! How willing we should be to meet any condition to maintain that relationship!

Do you remember the story of the merchant who set out to search for valuable pearls? When he found one pearl that was of great price he went and sold all that he had that he might purchase it. Christ is the pearl of great price. He is worth everything we are or own.

God knows each of us. He wants each of us as His own. Will we be on His list that final day?

TABLE TALK: *It is interesting to find out how many people you know. See how many in your block you can name. Are there some near you with whom you should get acquainted?*

AUGUST 29

When Shadows Disappear

And I will bring the blind by a way that they know not; in paths that they know not will I lead them; I will make darkness light before them, and crooked places straight. These things will I do, and I will not forsake them. Isaiah 42:16.

Though Helen Keller is blind to the sun which shines in the sky, the eyes of her soul enable her to capture a sunshine for her life which no one can take from her. The darkness which has crowded about her on every side has not blotted out the sunshine in her heart, for this little sentence sums up her philosophy: "Keep your face to the sunshine and you cannot see the shadows." It is a wonderful thought to take with you today.

If you keep looking to God, who is the Light of the world, the shadows will disappear. There will be a brightness about living which you can always possess, because in Him is "a lamp unto your feet," lighting the pathway you walk day by day. It is a wonderful assurance to have His word and promise that this light will never go out.

There was once a group of friends who started out together to climb a rather steep mountain. One of them became ambitious and hurried along ahead of the others, so that finally he became separated from the group. It was not until they had climbed over a steep wall that they found their friend again. He was sitting on a large rock looking out over the beautiful scene. As the others approached he spoke up and said, "Now that you are here let us all go up a bit higher." Together they could scale the dangerous heights ahead and see even rarer views.

So often God's way seems too slow for us. We cannot wait, so we hurry on only to discover as we meet some impossible situation that we cannot face it alone. It is then we realize that we cannot achieve the greatest victory without His presence. But with Him we climb to heights of undreamed beauty.

TABLE TALK: *You have heard other stories about Helen Keller. Tell them. What qualities does she possess which would be desirable in all of us?*

AUGUST 30

He Wants You!

And I will give them a heart to know me, that I am the Lord: and they shall be my people, and I will be their God; for they shall return unto me with their whole heart. Jeremiah 24:7.

A little girl living in a beautiful home was stricken with an incurable disease. She was destined to remain a helpless cripple. Her life was to be lived in a wheel chair. She had been accustomed to interesting travel and interesting people, and now was doomed to sit at home, alone.

Her mother, however, kept on with her traveling. Thoughtfully she would remember to bring some luxurious gift for her little crippled girl at home.

Once she was gone for a period of several months on a visit across the ocean, and when she returned she brought her little daughter an especially valuable present. When she gave it to her, the little girl merely shoved it aside. The mother said, "Well, darling, aren't you even going to open it? It is a very expensive present. I want you to know that I paid a lot of money for it." Finally through the tears the girl was able to sob, "Mother, I don't want things—I want you!"

So often we try to appease God and satisfy our own conscience by the giving of a gift of money or by the use of our talents for the church. Too much of our devotion is superficial. God is not primarily interested in the things that we give Him. He wants us. He wants to rule as King on the throne of our hearts. He wants us never to be separated from Him and there is sadness in His heart when we wander off into the far-off country. He is lonely until we return. The gifts we offer Him and the promises we make but do not keep mean little. He wants us. He wants our hearts and our lives dedicated to a full life for Him.

Today the eternal Father is seeking you. Once He has possession of your heart He will give in return a life with immeasurable happiness. He is saying, "Son, give Me your heart." Will you give it to Him?

TABLE TALK: *The giver is more important than the gift. Have you given yourself completely to your Master?*

AUGUST 31

Inferior Products

Count it all joy; my brethren, when ye fall into manifold temptations; knowing that the proving of your faith worketh patience. James 1:2-3.

A wealthy man loved to build beautiful houses. He had a contractor friend who always did his work and, as the years passed on, he grew to have complete confidence in him. He trusted his honesty and his integrity to the extent that he did not even think it necessary to check on him in any way.

One day, this wealthy man went to his contractor friend and said, "John, I want you to build another house for me. I am depositing $30,000 in the bank, and I want you to build the best house you can, for that amount of money. I am going to be gone during the whole time you are building this house, but when I come back, I will look it over."

Then the contractor started construction. In his conscience a furious battle began to rage. Although his rich friend had always paid him an honest fee, here was his chance, the evil voice persuaded, to make some extra money. After all, no one was watching him. He could use second-grade materials where they would never be seen. No one would ever know the difference. "Right" tried to battle "Wrong," but in the end, evil was victorious.

Finally the house was completed. It was beautiful to behold. The outside was just as it was supposed to be. No one could tell that it contained inferior products. The rich man returned from his journey, and he too, was very pleased at the result. He could not tell that trickery had been played on him. After complimenting John for the job that he had done, he turned to him and said, "My friend, I have always paid you a fair price for the work you have done for me. But I am getting older and have plenty of money on which to live. I have decided to give you, as an extra gift, this house."

We should always remember that today we are building the house we are going to have to live in tomorrow. Build well!

TABLE TALK: *Discuss the danger of using inferior products in any product or project.*

SEPTEMBER 1

A Little Child Shall Lead Them

From a babe thou hast known the sacred writings, which are able to make thee wise unto salvation through faith which is in Christ Jesus. 2 Timothy 3:15.

There is always fear in the heart of a mother when her child is suffering. The terror increases as various questions come to her mind: "Have I done everything possible? Have I given my child the best medical care? Have I done anything to cause the situation?" A mother would rather suffer herself than to have some harm come to her children. Throughout most of our land this same love abounds in the hearts of parents. Most children in our country are well fed and physically cared for.

This is not the case in all parts of the world. There are those who are homeless because of war. Others are suffering from the lack of food and medicine.

Physical suffering is terrible but of even greater danger is the neglect of the soul. A child cannot be fed once and then be forgotten. He gets hungry every day. His needs are the same spiritually. And even in America, the land of material plenty, there are parents who starve their children spiritually. They do this when they fail to nourish them with the Bread of Life.

One Sunday morning a certain father, a prominent business executive, was sitting in his bathrobe reading the morning newspaper. His little girl came running down the stairs and he noticed that she was not dressed for church school. "Darling," he said, "you will have to hurry and get ready, or you will be late for church." "I'm not going today," she announced. "Why, of course you are," replied the father. "It is good for you to go to church." "Well," answered the girl, "if it does a person good to go to church, why don't you ever go yourself?" That gentle rebuke from a little child led that father into the Christian way of living and he has become an active soldier of God.

"The needs of these children cannot wait," writes a Nobel prize winner. "We cannot answer tomorrow. The child's name is Today."

TABLE TALK: *The problem of the spiritual nourishment of children is great. What can you as a family do about it?*

245

SEPTEMBER 2

Fair Weather Ahead

With whom my hand shall be established; mine arm also shall strengthen him. Psalm 89:21.

In Sault Sainte Marie, Michigan, there are famous locks connecting Lake Superior with Lake Huron. Superior is twenty feet higher than Huron, and the two are connected by St. Mary's River. The shipping on the Great Lakes could never be carried on from Duluth eastward unless man had made these locks, which let enough water in and out to raise or lower the ships from one level to the other. Man alone could never have figured out a way to lift one of these huge and heavy boats, if he did not have the properties of God-created water to help him.

Our lives are like a series of locks. As we go from childhood to youth and from youth to adulthood, we have many periods of change, when we must rise from one level to another. Parents, teachers, and friends, all try to encourage and help us. However, in the final analysis, it is God through Christ, who comes close to us, and says, "If you take my outstretched hand, and hold it tightly, together we will pass from one level of life to another, and each day we will climb higher."

To the Christian there is always promise of fair weather. There will be sunshine to make some day bright and cheerful. There will always be rainfall enough to make our lives grow. There comes warmth sufficient to bring an abundant harvest. In God we find the fulfillment of all happiness, and nothing can take this joy from us.

The story is told of a man whose shop burned down. He arrived at the ruins the next morning, carrying a table. He set it up in the midst of the debris, and above it placed this optimistic sign, "Everything lost, except my wife and children, and my hope. Business resumed tomorrow as usual."

The joy which is in Christ is like that. It rises above the troubles of the world, and sets our focus upon the things which are truly valuable. Faith is confident of fair weather ahead.

TABLE TALK: *Can you think of instances in your life or in the life of someone you know where hardship caused man to rise to a higher level with the help of God?*

SEPTEMBER 3

Counting the Cost

The fear of the Lord is the beginning of knowledge: but the foolish despise wisdom and instruction. Proverbs 1:7.

For many years an unfinished building stood in one of our cities. It was located beside a very beautiful lake. It was advertised that it was to be the most exclusive club in the entire world. Architects made elaborate drawings, contractors were hired, contracts were signed, and yet for many years the building remained unfinished because the builders had not counted the cost. Bankruptcy and total loss were the result. Centuries ago a group of men made the same fatal mistake. The unfinished tower of Babel stands as an everlasting tombstone over the defeated lives of those who begin to build but do not count the cost.

Beginnings are important. Football games may be lost on the very first play, and yet it is more likely that the team that has the greatest staying power will come off the field the victor. The child who has the opportunity of being raised in a Christian home under favorable circumstances has a good beginning that can mean much to him later in life.

Most important is what one makes of opportunities. There have been those who have been abundantly blessed in childhood by kind and loving parents, who still have taken the wrong road. As a result, they have not become what they could have become. They were unwilling to count the cost.

The day that you committed your life to God was a good beginning. You promised Him that you would remain faithful, that you would read His Word and pray, and daily be conscious of His presence in your life. Perhaps you were deeply impressed and still remember the moment when you said, "Lord, I will follow Thee." What has happened since? Have you grown in grace each day or have you stopped building because you have failed to count the cost? The Master says, "If any man would come after me, let him deny himself, and take up his cross." Have you counted the cost?

TABLE TALK: *Discuss how each of you began to learn of Christ. What important role does Sunday school play in the life of the church?*

SEPTEMBER 4

Obey the Rules

Train up a child in the way he should go, and even when he is old he will not depart from it. Proverbs 22:6.

On a visit to the winter quarters of a circus at Sarasota, Florida, a little boy was standing with his brother feeding peanuts to the elephants. Suddenly one of the elephants called Dolly snaked her trunk under the guard chain and grabbed the tot around his waiste. Before anyone could interfere, the elephant threw him to the ground and stepped on him, crushing his skull.

The general manager of the circus said the boy ducked under the guard rope to pick up some peanuts he had dropped and apparently the elephant became excited. So the little boy, trying to save some peanuts, went beyond the limits of safety and lost his life.

Such a tragedy happens to many in a spiritual sense. For a while, everything goes well. We live without restraints and inhibitions. We begin taking chances. Perhaps we go beyond the limits of safety. Tragedy results.

There are certain disciplines that must be followed if life is to be saved and secured. The engine must stay on two narrow ribbons of steel if the train is to reach its destination safely, and life must stay on the right track if heaven is to be our goal.

Our hearts go out to the parents of the little boy who saw their loved one snatched away by death. But there is greater tragedy than that. Think of the parents who live idly on, unconcerned about the spiritual death which can come to their children if they are not nurtured and taught the way that they should go. What blessings result when parents give their children the inspiration of knowing God as a real friend, so that they acquire true spiritual understanding! Consider little Wendy for example. Early in the morning, on the day when her sister was to be baptized, she was found standing by the little cradle singing, "Happy birthday, dear Pammie." She had caught the significance of what it means to be a child of God!

TABLE TALK: *Are there any children in your neighborhood who, though physically well provided for, need spiritual care? What should you do about it? Discuss.*

SEPTEMBER 5

Why Not Choose Life?

But thou, O man of God, flee these things: and follow after righteousness, godliness, faith, love, patience, meekness.
1 Timothy 6:11.

Some of God's children find wealth and prestige in their lifetime while others have only the bare necessities. Some have many friends, others have only a devoted few. Some live in beautiful mansions, others in humble cottages. In this lifetime, the lines are sometimes drawn deep and clear. Some day God will erase them all. He will know only one line of difference. It is the one that separates those who have chosen to serve Him and those who have not.

No doubt, you have often seen a group of neighbor boys on a vacant lot getting ready to play a game of baseball or football. A couple of fellows are picked to choose up sides. They decide what side each boy is on by saying, "You are on this side, and you are on that side." But it is not that way at all in this game of life. You choose which side you want to be on. The decision is yours to make. You must give answer to the question that echoes across the ages from the very beginning: "God has chosen you. Do you want to be on the Lord's side?"

An artist once spent long hours painting the back of a man who was turning away from the presence of Christ. His friends could not understand why he should depict such an unusual scene, but the artist merely replied, "He went away sorrowful for he had great possessions." He had chosen to keep his earthly goods, his wealth, and his riches, rather than to accept God. So he turned away from the everlasting blessings of heaven.

Can you imagine anyone turning away from the Master's love and mercy? Can you imagine a drowning man throwing away his life belt, or a wounded man pouring a life-giving medicine upon the ground? Remember, as you serve God you exchange your sinful life for an eternity of joy. Why not choose life?

TABLE TALK: *Discuss instances of people who have thrown away their possibilities of real happiness and joy in living, because they chose to follow after the lure of money and a supposedly "good time."*

249

SEPTEMBER 6

Choose Wisely

Enter ye in by the narrow gate; for wide is the gate, and broad is the way, that leadeth to destruction, and many are they that enter in thereby. Matthew 7:13.

In one of the Old Testament books there is a verse that tells us that "the highways were unoccupied and the travelers walked through byways." One immediately wonders why the highways should be untraveled. Was the bridge out? Were the highways undergoing repair? Were the byways and the side roads so much more beautiful? Even so, it seems people who are in a hurry to go from one place to another scarcely have time to observe the beauty along the way. So that could not be the answer.

What was the reason? There were bandits and robbers who infested the highways. One caravan after another had been stopped and looted by thieves coming out of ambush along the way. It was unsafe to travel the main roads, then, because of the danger of attack by ruffians. There are still broad highways to avoid and besetting dangers to guard against. "Wide is the gate, and broad is the way, that leadeth to destruction," writes the Gospel author, and it is a word appropriate for our day. One would expect the well-kept, smoothly paved highway to be the safe and preferable one. But the fact that it is wide and smooth can be a contributing factor in making it the most dangerous for travel.

When things come our way too easily we are likely to have little understanding of our neighbor who may be suffering under a lot of difficulty. Unless we know what it means to be out of some of the necessities of life we probably will never make any sacrifice to provide for someone who is in need. We can become very thoughtless out there on that broad highway.

Far more tragic, of course, is the fact that the broad way does not lead anywhere. Some day the jolt will come if we take that course. We will have been robbed of our souls. Only the narrow way leads to life. God give us the courage to choose wisely.

TABLE TALK: *Is there a section of town which you avoid? Why? What can you do to better the slums of your city?*

SEPTEMBER 7

You Are a Witness

Ye are my witnesses, saith the Lord, and my servant whom I have chosen; that ye may know and believe me, and understand that I am he: before me there was no God formed, neither shall there be after me. Isaiah 43:10.

Sometime ago a Sunday school of a large church set out seeking new children. The church school teachers had been asked to seek out the children who had no spiritual home. One day, as a certain teacher was walking down a busy street, he stopped to speak to a young lad who was shining shoes. After a bit of conversation he asked the boy, "Sonny, are you going to Sunday school next Sunday?" It did not take long for the lad to answer "No." But the man kept on encouraging him. "We have papers for everyone that comes, with a lot of colored pictures." Still the boy would not come. "We have good music and everything you would want to have a good time." But the lad just shook his head. Disappointed the teacher turned away and began to walk on down the street.

He had not gone very far when he heard hurrying footsteps behind him, and turning around he saw it was the boy to whom he had talked. With an earnest, eager look the young lad asked, "Mister, are you going to be there?" "Yes, I am there every Sunday," replied the teacher. "Then I will be there, too," answered the boy.

The church school paper, the music, and all the other things for having a good time were just a part of the spirit which interested that young lad. It was the kindness and understanding of the teacher that really won him.

You are called upon to be a Christian witness. That means you must live Christ in everything that you do.

TABLE TALK: *Have there been times in your life when you have excused yourself from stopping to help others who may have been in need, to give someone a kind word of encouragement, or to soothe a sobbing child, by saying, "I'm too busy"? Those are the very times when you could have been a very effective witness, but failed. Will you not resolve to do differently next time?*

SEPTEMBER 8

The Master Organist

Then shall the King say unto them on his right hand, Come, ye blessed of my Father, inherit the kingdom prepared for you from the foundation of the world. Matthew 25:34.

So many people have no real music in their lives. They have never come in contact with the great Musician who can cause melodious anthems to swell from the soul. He is willing to enter the heart of everyone. What a tragedy it is that so many refuse Him!

In one of Europe's great cathedrals, a man who was the organist for many years retired. During his entire time of service he had tenderly cared for the instrument, which he had learned to love. And so he was made custodian of the organ. The people of the congregation knew how well he would take care of it.

One day a rather distinguished man wandered into the cathedral, saw the custodian standing by the organ, and asked of him the privilege of playing the instrument. "No, I can't let you," he was told. "I am very sorry." The man persisted in his request. Finally, though he was very hesitant to do it, the custodian granted him the privilege. And then, as the man began to play, he stood there spellbound, for he heard music the like of which he had never heard before in his life. It gripped his soul. Big tears rolled down his manly cheeks. When the musician had finished playing, the custodian turned to him and said, "Please, sir, tell me, who are you?" The man quietly answered, "I am Felix Mendelssohn."

It is said that for years afterward this custodian would recall this incident and was heard to say again and again, "Just suppose I had refused to allow him to play on the organ."

Jesus, the great Musician, wants to bring harmony into your living. He passes by again today. He will hear you if you but pray, "Come into my heart, Lord Jesus."

TABLE TALK: *Discuss times when you have been thrilled by the music of a real master, an organist, a pianist, a symphony orchestra conductor. How can this be applied to your life with the Master Organist?*

SEPTEMBER 9

Where Is Your Prayer Corner?

And after he had sent the multitudes away, he went up into the mountain apart to pray: and when even was come, he was there alone. Matthew 14:23.

A Negro woman who lives in the northern part of our country is known by everybody in her community. A very interesting story reveals her triumphant spirit. Years ago she and her husband with several small children headed toward the West from Pennsylvania. Finally they reached the great north woods. By her own testimony, their total possessions were a hundred-pound sack of flour, a dollar in currency, and faith in God. They homesteaded about four miles inland from the road along Lake Superior now known as the North Shore Drive and felled the trees to form a little clearing where they planted their first little garden and reaped their first crop.

But rugged days were ahead. It was not an easy task to feed and to clothe and to house their large family of sixteen children. But by persistent effort and a willingness to sacrifice it was accomplished. The original cabin still stands. Later, of course, another house had to be built to make room for the growing family.

As one hears this story of the years through which this woman has lived it is almost impossible to believe what she has accomplished and how she has been able to do it. That is, until she gives the answer. Her eyes sparkle and her face beams as she tells the secret. "Come with me," she says. And then she leads you to a little spot beside a tree. "This is my prayer corner. Whenever there seem to be problems, as there have been so often, that I couldn't face alone, I would come here and talk to Jesus and He would tell me how I would be able to conquer them. Never once did He fail me."

Nor will He ever fail you. He is the kind of a friend that keeps His promises!

TABLE TALK: *Can you think of any similar story about a family such as this? Tell about it.*

SEPTEMBER 10

Our God Is Love

And thou shalt love the Lord thy God with all thy heart, and with all thy soul, and with all thy might. Deuteronomy 6:5.

Every morning a pudgy, little kindergartner slowly and laboriously boarded a certain school bus. Because of her size it would take her an extra long time to haul herself into the bus. The driver was always very patient about waiting for her to complete the operation. The last day before Christmas she got on as usual, went through the business of pulling off her mittens, finding her token, and dropping it into the box. Then she thrust a package at the driver and a shrill five-year-old voice delivered her obviously home-instructed speech, "Merry Christmas, and thank you for taking such good care of me." Then the youngster gazed at the driver and added this unrehearsed postscript, "And I just love you!"

I am sure that the bus driver, and everyone else who heard this little girl, were thrilled at this expression of gratitude. I likewise think our heavenly Father must often yearn to have His children express their thanks in words such as hers.

So often we are reminded of what He does for us. There was a story not long ago of a man who started on a shoestring but whose business venture ended in success. An attack of polio left one arm handicapped, a leg in a brace, and his back supported by another brace. For twenty years he could not sit up in a chair and the doctor said he would never walk again. But his faith in God, plus his own will, enabled him to testify now, almost casually, "But I am walking today!" His living is an example of one who kept loving God in spite of physical handicap and God saw him through.

Today this man's life testifies to the fact that if we meet the conditions, the great Creator never fails in any promise that He makes us. Our God is Love. We should likewise love the Lord with all our heart.

TABLE TALK: *Call to mind examples of people who have been handicapped and have not given up their faith in God, and who have ultimately been able to achieve victory.*

SEPTEMBER 11

The Man Who Died for Me

The Son of man came not to be ministered unto, but to minister, and to give his life a ransom for many. Matthew 20:28.

It was a stormy night outside, but all was peaceful in a certain home in a quiet suburban community. Two little children had been safely tucked into bed for the night—at least, that is what the mother thought. Just five minutes later a fury far greater than the storm suddenly struck this quiet home.

Above in the sky, an airplane had been trying to find its field for a safe landing place. But something happened. It lost a part of its wing, causing the plane to strike this home, turning it into a blazing inferno, and killing not only the passengers and the crew of the plane, but the children as well.

As one stood at the scene of this great tragedy, he could not help but learn a lesson from the gallant firemen who were risking their lives in an attempt to save others. And in seeing them, be reminded of Him who gave His only Son, that we might live.

One day a woman went to the corner store to do the family shopping. She left her little baby tucked in the crib. On her way back, she heard the screaming of the fire engines, and the thought occurred to her that it might be her home. She hastened her step, and much to her dismay, found that it was. She made an attempt to rush to the burning building but a fireman stopped her. "I've a baby upstairs, and I must save him," she cried. But the fireman said, "I'll go." And up into the flaming building he went, in time to drop the baby safely into the net below, but he lost his own life.

Some twenty-one years later a young lady was standing at a graveside weeping. At the head of the grave was a bronze statue. "Was that man your father?" she was asked. "No," she replied. "Was it your brother?" "No." "Then why are you weeping?" "That's the man who died for me."

Christ gave His life that you and I might live.

TABLE TALK: *Christ died for you. Daily others sacrifice for your happiness. What are you doing for others, for Christ? Discuss.*

The Safety Man

Be ye kind one to another, tenderhearted, forgiving each other, even as God also in Christ forgave you. Ephesians 4:32.

One day our college was engaged in a very important football game. The two teams were evenly matched, but our side held a very slender lead, and we were trying as best we could to protect it. The game was almost over and we were pretty confident that we would be victorious. Suddenly the opposing team's star fullback broke through the line, ran past all of the defenders until there was one man between him and the touchdown. He was a little fellow only about half the size of the one coming at him carrying the ball. Now it was all up to him, and how magnificently he performed his task! He lunged with his frail body in one of the most beautiful tackles ever seen. He seemed to be inspired beyond his capacity, because he had come to the realization that he was the only one who could save victory for his team.

We may sometime find ourselves in the same position as that football player. We may be the only person who can give the help whereby victory will come to some soul. If we fail in our duty, perhaps there will be no one else to take our place.

Perhaps the task seems much too large for our meager capacities. But if ours is a living relationship with God, there comes to us a power beyond our dreaming. The strength of the Almighty, which the occasion demands, makes us capable of conquering any situation.

In football the player I mentioned is called the "safety man." Why not be a "safety man" in life? You will then give yourself to the task of securing victory for those who might be standing on the verge of defeat. By your kindness and tender-hearted consideration you may help someone who is in great need of friendship.

TABLE TALK: *Discuss instances of how a single act of kindness by some friend made the difference between victory and defeat in your life.*

SEPTEMBER 13

We Have a Destination

For I am persuaded, that neither death, nor life, nor angels, nor principalities, nor things present, nor things to come, nor powers, nor height, nor depth, nor any other creature, shall be able to separate us from the love of God, which is in Christ Jesus our Lord. Romans 8:38-39.

Airports are very interesting places, especially international depots where people from all over the world come and go. An unforgettable incident occurred at such a place several years ago. I was a part of a group of eleven Americans who were making a study tour of the new state of Israel. We were standing at midnight at the airport in Rome ready to take a flight over the Mediterranean bound for the port of Lydda, the air base in the new state of Israel. It was a nonscheduled flight and the equipment was very poor. Some of us wondered whether we would ever reach our destination. The pilot when asked if we would make any stops along the journey replied, "Well, that depends on whether we think we might be running out of gas." His words were not very reassuring to say the least. However, everything went well.

Life is much like an airplane journey. Before the takeoff there is much preparation that has to be made. The plane has to be checked carefully, the pilot has to chart the weather conditions, and even when the plane has been taxied to the starting position, the "warm up" of the motor is part of the procedure. There must be much preparation for living, too. Disciplines and training are a part of the course if the goal is to be reached.

One watches a plane take off into the sky and it grows smaller and smaller until it is lost to sight. But it is not gone. Somewhere beyond, there is a port, and others who are waiting there suddenly see it appear. Life is like that, too. At death we say, "She is gone." But heaven says, "Here she comes."

TABLE TALK: *Discuss how you can prepare your life to assure its arrival at its eternal destination. Note the difference between the death of a Christian and an unbeliever, how there is hope and happiness for the Christian but despair and sadness for the unbeliever.*

SEPTEMBER 14

Friendliness Is Contagious

As ye would that men should do to you, do ye also to them likewise. Luke 6:31.

During some seasons of the year, the children of the community may be afflicted with certain contagious diseases. Parents try to be careful but somehow the children seem to catch measles, mumps, or chicken pox anyway, as they play with their friends, study at school, or shop at the super market. Most often when we think about the word contagious it is in connection with something we do not like or want. But there is something which should be a lot more catching than diseases.

Can you think of anything more contagious than a smile? We simply cannot stay angry with a person who answers back with a friendly sincere smile. When we go down the street and meet a friend who gives us a smile and a cheery greeting his friendliness is catching. It helps make us want to do the same thing in return.

On a college campus there is a "hello" walk on which it is traditional to speak to any student who might be met along the way. It is not long after one becomes a part of the campus that the greeting is a habit. The warm friendliness one meets is contagious.

And so it is that our love for Christ and His way of life should be contagious, too. People who do not know Him can catch the glow from us. Our actions can help them to want to learn to know Christ more personally. We should be so filled with love and enthusiasm for the Master that others will say, "I want to know Him, too. If He can make people that happy, I want also to know that partnership."

Remember today that you will be influencing someone along the highway of life. May the Christ within you cause your heart to sing so that you will radiantly glow wherever you go.

TABLE TALK: *Resolve that the next few days you will wear a smile and then later discuss the results. What do you think will be the effect?*

SEPTEMBER 15

Who Are You?

And have put on the new man, that is being renewed unto
knowledge after the image of him that created him.

Colossians 3:10.

An inquisitive child playing on the sidewalk will look up at a
passer-by and say, "What's your name? Who are you?" It is
a question one is asked, perhaps not always verbally, every day
as one walks down the street.

You are a sacred personality created in the image of God. We
have often thought too cheaply of lives, sacrificing them by the
thousands in war without thinking about the value of the human
souls thus given. Each one of us has the stamp of the divine
upon us. We mean something to God. After His likeness we
have been made, and because of our worth in His sight, Christ
died on the cross to save us.

We are sacred personalities living in a cycle of time. Perhaps
many times you have wished that you had never been a part
of this twentieth century. There seem to be so many problems
that we must face. But real living is the result of being challenged by the impossible.

We are sacred personalities living in a cycle of time, with a
geographical location. Have you ever thanked God for living
in a country like America? Think of the advantages we have
over those who live elsewhere. No nation on the face of the
earth has been so abundantly blessed.

We are sacred personalities living in a cycle of time, with a
geographical location, endowed with certain talents. To some
are given five talents, to others two, and to still others only one.
Each of us has been given something, and God will judge us only
as we have used our talents in proportion to what we have been
given.

It is well to consider our sinfulness and need of the Saviour.
It is well, too, to consider the soul's worth, for which Christ died.

TABLE TALK: *Have you ever stopped to consider the po-
tentialities you possess because of God? Recount your priceless
possessions such as health, sight, mind, etc. How are you using
them? Are you trying to develop them?*

SEPTEMBER 16

Richer at the End of Each Day

Understanding is a wellspring of life unto him that hath it: but the correction of fools is their folly. The heart of the wise instructeth his mouth, and addeth learning to his lips.

Proverbs 16: 22-23.

Every day through most of the year millions of youngsters make their way to school. Thousands of teachers are there to meet them. The blackboards are marked, examinations are taken, and students are either passed or failed. It is wonderful that our boys and girls have a chance to learn the things that will help them grow up to become good citizens.

But the truly great educators agree that real education must begin at the center. We must teach the youngsters how to live rather than just how to make a living. It is strange to discover that many adults with years of schooling and experience behind them still have not learned the real secret of living. They may be successful businessmen or capable housewives but there is an absence of things which are worthwhile and living and lasting.

You remember that old adage, "You learn something new every day." It is a good one. It is well to set as a goal to be richer at the end of each day. Richer not only in terms of facts and figures, but more important, richer in the treasures that really count. Each day we should spend time to learn more of the wisdom of God. There must be times set aside from the busy schedule to talk to God so that we may be reassured by His promises and directed by His commandments. Each one of us can make an attempt to make our life famous and successful but only the Master can make it worthy of eternity.

Each day you find yourself in the schoolroom of life. Let the Master be your teacher. He will lead you in the pathway of faith and along roads of loving service to your fellow men. You will find yourself richer at the end of each day.

TABLE TALK: *What new idea or fact have you learned in the past few days? How can you put it to use?*

260

SEPTEMBER 17

The Virtue of Patience

He setteth up on high those that are low, and those that mourn are exalted to safety. **Job 5:11.**

A Pennsylvania woman was one day brought to a hospital. She had to go there only because she had tried to be kind and helpful. She had observed a minor highway accident, and had stopped her own car and gotten out, deciding that someone ought to direct oncoming traffic. For a few moments she had the situation well in hand, but then one driver failed to heed her signals and went crashing into one of the wrecked cars, which in turn hit her. The would-be-kind lady was taken to a hospital.

Sometimes it seems that when we show kindness and consideration to others it turns into dissatisfaction and regret. Perhaps we offer our services to people and get only sneers and bitter remarks in return. We begin to wonder if it is worth while to be generous and thoughtful any more. Undoubtedly many kind things that we do go unappreciated and seemingly fail to accomplish their purpose. But living in the Master's spirit never loses its worth even in an ungrateful world. Merely by showing patience and perseverance a great deal can be accomplished.

A young student once became disheartened because of the difficulties of his studies and the long years it took to finish school. He threw down his books in despair and went back to the crude and backward settlement which was his home. There he saw a woman rubbing a bar of steel on a large rock. He asked her what she was trying to do. He was told that she wanted a needle, and thought she would rub the steel until it was small enough. It seemed utterly ridiculous to the young man, but it was an example to him of what patience is.

Christ did not ask anything in return when He went about doing good to His fellow men. Most of the time He received nothing but ridicule but that did not keep Him from living abundantly. Never did He lose His perspective. Patiently He sought His goal. Because of it He finally gained the victory.

TABLE TALK: *Discuss how patience in dealing with the unappreciative and disgruntled might be successful.*

261

SEPTEMBER 18

Valleys and Mountains

Speak to the earth, and it shall teach thee; and the fishes of the sea shall declare unto thee. Job 12:8-9.

Sometime or other you no doubt have stood on the top of a high hill and looked about you for many miles around. Perhaps you saw green fields spread out like a patchwork quilt. And in the distance a river winding its way through the valleys. At the foot of the hill a highway might have been seen stretching out its concrete arm toward the town which lay a few miles beyond. From the hilltop the universe was a masterpiece which had been created by the great Artist above.

Then perhaps you went down the hill into the valley below. Here there seemed to be another world. A farmer was hard at work plowing one of the fields which you had seen. The river flowed endlessly by with its rushing current. Along the highway trucks and cars swiftly passed trying to reach their destination. Here was a picture of hard work and busy people.

The scene in the valley was not nearly as impressive as the beautiful view from the top of the hill. But nevertheless both were parts of the picture of real life. All of us are expected to work hard and accomplish in a lifetime all that God has given us the strength and the talents to do. We must never forget the everyday obligations we have; but there must always be mountaintop experiences, as well.

There must be a time when we can go with Christ to the hilltop to spend a few moments listening and talking with Him. In kindness and love He can soothe our weary minds and heal our aching hearts. He inspires us to go back to the busy streets of life with new courage and new strength to face the tasks which He is counting on us to do. From the beauty and peace of the mountaintop we will go into the valley of life with the spirit to work harder than ever before in the Lord's vineyard and to bring the good news of salvation to all men.

TABLE TALK: *Have you ever felt inspired by the beauty of nature? Plan a day when the whole family can go somewhere together.*

SEPTEMBER 19

God's Pay Day Will Come

And I have been with thee whithersoever thou wentest, and have cut off all thine enemies from before thee, and I will make thee a great name, like unto the name of the great ones that are in the earth. 2 Samuel 7:9.

History will never forget the name of George Washington Carver. He was not only a masterful scientist, but also a true humanitarian. He won his way into the hearts of countless men and women all over the nation.

Sometime ago he was offered a job that would have paid him $100,000 a year in salary and provide him the very best modern laboratory that money could buy. But he chose to stay at his common task, which paid less than $2,000. There was something more important to this man than a big salary and a beautiful home. He knew he was doing what he was meant to do.

There are countless heroes whose names we never hear who give up fame and fortune to live a life that is dedicated to something beyond the monetary range. Somewhere today there is someone who turns down an unfair deal in favor of honesty. Someone else will forget his own needs to help another get a new start in life. Somebody today may give up the chance to become famous rather than compromise with his Christian beliefs. Maybe that somebody will be you. It is regrettable that so many who try to be famous in the earthly world end up known for their infamy. There are heroes that history books may overlook, names that will never be etched on gold plaques or great monuments. Long after these plaques have worn away and the monuments have crumbled to the ground the heroes of the spirit will live in the eternity of heaven.

Maybe at times you have had doubts about whether it is worth while to work for goodness and brotherhood and all the things that God has said will make our world better. Sometimes all you receive is ridicule and rebuke. Never forget that God's pay day will ultimately come and living for Him assures you of richness and reward.

TABLE TALK: *Discuss the things beyond salary and hours that are important when you are seeking employment.*

SEPTEMBER 20

The Master Wants You

Even so let your light shine before men; that they may see
your good works, and glorify your Father who is in heaven.
Matthew 5:16.

One of the most beautiful streets in the world is in Paris, a
city of impressive boulevards lined with flowers and great buildings. At the end of this street stands the imposing statue of
Napoleon Bonaparte, the mighty warrior. At the other end stands
a modest statue of Louis Pasteur, the scientist. The tomb of the
warrior depicts hate and a continent in conflict; the statue of
the scientist symbolizes good will and understanding, a hand
reaching out to help humanity.

Some time ago the people of France were asked to choose from
among her illustrious sons the one most worthy of lasting fame.
The name of Pasteur led all the rest. Here was a man who
worked and lived for the things that he knew were good and
eternal, who worked to save lives from disease and destruction.
And he lived to tell about Him who saves lives for all eternity.

The great armies of the world equipped with their forces of
destruction will never be able to save our civilization. Neither
will we be able to uncover a mechanical means capable of doing
it. Only as each one of us dedicates his life to witness for the
Master will it be possible.

As a man stood watching an old artist working at the potter's
wheel shaping a bit of clay, he asked, "Why don't you use
machinery to do that?" The old man simply replied, "We have
tried all kinds of machines but they just don't seem to work.
Somehow it needs my own touch."

God has chosen you to witness for Him. You cannot shift the
responsibility to anyone else. A different everyday task is given
to each one of us. Some of us are engineers, some laborers, some
housewives, others students. But all have the capacity and the
obligation to tell others each day in our speech and living of
the Master of eternal life.

TABLE TALK: *Discuss the possibilities you have for witnessing for Christ just by your everyday actions, at the office,
in school, at home, at play, in your social circles.*

SEPTEMBER 21

God Is Our Guide

And the Lord, he it is that doth go before thee; he will be with thee, he will not fail thee, neither forsake thee: fear not, neither be dismayed. Deuteronomy 31:8.

A little boy was standing with his great shepherd dog at a busy intersection. A man near by noticed that the lad wanted to cross the street, but the dog held him back. Finally the dog led the boy safely across to his destination. Then the man saw that the lad carried a white cane, indicating that he was blind. He became fascinated by what he saw, so he hurried his step and joined the lad, and entered into conversation with him.

"Have you been blind long?" the man asked. "Not all my life," replied the lad, "but I had an accident which made it impossible for me to see at all." "This dog seems to be a good friend of yours." "Yes," replied the lad, "Prince and I are good friends. I don't go any place without him. As long as I do what Prince wants me to do I never get into any trouble at all."

Many times each day we stand at the crossroads and must decide which way we should go. Tempting voices would seek to lure us away from the high road of God's way. Sometimes we are confused. We do not know where to turn or what to do, that is, unless we know this real partnership with the Master. For if we would only learn the secret of never going any place without Him, we would with the little blind boy be able to make this confession, "As long as I do what the Master wants me to do I never get into any trouble at all."

A young man came to his minister. He wanted to know what he could or could not do. He did not want to compromise his Christian faith and so he wisely sought the advice of his pastor, whom he had learned to trust. The reply of the wise minister was this: "You can go any place and you can do anything as long as you can take Jesus with you."

When we are faced with the perplexing choices in life, we should remember to ask what the Master wants us to do.

TABLE TALK: *Have you wondered at times what you should do as a Christian? Have you been tempted to do things that are questionable?*

SEPTEMBER 22

Do You Ever Feel Lonely?

And if children, then heirs; heirs of God, and joint-heirs with Christ; if so be that we suffer with him, that we may be also glorified with him. Romans 8:17.

A little girl was left an orphan by the sudden death of both her father and her mother. Some friends of the family cared for her, though they never officially adopted her. It was a rather unfortunate arrangement, for a bond of love did not seem to exist between them, and as a result there was constant unhappiness, especially on the part of the little girl. She covered over many of the hurts of her heart by trying to lose herself in giving unselfishly to others.

She loved her church and was the most brilliant student in her confirmation class. But one night she ran away from home. The surrounding countryside was searched. Finally, early the next morning, she was found in a ditch where she had slept part of the night. As she was brought back she cried her little heart out as she told her story of intense loneliness. "I feel as though I belong to nobody," she pitifully cried.

How different her living became when she was placed in a different home and felt the security of loving arms around her! It would be hard to believe how even her appearance changed as her outward radiance indicated the confidence which we know she had in her heart.

Are you ever lonely? Do you ever feel that nobody cares? Are you ever tempted to run away? Whenever these moods come upon you, remind yourself of the great fact that you are not an orphan, nor are you ever alone. You belong to somebody and His is a love that will never let you go. You are united with the great God who created you. You are made in His image. When sin came to separate you from Him, He gave His very own Son to die on the cross that you might be brought back to Him and not only receive the assurance that you have been forgiven but also the joyful knowledge of belonging.

TABLE TALK· *Stop to think about all the homeless children in this world, victims of war, orphans, children whose parents do not want them. What can you do for some of these?*

SEPTEMBER 23

Be Prepared

And he that sent me is with me: he hath not left me alone; for I do always those things that are pleasing to him. John 8:29.

The motto of the great Boy Scout organization is: "Be Prepared!" Many times in life you have discovered how good that advice is. In times of prosperity it is well to lay aside material means in order to "save for a rainy day." As we read the Word of God and pray we build up spiritual resources that stand us well in the time of trouble. As we walk hand in hand with God we are in the presence of One who will always give us victory. And if He is with us we never need to worry.

A county superintendent once visited a rural school. She noticed the desks of the children were very untidy. As she was about to leave she told the children that some day she would come back. She would not tell them when she would return, but when she did, she intended to bring a prize for the one whose desk was the neatest. After school that day a girl who had the reputation of being the most untidy in the room declared to the rest of her schoolmates that she was going to win the prize. In utter amazement her class exclaimed, "How do you expect to do that?" "I've decided to clean my desk at the end of every week," said the girl. "But what if she should come at the beginning of the week?" The little girl thought for a moment and then answered, "Then I will decide to clean my desk at the end of every day." "But what if the visiting teacher should come at the beginning of the day?" Once more the girl thoughtfully pondered and then suddenly exclaimed, "Well, then I guess I will just always keep my desk clean!"

We never have to worry about when Jesus will come again if we always keep our house in order. If we live each day to the best of our ability and then at night honestly, willingly, and penitently confess our sins, we will always be prepared so that whenever He comes, the great prize which He offers because of His love will be ours.

TABLE TALK: *Mention instances of how fortunate people were when they had made preparations for emergencies, and how unfortunate they were when they were unprepared.*

Are You Listening?

Today if ye shall hear his voice, harden not your hearts, as in the provocation, like as in the day of the trial in the wilderness. Hebrews 3:7-8.

When I was a boy I was fortunate enough to have a loving mother and father who took care of my every need. How dependent I was upon them! They fed me, clothed me, gave me a home in which to live, and they did not expect that I pay them a thing for all of those services. They did this for me because they loved me. They wanted nothing in return.

When I left for college I discovered how really dependent I had been upon them. I never had had to worry about getting up in time because Mother or Dad would always awaken me, but now being away from home, I had to rely on an alarm clock.

I used to set it at a certain time in the morning, in time for my first class. I soon found myself getting into the habit of turning it off and going back to sleep. Many days I slept too long, so I conceived of the idea of having two alarm clocks, one to ring at an early hour, and the second to reawaken me so that I would not be late for school. Finally, I slept through them both, and decided that if I was really to get to school on time, I would have to readjust my way of living.

God was very wise when He gave each one of us a conscience, a little bell to warn us against doing wrong and to let us know when we have done wrong. Whenever we are faced with this kind of temptation a voice tells us, "No, you shouldn't do that!" Sometimes we listen to that voice, and sometimes we do not. Have you ever stopped to think that our consciences are like alarm clocks? If we do not pay attention to them, they may sometimes speak to us and we will not even hear them.

And remember, God is most unhappy when we will not listen to His voice. We must learn to listen to God and carry out His wishes. Only then will we readjust our way of living to a happy and fruitful life.

TABLE TALK: *Mention instances when God has directed what you should do by speaking to you through the voice of conscience.*

SEPTEMBER 25

We Know There Is a Paradise

For I reckon that the sufferings of this present time are not worthy to be compared with the glory which shall be revealed to usward. Romans 8:18.

A little girl much loved by her family and friends seemed as close to being without fault as any human could be. Thoughtful and considerate, she had learned at an early age to love her God above all things, and also to love her neighbor. She enjoyed living to the fullest, and very frequently as she went about her house she would say, "Isn't God good to us?"

One Sunday in church school she was especially impressed by the lesson concerning paradise and the "house of many mansions." Later at home she went to her father, whom she loved, and said, "Daddy, how can it be possible that God has made such a wonderful place as paradise for us when we do so many bad things and hurt Him so often?" Hard as he tried to convince her, there still seemed to be doubt in the child's mind.

The very next day she went off to school but as noon approached she became sick and was taken home. In the afternoon she lapsed into unconsciousness. Her family waited in anxiety by her bedside hoping she would speak. Then toward midnight she looked into her father's eyes and said, "Daddy, I know there is a paradise in heaven."

It seemed as if she had received a glimpse into the great beyond. And now before the angels would take her from this world, she wanted to leave with her loved ones the assurance that all was well with her soul.

In all of our lives there come moments of doubting when we wonder how God could be so good to us in spite of all the sins that we have committed. We live in fear of the future and shudder at the thought of death. Each day would have more meaning and contain more true living if this assurance were ours: We know there is a paradise, a place of perfectness without sorrow and sin and death.

TABLE TALK: *Discuss how you feel about heaven and death. Remember that death can be a beautiful experience only if you are a Christian, because then you are assured of paradise.*

SEPTEMBER 26

Go Work Today

He said unto them, The harvest indeed is plenteous, but the laborers are few: pray ye therefore the Lord of the harvest, that he would send forth laborers into his harvest. Luke 10:2.

There are so many ways in which we can be of service in God's kingdom work. Going His way opens up countless avenues which we can walk where we can be a blessing to our fellow men.

For example, here is an executive in a large concern who had never before systematically read the Bible but now he had resolved that he would. He had sought the advice of his pastor, who directed him in the purchase of a modern translation. Not only is he still reading the Bible himself each day, but he has placed a copy in the office or home of almost every other executive in that company. In his growing partnership with the Master he has led many families into the Christian church. Men to whom he has talked bear him this witness, "He is the first business executive I have ever known who has spoken to me about Christ and the church."

Or here is another. Her work as a beauty parlor operator is her avocation, for she had made her vocation working for the church. She has a radiant disposition, for she not only begins her day with God but walks through the day directed and guided by His presence. Women come to her not only to have their hair taken care of, but to hear her beautiful philosophy. They become influenced toward God by her consistent testimony.

Or consider the friendly couple who are the caretakers of a certain church. In a real sense they are ministers, for concerning their manner of life it can be truly said, "They go about doing good." In reverence and humility they care for God's house. They have made of their work a mission. Many people each week cross their paths and never does anyone fail to catch the vibrant spirit which they manifest and which indicates their love for the Master they so willingly serve.

There is much work to be done. God is depending on you.

TABLE TALK: *Do you know any businessman who practices his faith in this manner? How can you make Christ evident in your work?*

270

SEPTEMBER 27

Count Your Blessings

Now faith is assurance of things hoped for, a conviction of things not seen. Hebrews 11:1.

A young Marine will never be able to kick a football as he did when he was a star high-school player a few years ago. He lost seven toes by Chinese bullets and Korean frostbite. His baseball future also seems dim. His left arm is still numb from a Chinese gun blast. Yet the twenty-one-year-old corporal, now home again, is one of the happiest young men in his community. His courageous spirit is a constant lesson to those about him.

Wavy-haired, square-shouldered, Dick tells the story with scant emotion. He grins lightly when he tells of the bullet that entered his side, struck the lung, then bounced back fracturing three of his ribs before finally going out his back. And he is collected as he tells about his being wounded the second time. Then he lay in the snow bank for "I will never know how long" before walking a hundred yards for help. When his mother shows visitors Dick's purple heart he simply smiles and says, "Aw, I am no hero!"

This young man is typical of many who are each day conquering major catastrophes. How insignificant some of our concerns become in the light of the suffering and hardships that others have to face. We should remember that our complaining and worrying not only render us incapable of meeting problems, but they also influence the spirit of those about us. How often one becomes depressed at hearing other people complain! Life just seems to turn drab. On the other hand, what a soul-warming experience it is to find courageous souls, like the soldier boy mentioned, who make the best of any situation!

The greatest of all men suffered the most yet endured and gained the victory. Following Him we are given strength to bear whatever burdens may come. We know that then "all things will work together for good."

TABLE TALK: *Comment on the effect that the parents' state of mind has upon the children's spirit.*

SEPTEMBER 28

Look—Listen—Live

He therefore that supplieth to you the Spirit, and worketh miracles among you, doeth he it by the works of the law, or by the hearing of faith? Galatians 3:5.

There once lived a man by the name of Zaccheus. Being very short of stature, he was concerned about how he should be able to see Jesus when He passed by. Someone tall might stand in front of him. So he resolved to climb a tree, where he could see. Three things happened.

First, Zaccheus looked. Maybe it was curiosity, but likely more than that. He was seeking the Saviour. The remarkable part of the story is that Jesus looked, too, and their eyes met. So often we become confused and wonder how we can find God, as if He were hiding in some unknown place. That is not the case at all. God is omnipresent. This very moment if you would but turn to Him you would discover that His eyes are upon you.

Then Zaccheus listened. Jesus had something to tell him, even as He has something to tell us today if we would only take time to be still and hear His voice. "Zaccheus, come down from that tree," the Master said. "I want to visit you in your home." Zaccheus climbed down from the tree as with great joy he accepted the invitation of the Master.

The third thing that happened is the most remarkable of all. Zaccheus looked and listened, and now he lived. Two miracles happened to him. The first was that he saw how sinful he was and how much in need of a Saviour. The second was important, too. The miracle of a changed heart demanded that he also alter his life, and so he promised the Master that he would not only make restitution for all that he had done wrong, but that he would henceforth be a different kind of a person.

We, too, can have the same experience as Zaccheus, if only we come into the presence of Christ, recognizing our imperfections and resolving to live a better life.

TABLE TALK: *Discuss the people you know who are really living to the full. Take a look at your own life to discover what is lacking. Then look at Jesus, listen to His words of promise, and discover what it is really to live.*

Prove Yourself to God

Oh give thanks unto the Lord, call upon His name; make known among the people his doings. Psalm 105:1.

I was standing one day in the city of Jerusalem. Ever since childhood one of my ambitions had been to walk the highways upon which the Master had traveled. Now I had just come from Nazareth, having seen the place where Jesus was supposed to have worked beside His father in the carpenter shop. Now my guide pointed to the place called Calvary, that little low hill upon which the cross once stood.

Great emotion filled my soul as I seemed to see Him there dying on that cross for me, and silently I prayed, "Thank You, Lord, for saving my soul." I am sure that I heard a response from His lips echoing down the corridors of time. It was this: "Son, go out and prove that your life has been worth saving."

I have often thought about that experience. Salvation is a free gift from God, to be sure. But if it means anything to us, we will give evidence of it by our living. We prove that our lives have been worth saving only as we go about doing good, even as He did.

What the Master demands of us is more than mere lip service. He was always severely critical of those who spoke one way and lived another. What He demanded from His followers above all else was a practice consistent with their speech.

The early disciples made the great impact they did upon the world of their day not so much because they were brilliant orators—most of them were ordinary people like you and me—but because others were attracted to their way of life as they demonstrated what it meant to be in partnership with God. They put into practice the Christian virtues so that people saw evidence of their faith

We prove that our life has been worth saving as we seek to follow Jesus. That makes us kind and helpful to others. We prove to the world the dynamic that is within us as we build houses of hope in the lives of others desperately in need.

TABLE TALK: *Discuss specific things you can do each day to prove to God that you are sincere in your Christian faith.*

SEPTEMBER 30

You Make the Decisions

He that giveth heed unto the word shall find good; and whoso trusteth in the Lord, happy is he. Proverbs 16:20.

A commanding officer stood at rigid attention at an airfield where he was stationed. He had trained a group of young men in the art of flying. Now one of them was climbing into his plane for his first solo flight. The officer was tense as the boy taxied the plane out to the runway. There he put on his brakes and raced his motor, as he prepared for the takeoff. When the signal came from the tower, the plane sped down the runway, climbed into the air, circled to gain proper altitude, and leveled off at eight thousand feet to sail smoothly on into the far-off horizon. Then for the first time the commanding officer relaxed as he smiled and said, "Well, he's on his own now."

It must be quite an experience to make your first solo flight in an airplane but certainly it would be foolish to attempt it had there not been countless hours and months of discipline and training under competent teachers. That is the price that has to be paid to achieve any success in life. That is the reason it is so important that children be trained in the way that they should go.

How quickly the years pass by. The school years come to an end; our children leave home to take their place in the field of life. As parents we must say, "You are on your own now." Whether or not the venture will be successful will depend upon the training we have given them. Whether or not we can relax like that older army officer as he saw his student successfully pass the examination, will be determined by our willingness to take the time to teach our children the important things of the spirit.

No one is properly equipped to be on his own unless there is within the presence of Him whose companionship is real.

TABLE TALK: *Can you recall the time when you were "on your own," perhaps your first day of school, your first job? How did you feel? What assurances did you have?*

274

OCTOBER 1

Now I Belong to Jesus

But he answered and said, It is written, Man shall not live by bread alone, but by every word that proceedeth out of the mouth of God. Matthew 4:4.

It was a Sunday evening at the close of a camping week. A group of young people had separated themselves for a time from the busyness of city life to pray and worship together and to be reminded of the partnership which could be theirs with God.

The closing service took place in the chapel located on the shore of the lake. The whole front of the chapel was a picture window and the altar setting was a lake in the forefront and a beautiful wooded hill beyond with the sky above it. The lights were turned off and the moon rose in all its splendor causing a pathway of golden light down the hill, across the lake, and through the window to the faces of the young people who were worshiping here. It was as if God were reminding them that there is always a way open from Him to man. Silently the group remained as they saw this unforgettable sermon. Then suddenly they broke into song: "Now I belong to Jesus, Jesus belongs to me; not for the years of time alone, but for eternity."

What can be worth more than the knowledge that we belong to God? And how necessary it is that we have the assurance that we need not be separated from Him.

We live in a day in which many are proud of their achievements. We have created so many inventions. So many luxuries are available to each one of us, opportunities abound on every hand. Each day the standard of living increases. But as ever before, we need to remind ourselves of the fact that man does not live by bread alone. We cannot save ourselves. Alone we are of little consequence. But when the miracle of belonging takes place and we allow God to control our lives, then the least of us can be of importance in the work of His kingdom.

TABLE TALK: *Discuss instances in which you are completely dependent upon other people. Have there been times when you have thought that you could get along without God, and have discovered it is not possible?*

OCTOBER 2

God Is the Creator

Be not therefore anxious, saying, What shall we eat? or, What shall we drink? or, Wherewithal shall we be clothed? . . for your heavenly Father knoweth that ye have need of all these things.
Matthew 6:31-32.

One evening a man invited a group of guests to partake of a very sumptuous banquet. He had them seated in a large room. At one end he had placed a screen and at the other a projector. Before the first course was served, he showed some pictures of people toiling among the rocks in the misty cold. They were gathering up oysters. After he had shown in these pictures all of the work these men had to do to make possible this one course, he served the oysters to his guests.

Then before he served the next course he showed pictures of the farmer tilling the soil, planting the seed, working in the field to raise his crop. He showed pictures of grain being taken to the mill, of flour being produced, and of the countless numbers of people working the various processes that made possible the food which they were about to eat. As every course was thus presented by pictures, an indelible impression was left with those present of our dependence upon one another in the business of daily living.

After the last course had been served the host flashed on the screen a single hand which everybody recognized as symbolizing the hand of God. Each one was reminded again that none of these things would be possible if God should for one moment withdraw that provident hand of creation which "daily provides abundantly for all the necessities of life."

As children of the heavenly Father we never have to be afraid that He will forsake us, for this is His promise: "Be not therefore anxious, saying, What shall we eat? or, What shall we drink? or, What shall we put on? for your heavenly Father knoweth that ye have need of all these things."

TABLE TALK: *Mention instances when you have been worried about what may happen tomorrow? Or are there things you are worried about right now? God is still watching over you, caring for you, providing for you. You need never worry.*

OCTOBER 3

Not Only a King, but a Father

Fear not, little flock; for it is your Father's good pleasure to give you the kingdom. Luke 12:32.

Is God set apart, or is God a part of our lives? One of the greatest miracles of life is the knowledge that God through Christ identifies Himself with us. We can become at one with Him. The Atonement is proof of this promise.

We believe in a majestic God, but too many of us think of Him sitting on a golden throne like an earthly king far detached from His people. Rather, He is the kind of a king that comes down to walk the streets and the byways of life, daily acquainting Himself with the needs of His children, being concerned about them and always willing to help them. He wants to know about our sufferings. He wants to be told about our mistakes. He wants us to share with Him even our little cares and worries and He seeks to identify Himself with us in our problems so that He can give us the help that we so desperately need.

Once in olden times a little boy was standing in a great throng of people watching a parade pass down the street. Finally there came a great chariot with many guards walking on each side, for seated high upon that chariot was an emperor returning from his fields of conquest. The little lad broke through the guard and approached the king, but the guard stopped him as he said, "You can't get on this chariot. It belongs to my emperor." The little boy replied, "He may be your emperor, but he is my father!" Then they let him climb to his father's lap.

God is not only our King; he is also our Father. Fear not, therefore, little children, and be not dismayed, for each day God is present with you to lead you in the way that you should go. Let that be your first thought when you awaken in the morning. Think of it often through the hours of the day and at night when you lay your head down to rest. Have faith to believe that He is your Father and that you belong to Him. Remember He has made you in His own image, redeemed you with His own Son.

TABLE TALK: *How do you treat your best friends? Do you talk to them? Do things for them? How many times have you stopped to talk today with God?*

OCTOBER 4

Look at Your Blessings

Cast thy burden upon the Lord, and he will sustain thee: he shall never suffer the righteous to be moved. Psalm 55:22.

So often we complain and wish for the many things that we do not possess. We rob ourselves of the joy which could be ours if we would only be grateful for the things we have. Perhaps we are more fortunate than we sometimes think. We would be wise very frequently to appraise our blessings. For if we did, we would be much more grateful for what we have.

A man had decided to sell his farm. He went to town and selected a real estate firm to list it for him. They came out and looked over his property and wrote a description of it for advertising purposes. As the farmer looked over the description his eyes got bigger and bigger as he kept reading. Finally as he came to the end he turned to the real estate agent and said, "I have decided not to sell this farm; this is exactly the kind of a place I have always been looking for. I didn't realize I had it."

When you are tempted to complain that your troubles are greater than anyone else's and your burdens are heavier than those of your fellow men, think of the legend about how God invited all of His complaining children to come and each place his greatest trouble or worry or burden in a big pile. Then God allowed all His children to look upon this great mountain of trouble. He invited each one to choose from among the burdens the one he would prefer. The legend says that each one took the same burden which he had himself laid there.

Sometimes it is good for us to compare our state with that of our fellow men, especially with those who have greater burdens to bear than we. About us each day are heroic souls who are carrying heavy crosses. Yet they are not complaining; rather, are they singing praises to God who keeps giving them the strength to endure. There are people who are suffering from great physical ailments; yet they are living radiantly, testifying to the sufficiency of the grace of God. It can be so for you also!

TABLE TALK: *Stop to consider how many real burdens you have, and then think of your neighbor and realize how fortunate you really are.*

OCTOBER 5

The Miracle of Becoming

But as many as received him, to them gave he the right to become children of God, even to them that believe on his name.

John 1:12.

This is the promise of the "Miracle of Becoming." As many as received him, to them gave He the right to become. And it can happen to you! But only if you have faith to believe, and only as you meet the conditions by turning over to Him what you have or what you are so that by His power He can create something tremendously great.

The difficulty with most of us is that we do not believe it can happen. We spend our time complaining about our lot in life rather than using what we have for good. Suppose Abraham Lincoln had said, "I was born in a log cabin. I had limited opportunities as a child. There is no chance for me to become anything and therefore I won't try." Suppose Martin Luther had said, "The world has not treated me fairly. I have tried to be honest with my conscience and do my best, but in spite of it all I am an outcast. So why should I make any contribution to human life?" Suppose John Bunyan had said, "They threw me into Bedford Jail. I am being unjustly punished. Why should I try to be helpful to my fellow men?" But none of these men said any of these things. Therefore, great things resulted.

Abraham Lincoln created an opportunity to educate himself and became a great president of our nation, who left with us principles which we still hold dear. Martin Luther was not satisfied until he could restore to the world the forgotten concept of religious freedom that "the just shall live by faith." John Bunyan created a "Pilgrims' Progress," being willing to accept the circumstances about him and used them for good.

Perhaps your name will not attain the greatness of those just mentioned, but any soul will be great that has the faith to believe the promise that if we give Him our life, such as it is, He has the power to make it become something of great worth.

TABLE TALK: *Mention several people who have made a name for themselves through sheer determination. Discuss how and why they have done so.*

OCTOBER 6

The Road of the Loving Heart

The fool hath said in his heart, There is no God. They are corrupt, they have done abominable works, there is none that doeth good. Psalm 14:1.

Have you ever noticed how desolate trees look in the bleak days of winter when they stand seemingly lifeless, stripped of all their glory? And then the miracle happens! The Creator touches these trees with the breath of spring and they become clothed in their garments of green. As we witness such happenings we are prompted with the Psalmist of old to say: "The fool hath said in his heart, There is no God."

But the greatest miracle is when the great Redeemer touches the human life dead in trespasses and sins, strips off the filthy garments of unrighteousness, and reclothes that soul in the raiments of His glory. When this experience takes place in the human soul something results. As the individual feeds upon the word of God and comes to the heavenly Father in prayer, he begins to exemplify the spirit of the Master in his daily living. Day by day this reclothed person becomes a little kinder in his action toward others. He ceases to speak harshly and guards himself against judging others, having come to the conclusion that judging belongs to God. He seeks to lend a helping hand to those in need as he walks among them. The result is that day by day his life becomes more glorious. For the more he invests of himself the greater are the returns that come back to him.

Henry Ward Beecher tells about seeing a newsboy one cold wintry morning standing on a corner shivering in the inclement weather. He reached into his pocket and gave the boy a few coins, then patted him on the shoulder, and said, "It is a mighty cold day, isn't it, Son?" The boy smiled as he replied, "Well, it was, sir, until you came along."

Try putting a little more love into your living. For if you do, you will discover that you will love life more than ever before. For the Master's way is the road of the loving heart!

TABLE TALK: *Mention people you know who exemplify radiant Christian living.*

OCTOBER 7

Forever Keep the Vision

Whosoever believeth that Jesus is the Christ is begotten of God; and whosoever loveth him that begat loveth him also that is begotten of him. 1 John 5:1.

One morning an Indian chief sent his three boys into the mountains. He told each of them to bring back some trophy indicating how far he had gone. Then he waited for their return. In the early afternoon the first son returned. He held in his hand a piece of bark, which indicated he had reached the timber line of the mountains. Toward supper time the second one returned. He held in his hand a piece of rock showing he had reached the stone line of the mountains. It was late evening when the third returned home, and when he arrived he had nothing in his hand. His clothes were torn, and it was apparent that he had had a very difficult journey. But his face was so radiant that his father knew he must have had an experience well worth the cost of his difficult and trying journey. Softly and silently the lad began to speak: "I have brought back nothing, but I have seen the sea and it keeps beckoning me on!"

The Great White Host in heaven above testifies to the glory life can hold. They have reached the goal because they caught the vision which kept beckoning them on until eternity became their home. So often we fail to receive the most out of life because we stop at some halfway point, unwilling to pay the price of the hardships we must face and the trail blazing we must do to reach that far summit. But once you have really caught the vision, it will inspire you to pay any price to attain the goal. For the glory which has been revealed to you keeps persuading you to continue climbing. Remember you do not travel in your own strength, for when human resources run out God's power is always there to help you carry through.

Never be so foolish as to allow the material things of the moment to cloud the vision of those things which are eternal.

TABLE TALK: *Mention people you know who have set high goals for themselves and who have failed to reach them because they were not willing to pay the price. Mention others who have achieved their goals because of perseverance.*

OCTOBER 8

Flight for Life

And when she had said this, she went away, and called Mary her sister secretly, saying, The Master is here, and calleth thee.
                                                                    John 11: 28.

Not long ago there was a picture in the daily newspaper of a mother and her three-year-old boy, and it carried this headline: "Flight for Life." The two were going by plane to New York so that the little lad who was suffering from leukemia might be treated with a rare new drug. The doctor had predicted that the boy would have but three to six months to live unless they would be willing to take this flight. It was necessary to go to New York, where the drug was to be found and the treatment was given. Had the mother and son stayed at home the boy would have faced certain death. But they did not do that. They paid the price, met the conditions, and found a cure.

All of us are concerned for the welfare of the human body. A parent does not hesitate to spend his entire fortune or to borrow money if need be, to preserve the physical welfare of his child. We become very unselfish when a loved one is sick and is in need of medical care. That is the way it should be.

But why is it that people are concerned about things that can harm the body and seem to be so unconcerned about those which harm the soul? Why is it that so few are willing to pay the price of the spiritual "flight for life?"

Just think of what God offers us: A journey with Him. The price? Your willingness to go and your total commitment of life to Him. It is at his point that many of us falter, trying to keep one hand on the things of the world and the other hand in God's. We must leave everything behind if we are to go with Him, for He is a Pilot who enables us to soar above the transient things of earth through the storms of life to the glory on the other side. He is well acquainted with the difficulties along the way, but likewise He is sure that He can lead us safely to our destination.

TABLE TALK: *Have you heard of people who are ill, who refuse to see a doctor, and yet pray for a miracle? Have you also known people who want something desperately, and yet refuse to do anything to obtain it except wish for it?*

OCTOBER 9

A Universal Language

If I speak with the tongues of men and of angels, and have not love, I am become sounding brass, or a clanging cymbal.
1 Corinthians 13:1.

A state welfare director, a social worker himself, warned his associates one day that they were in danger of destroying their power to communicate with people. "There are too many 'wooly phrases' and padded words in use," he said. He gave this as an example: "To be emotionally well integrated one must be able to participate in one's environment with the minimum amount of conflict. Put simply, which is the only way to put it, this means that to be happy you must enjoy taking part in the life around you." He also took a sarcastic jab at his fellow workers for using too much technical jargon. He suggests that social workers should follow the example of a Texas congressman who after two days of listening to the many-syllable words of psychiatrists and social workers at a National Welfare Conference, opened his speech with this remark: "You will have to excuse me for using words that you can understand."

The Saviour spoke in our language. He talked so simply that even a child could understand Him. His purpose was that all might have the opportunity of knowing the way of truth and life. He did not want to lose His power to communicate with ordinary people and so he used a language which could be understood by all. When a sinful woman wept penitently at His feet, He spoke words whose meaning was clear: "Your sins are forgiven. Go and sin no more." When the disciples asked who was to be the greatest in the kingdom, He placed in their midst a little child and said, "Of such is the kingdom of heaven." His language is as understandable today. It is the language of love.

TABLE TALK: *Which has impressed you more—a speaker who talks in intellectual phrases, or one who speaks simply and sincerely? Also, do you know people who talk about doing good things and never do, and others who never flaunt their works but always go about doing good? Which would you choose as a friend?*

OCTOBER 10

Is It Worth the Price?

I pray not that thou shouldest take them from the world, but that thou shouldest keep them from the evil one. John 17:15.

A house was on fire in Oklahoma City. Carolyn, a little two-year-old, was sleeping in one of the bedrooms. Fireman Bob crawled into the building. He was smoke-blinded, but he was glad to lay hands on a little form wrapped in a blanket. "When I pulled the bundle off the bed, I heard a little cry," he reported afterwards. "But when I got it outside I discovered that I had made a tragic mistake. It was only a big doll." The real little girl perished.

Fireman Bob is not the only one who has made this tragic mistake. He thought he was saving a life—in fact, he risked his own life to do it. But instead, when the smoke had cleared from his eyes, he had a plaything in his arms. How often we are deceived by smoke-filled eyes! Our vision becomes beclouded by the things of the world. We think we have hold of something only to discover that it is of little worth, a mere plaything.

When the Titanic was going down, everyone on board was told that he would have a few minutes to go back to the stateroom. One of the women passengers rushed to her cabin. She saw on the table her costly jewels and beside them two oranges. What should she choose? She did not hesitate long. What good were her precious jewels if she became hungry on the life boat? In a matter of life or death, oranges would be of more value than diamonds.

It is well under any circumstances to remember that we should not buy something just because it is cheap. It may be very costly in the long run. Neither should we sell our souls for any price. Live close to the Master that your vision may be kept clear. For if you go your own way without Him it is possible that in the end, like Fireman Bob, you may have in your possession merely a plaything and your real soul may have perished.

TABLE TALK: *Discuss the folly of dedicating your life to a worthless cause. What cause is worth life dedication?*

OCTOBER 11

Be Honest with Yourself

And Jesus said, Neither do I condemn thee: go thy way; from henceforth sin no more. John 8:11.

One day a woman who had committed a great wrong was brought into the presence of Jesus. They wanted Him to condemn her, but He turned to them and said, "He that is without sin among you, let him first cast a stone at her." When they heard it they went away one by one and Jesus was left alone with the woman standing before Him. He looked at her and said, "Where are they? Did no man condemn thee?" She answered, "No one Lord." Then Jesus said, "Neither do I condemn thee: go thy way; from henceforth sin no more."

Could there be a more touching story of living forgiveness than this one? And where is there a more pointed lesson for the one who sets himself up as a judge of his fellow men?

There was a woman who had little concern over the state of disorder in her house. Her kitchen often looked as if someone had taken a giant beater and stirred up the pots and pans, fruits, vegetables, and dishes, then simply let them be wherever they happened to land. One day she was out driving with some friends and they decided to stop in for a minute at the home of a very close friend of all of them. As the car was drawing up to the curb outside the house, the woman of the very casual housekeeping habits commented, "Well, this is one place where you never know how the house is going to look when you step inside of it." She recognized this situation in another's house, but was quite unaware of it in her own.

What sharp vision we have for the faults in others, but what rose colored glasses we often slip over our eyes when we consider our own wrong doings! We are quite blind to our own weakness. A keen sense of our own sinfulness will drive us to a deeper appreciation of the mercy of God. God help us to be alert to our own faults.

TABLE TALK: *Have you ever been quick to criticize someone else without stopping to consider that you may be guilty of the same faults? Next time you think of criticizing someone, why not say something constructive instead!*

OCTOBER 12

Headed Toward the Sunrise

Thy sun shall no more go down; neither shall thy moon withdraw itself; for the Lord will be thine everlasting light, and the days of thy mourning shall be ended. Isaiah 60:20.

For travelers from the United States it is a fascinating experience to fly the Atlantic in mid-summer. The stewardess informs them that they are about to take off for Iceland on a night flight over the North Atlantic, that the sun will set about nine o'clock, and that they will see the sunrise again only three hours later. The farther north one travels, the sooner will one reach that point where the sunset and sunrise are one. The only way to reach that point, of course, is to travel toward the sun.

That is the direction toward which every Christian life is headed, toward the Sun of Righteousness. There is always a goal and a destination ahead. This gives real zest to life's journey because then we have a real purpose in view. There are sunny hours when it is bright and finding the course is made easier. The traveler can enjoy the beauty of the sea, the sky, the islands, and the icebergs. But part of the way is through darkness. The sun is not visible. Yet every passenger knows this is a temporary state of affairs for the sun will rise again. It is still in the heavens. If it were not, the earth would no longer have life upon it. But it is dark now and the plane is completely dependent upon instruments to keep to the course.

Life is like that, too. We cannot always see our way clearly. It is dark and conflicting storms whirl about us. We find disappointments, both in ourselves and in others. Things indeed sometimes look very black. But God has provided adequately for every situation in life. Even though darkness seems to encircle us at times He has given us the instruments by which we can forge ahead. I like to think of faith as our capacity to turn to the divine radio waves which keep us on the way. God will take care of us if we but have the will to entrust ourselves to His hands.

TABLE TALK: *Have there been times in your life when troubles and disappointments made you wonder if ever the sun would shine again?*

OCTOBER 13

A Lifetime Business

And he said unto them, How is it that ye sought me? wist ye not that I must be about my Father's business?
Luke 2:49. (A. V.)

Some years ago an old man was given the job of painting the face of a town clock. But it was not to be an ordinary job for on the clock he was to paint a motto that would be worthy of his village, and he was to choose the words himself! He found it a difficult choice to make. Frequently he visited the mayor of the town to ask his advice. Finally, the mayor became impatient with the old man and told him to go about his own business and see to it that the clock was painted. Then it came to the old man: "Go about your business." That was the motto he would use. What better counsel as one asks the time of day?

We are so often reminded these days of that little sentence, "It is later than you think." Maybe it is. But it does not matter how early or late it is. The important thing is that it is late. There are history-making hours. We can be sure that the historians will take a lot of pages to record the events of this age.

We Christians need to take much heed to plan our strategy. We cannot wait any longer. We must go about our business today. And our lifetime business is living for Christ. It must be our concern whether or not our neighbor goes to church. It must be our concern whether or not business is carried on honestly. It must be our concern that the armies of Christ are greater than the armies of the world. This is the hour when the church must make its mark upon the world. Only as the Christian spirit fills each home and each heart will this come about.

Your life is meant to shed light upon the darkness of this struggling age. It is you who must be the missionary, wherever you go telling the world of a Saviour who has the power to redeem, drawing your neighbor to the things eternal.

TABLE TALK: *Have you ever tried to excuse yourself from trying to point someone else to the Christian way of life, by saying "I am not my brother's keeper?" If you have the light, you are obligated to spread it to others. Name ways in which this can be done.*

OCTOBER 14

Always a New Beginning

Wherefore if any man is in Christ, he is a new creature; the old things are passed away; behold, they are become new.

2 Corinthians 5:17.

If you have ever visited the oceanside you may have watched people making drawings in the moist sand. Many of them are clever works of art, pictures of castles or churches, or portraits of famous men and women. But suddenly the tide comes in and the lines are washed away. The drawings disappear and the artist must start all over again.

Sometimes our own lives seem to be such a series of defeats and new beginnings. Our happiness seems to be washed away by everyday troubles and we are left to start all over again. But because of God there is always the possibility of a new beginning. Because of Christ our Saviour we can live today with new hope and courage; because a King came to earth to die for us and to give us His power, we can forget the trials and tribulations of the past and receive courage to lift our eyes to a new and better day.

God has many preachers who never set foot in the pulpit—the sunrise, the new-fallen snow, the flower burst into full bloom. They all tell us of God's love, which makes all things good and pure if only we yield to His plan. Every darkness is broken by the sun. The landscape is brightened by a blanket of white snow. A tiny flower can cheer up a lonely room. Everywhere we look God gives us evidence of His true goodness. His love for the earth is expressed in the beautiful things of nature; His love for man is expressed in the beautiful spirit of a Christian who goes about doing good.

But the most wonderful blessing of all is that He can take a bitter and bruised soul and make out of it something of eternal value. He can take your life and make it new again. He can turn sins into forgiveness and hatred into love. He can lead you into the land of beginning again, where there never need be a dark moment.

TABLE TALK: *Name instances when you have been discouraged, and suddenly your path was illumined.*

OCTOBER 15

In Debt to God

For ye were bought with a price: glorify God therefore in your body. 1 Corinthians 6:20.

A little girl visiting London very much wanted to see the Queen. One day she started off by herself and walked to the gates of the palace. There a sentry stopped her and asked what she wanted. She promptly told him she would like to visit the Queen. The soldier laughed, pushed her aside, and told her to be on her way. The little girl turned and as she walked along down the street past the palace walks, she began to cry. Suddenly a kind man stopped her and asked her why she was crying. After she had told him, the man took her hand and together they walked back toward the gate. The sentry came to attention and the two passed through the gates, for that kindly man was a prince of the royal family. The friendly prince took the little girl to the Queen, who kindly and graciously received her.

Each one of us has the privilege of taking the hand of Christ and being led to God by Him. Though countless wrongs and shameful sins stand between us and our heavenly Father, we need not go away and be lost in the darkness. God's Son is ready to take those sins upon His shoulders and to clear the way which leads to forgiveness from the heavenly Father.

Some years ago a young lad became very sick. A certain doctor in faraway Australia was recommended as one who might possibly be able to save the boy's life. Though the fee was very large, the father was willing to use all his wealth in an attempt to save the boy's life. The doctor was sent for, and the boy's life was saved. The father mortgaged all of his property to pay the cost.

The greatest price ever paid for the saving of life was upon the Cross. But God our heavenly Father was willing to give His very all that His children might have the opportunity of living forever with Him.

TABLE TALK: *Recount times when there has been something you have wanted very much but have not been able to afford. The price for total happiness is a total commitment of yourself to God. You can afford the price.*

OCTOBER 16

Love One Another

Whosoever denieth the Son, the same hath not the Father: he that confesseth the Son hath the Father also. 1 John 2:23.

It is said that John lived the longest of all the disciples. Because he had known Jesus and walked and talked with Him, the people were anxious that he should tell them about the Master who had gone about preaching and teaching. And the aged John would turn to them and say, "Little children, love one another." To him there was nothing else that could better tell the story of Christ, for the Master Himself was loving and understanding and He wanted everyone else to be the same.

It is love that gives meaning to life, that makes flowers beautiful to our eyes, and that gives to the hours of each day something more than just the sound of the chimes indicating that time is passing on. When we love God there is sunshine on the darkest days and there are stars that shine on the blackest night.

The kindness and the goodness we show others is the overflow of our love for God. As we sing our praises to Him our hearts are filled with the spirit of sharing what we have with our neighbor, whoever he might be. Because we belong to God we may have the constant joy which persuades us to share with others. Christians are not known for their stinginess. Prompted by love for others, they are generous spiritually and materially.

A man walked into a florist's shop to buy some flowers. He picked out a dozen of the kind his wife liked best and told the man he wanted him to send them out right away. "Is she sick?" asked the clerk. "Indeed not," said the man, "she is just as well as you are." To this the clerk rather apologetically replied, "I am sorry, Sir, but usually the husband doesn't buy his wife flowers unless she is sick." Too often we put off doing the little acts of kindness until it is almost too late. God would have us show our love to those about us at all times so that we need never have reason to regret that we waited too long.

TABLE TALK: *Stop and think of all the unexpected things you can do to make someone happy, the little things that mean so much, and then resolve to do them, just because of love, not because you expect any return.*

OCTOBER 17

Faith Like a Little Child

Yea, though I walk through the valley of the shadow of death, I will fear no evil; for thou art with me; thy rod and thy staff, they comfort me. Psalm 23:4.

When my father came to America he settled in a little northern town in Wisconsin, where he operated a hotel. One day, he experienced a real conversion. The power of God entered into his life and as a result he became a road builder for Him. As the years passed on, a real transformation took place in him. More and more his faith became like that of a little child.

For forty years he worked long hours, six days a week, but he never missed church except for sickness. Nor did a day pass without the family gathering together for family devotions.

He never earned a college degree, but he progressed very far in the school of life. No one ever awarded him a doctorate, but I know heaven conferred many honors upon him. His name was not written in the newspapers, but because of Christ, his Saviour, his name is written in the Book of Life.

As life came to a close for him he did not proudly proclaim his accomplishments. Calmly he asked that his pastor be called, as he wished to receive the Sacrament of the Lord's Supper and be reassured of the forgiveness of his sins. After receiving the promise in simple faith, he walked with God to greet the dawn of the Eternal Tomorrow.

We all need a childlike faith in God. When we have it, it changes all of life. It colors everything about us. It makes living a growing experience. It gives us the right perspective. It puts us in our proper place in comparison with the magnitude of God. It makes us ever conscious of our total dependence upon Him and at the same time, gives us the assurance that He will always see us through, that He will take us by the hand and lead us even through the last "valley of the shadow."

TABLE TALK: *Do you know anyone who has been a living testimony to God's message? Discuss your need for being a living example of Christian beliefs.*

OCTOBER 18

Faith of Our Fathers

And the apostles said unto the Lord, Increase our faith.

Luke 17:5.

I recall walking one day up the Appian Way outside the city of Rome. I came to a little place on the highway which was marked as the spot where Peter was supposed to have seen the vision of the Master. The old legend says that Peter was leaving Rome by this route because he was afraid that the people would kill him on account of his faith. At this particular spot he was supposed to have met the Lord and, startled by the vision, to have asked Him, "Master, where are you going?" And we are told that Jesus replied, "To Rome to be crucified again." Peter knew what He meant. Immediately he turned around and went back to Rome. When the day of Peter's own martyrdom came, he asked that he be crucified with his head down and his feet up, because he felt that he did not deserve to be crucified in the same way as the Master.

We went on a little farther, to the catacombs, where each of us was given a little candle to light our descent into the darkness. Right there I learned a lesson. These little candles were sufficient to show us the way that we should go. You may not think that you have much to contribute to the kingdom of God, but remember even a little candle will help make the darkness disappear.

These catacombs, or underground burial places, through which we were now walking once served as a meeting place for the early Christians, where they could worship in secret. Many of their number were captured and brought into the great Colosseum, an arena which seated thousands of people, and here they were burned at the stake. They would rather die than give up their faith. Here, in the sacred place where I was now standing, many of them had been buried. Thank God for the faith of my fathers. But that faith cannot save me. It can only lead to the experience of salvation which I must have myself.

TABLE TALK: *How can you be a candle in the "catacombs" of the modern world? Is your faith strong enough to withstand a crucifixion by ridicule?*

The Miracle of Multiplication

This poor widow hath cast in more than all they that are cast-
ing into the treasury: for they all did cast in of their superfluity;
but she of her want did cast in all that she had, even all her
living. Mark 12:43-44.

A boy made himself famous one day when he gave the little
he had to the Master. It happened in the long ago. His mother
had prepared him a lunch, for He had decided to go fishing all
day. In his wanderings he came upon a crowd of people. There
were several thousand of them together. They were listening
intently as a man was speaking to them. Suddenly one of this
man's friends came up to the lad and asked if he would be willing to share his lunch with the people. The boy, being unselfish
and not even thinking of his own hunger or desires, immediately
gave him all that he had. The disciples in turn gave the
lunch to the Master who multiplied it so that it was enough to
feed these thousands of people. And when they had finished
eating there were baskets of fragments left over. The miracle
happened because a little lad gave all that he had to the Master.
It mattered not how small the possessions of the little boy were.

So often we attempt to excuse ourselves from Christian service
and giving by saying we have nothing to contribute or at least
not as much as some other neighbor or friend. We forget that
the important thing is not the amount, but the power of God.

The miracle keeps happening today. Another boy, a ten-year-
old of today, came up to his pastor one Sunday, held out a
clenched fist, opened it up and revealed ten dimes. "Here is some
money," he said, "for your radio broadcast. We listen to evening
devotions every night and I have saved this myself because I
enjoy hearing the programs so much." He was only a little lad;
the amount of money was not large, only ten dimes. And yet
the inspiration of such acts of devotion, multiplied by the power
of God in the hearts of many of His children, enabled that congregation to continue to support a tremendous radio ministry.

TABLE TALK: *Discuss what the children of the family can
do in the service of God through the church. Remember, each
little act is important.*

OCTOBER 20

Do You Ring True?

He that overcometh, I will give to sit down with me in my throne, as I also overcame, and sat down with my Father in his throne. He that hath an ear, let him hear what the Spirit saith to the churches. Revelation 3:21-22.

Luther Burbank became very famous because of a seemingly very insignificant accomplishment. He worked for long years just to develop more beautiful flowers and hardier trees. When his work was finished he was acclaimed a hero. Ever so often Mr. Burbank used to have what his neighbors called a $10,000 bonfire. Of 500 tiny plants he had grown, he would probably throw 499 of them into the fire. Or there might be 999 rose bushes that he would destroy just to keep one of them. You see, his job was to produce the very best trees and the most beautiful roses, and perhaps only one out of many hundreds met the high standards which he would set. He could have sold those second-rate plants, but he chose to burn them so that only the very best would be left.

If you live with Christ as your partner, then you must seek to uphold His unblemished reputation, His power to change lives, and His gracious goodness toward all men. You cannot afford to do anything for Him in a second-rate manner. His standards are the very highest and demand the very best that you can do. God insists that if you follow Him you shall live for Him twenty-four hours a day, seven days a week.

The reward for such a life is greater than you can ever imagine. If you give Him the few years which you call a lifetime, He will pay you back with an eternity. If you share with Him your material possessions, He will repay you in treasures many times more valuable than all the money in the world.

The Christianity that too many of us practice can be likened to a beautiful bell high in a tower. On Sundays and special holidays it rings to the glory of God, but the rest of the time it stands silent far above the reach of people that pass below. The least you can give God is the life that rings true each day.

TABLE TALK: *Analyze your activities of the past week. Have you always practiced true Christianity?*

OCTOBER 21

What the Partnership Means

Be strong and of good courage, fear not, nor be affrighted at them: for the Lord thy God, he it is that doth go with thee; he will not fail thee, nor forsake thee. Deuteronomy 31:6.

One day a boy ran to his father and said, "Daddy, we are partners, aren't we?" The father replied, "Yes, my son." "Well, then that means," continued the boy, "that you can reach your hand into my pocket and do anything that you want with what I have." "That is correct," answered the father. "And does that mean," the boy continued, "that I can reach my hand into your pocket and do anything I want to with what you have?" We can all imagine how disconcerted the father must have been by the boy's question.

But that is the kind of a partnership which Christ offers us if we are willing to go God's way. He wants to be able to reach into our lives and do anything He cares to with us. Sometimes that means the changing of our values, the lifting of our sights, and the elimination of selfishness, greed, and pride. It means that we have to be as clay in the hands of a potter allowing Him to shape our lives after His will. It means that we are new creatures.

In return, as our part of the partnership, He offers us the opportunity to reach our hand into the overabundance of His resources to use them for peace and happiness in our lives. That means that when sorrow comes we may stretch forth our hand toward God and there find the healing balm and the comfort that wipes away our tears. It means that when burdens grow heavy we may stretch forth our hand to Him and receive power in answer to our prayers. We can confidently declare, "I can do all things through Him who strengthens me." It means that when the summons of death shall come, we can stretch forth our hands to Him and take His hands so that we can leave this world in joy, and with this song of victory on our lips, "I will fear no evil; for thou art with me."

TABLE TALK: *Can you recite the Twenty-third Psalm? If not, read it and try to memorize it.*

Have You Kept Your Promises?

And call upon me in the day of trouble: I will deliver thee, and thou shalt glorify me. Psalm 50:15.

One day a Catholic priest came into his church and discovered that a certain statue of Jesus was missing from one of the altars. Hurriedly he rushed outside hoping to find the one who had taken it away. Much to his surprise as he looked down the street, he saw a little boy pulling a brand new red wagon and in the wagon was the statue of Christ. He walked up to the lad and asked him why he had taken it and the little boy replied, "I prayed Jesus that I would get a red wagon for Christmas, and I promised Him that if He answered my prayer I would give Him the first ride in it. And after I have kept my promise, I will bring Him back to the church."

So often in life when we want something desperately we turn to God in prayer and we tell Him that if He will just get us out of this emergency or grant us this blessing, we will really serve Him the rest of our days. Then when the dark clouds disappear and the sun begins to shine again we forget all about the promise we have made and go about our own self-sufficient ways, unmindful of our dependence upon Him who is the giver of all good gifts. Everyone of us can learn a lesson from that little boy. He made a promise and he kept it.

Those who know the real partnership with God are willing to meet the conditions which it imposes upon them.

A pastor was leaving the home of one of the stricken members of his congregation. The husband had suddenly been taken in death. A car drove up and out stepped a middle-aged woman who had suffered the same separation not many months ago. She looked expectantly at the pastor as she inquired of him, "Does she have it?" She had come to offer her help to one who was now suffering as she had suffered and she knew that if this friend would only keep looking up, that help would surely come.

"Call upon me in the day of trouble" is a promise. He will surely answer.

TABLE TALK: *Can you recall any other stories about children praying for something? A little child's faith in prayer can teach all of us. Comment upon this.*

OCTOBER 23

Taking the "If" Out of Life

And the rain descended, and the floods came, and the winds blew, and beat upon that house; and it fell not: for it was founded upon the rock. Matthew 7:25.

Have you ever thought of the phrase "taking the 'if' out of life"? The letters of the word "if" are the two middle letters of the word "life." The quest of the soul seeking victory is to take the "if" out of life. That means that we must build upon strong foundations and sometimes the cost appears to be greater than we are willing to pay.

As a great church was being built, tests were made to determine the carrying capacity of the ground beneath the excavating. It was discovered that though the wet sand might ordinarily be strong enough to hold the building, the only way to insure that it would stand secure in storm and flood was the driving of pilings deep into the ground. At great cost one hundred and ninety-three pillars were driven from fifty-five to sixty feet underground to undergird the foundation and make sure that the building would stand.

In life, there is only one foundation upon which we can build. If our house is to survive the storms that will come sooner or later we must build upon the Rock of Ages. In so doing we take the "if" out of life. No longer need we wonder as to the final results, for now the road can lead only to victory. There may be difficulties in building the house of life, but the great Architect will always be present to help us out of any dilemma that we might have to face. His advice will be like a roof that protects us from the elements of nature. Let the storms descend and the winds blow. Our house will still stand because it is built upon a rock. If we had built upon the sand, we could not have been so secure. In fact, we would have faced defeat. For the house which is built upon the sand will fall in life's crucial tests.

If we build each day the structure that is destined to be eternal, let us build well and be willing to pay the price that will secure our future.

TABLE TALK: *Retell the story about the man who built his house on sand. Matthew 7:24-27.*

OCTOBER 24

Resources of Unlimited Power

Let the word of Christ dwell in you richly; in all wisdom teaching and admonishing one another in psalms and hymns and spiritual songs, singing with grace in your hearts unto God.
Colossians 3:16.

When I was in Jerusalem I was told that a statue of Mary stands in the Church of the Holy Sepulchre. The tile floor in front of it is worn smooth by the pilgrims who stand there to worship. Upon the Virgin's neck have been cast costly necklaces and jewels and upon the altar coins and rings of silver and gold.

Gifts of gold and silver mean little to our God unless we have given Him our lives. He wants to walk and talk with us each day. When we allow Him to do this we discover what a wonderful pilgrimage we are on.

I know a middle-aged man who had not been near a church for fifteen years. Now he not only attends, but he attempts to live the gospel which he proclaims. One time he came to me and said, "Pastor, I want to tell you what has made a real difference in my life. A couple of months ago I started to read the Bible and I am already half through it. It is more interesting than any novel that I have ever read." I told him there would be much in the Bible that he could not understand, but that he should just keep reading it, opening his heart to God as he did so, and that God would then speak to him through His Word. Then he turned to me and said: "You will never know what a difference it has already made in my life."

There is a Presence that wants a song to be sung in your soul. Perhaps you have been in the far-off country. Maybe you have not been as loyal to Him as you should have been. Certainly you have sinned and should be very willing to admit it. You may even feel that you have been caught in the snare of the enemy.

But remember, it is not too late. The winsome, pleading Saviour stands before you today wanting to love you back into the Kingdom. Can you hear Him as He softly and tenderly calls you?

TABLE TALK: *When you dedicate your life to God, how can you give of yourself to the glory of His kingdom? What can you do for others, for the church, for your children?*

OCTOBER 25

The Lord Is My Light

For the grace of God hath appeared, bringing salvation to all men, instructing us to the intent that, denying ungodliness and worldly lusts, we should live soberly and righteously and godly in this present world. Titus 2:11-12.

Some place along the road of life one is forced to come to the realization that he cannot travel alone. That is, if he wants to be on a road that leads somewhere. Dark clouds of trouble blot out the light and we need a power beyond our own to give us the assurance that He is present as a friend by our side. If we are willing to receive Him, the Master reaches out His hand and offers Himself as our guide. He has climbed every mountain and walked through every valley where we are called to go. Together we can climb up and up with the view of life becoming more wonderful every step of the way.

These are not just idle words. They are convictions resting on the promises of Almighty God and upon the lives of countless Christians who have experienced in their hearts real happiness and joy. They testify to the results of a life that is lived hand in hand with the Master. The clouds in the sky may still come to cover the earth with darkness, but they cannot drive away the smiles from your countenance and the peace that is within your soul. For if you really believe that the things of heaven are greater than the things of the earth then you are rich in love and grace and mercy.

Oscar Wilde, a clever thinker of our modern age, has said that so many people know "the price of everything and the value of nothing." If godliness means more to you than worldliness, then life is really worth living.

Why not look through the eyes of God? Then you will see the sunshine which crowds out the shadows of all tribulation. God gives you a view of life from the mountaintop where the stars forever shine and where the pettiness and the little cares of this world are dimmed by the greatness of heaven.

The Lord is your light and your salvation. With God you can never be defeated.

TABLE TALK: *Discuss prices and values in terms of religion contrasted with worldly evaluations.*

OCTOBER 26

Do the Best That You Can

But desire earnestly the greater gifts. And moreover a most excellent way show I unto you. 1 Corinthians 12:31.

There is only one way whereby the world will ever discover lasting brotherhood and understanding. That is when Christ becomes the senior partner in every business, the king of every nation, and the ruler of every heart. The fire in every Christian's life must burn brighter than ever before. There is no other way to assure ourselves that tomorrow will dawn with a greater hope for every soul.

A busy man was hurrying out of a big city hotel and was whistling to himself as he walked along. A little lad was playing on the sidewalk and as the man passed by, the lad looked up at him and said, "Is that the best that you can whistle? I can do better than that." And then the youngster began to demonstrate the proof of his statement. And he was proud of his clear, loud tones. "Now try it again," the lad insisted. This time the man did so well that the youngster had to admit that he, too, was a pretty good whistler. The busy man smiled and hurried on his way, but he turned around just long enough to hear the youngster shout, "If you can whistle that good, how does it happen that you were whistling like you did before?"

Too many people are not giving the world enough of the song they possess. Those who make up the world-wide church of today cannot stand on the edge of the struggle speaking softly to themselves. Their voices must be heard across the nation proclaiming the message in loud and confident tones of joy and salvation for all men. They must speak clearly concerning the promise of peace and love that can be understood by every heart and life. They must stand in the middle of the struggle evincing their faith in a God that continues to make us more than conquerors.

TABLE TALK: *Have you ever done a task just well enough to get by, and thought to yourself, "Oh well, nobody will ever know the difference"? Did you feel the same satisfaction as over a job well done?*

OCTOBER 27

When There Is Music in Heaven

I say unto you, there is joy in the presence of the angels of God over one sinner that repenteth. Luke 15:10.

I have a sweet old friend whom I have known for many years. Through the course of the winter she was confined to her home. She called me one day and asked me if I could find time to give her communion. I went to her home and conducted the most unusual communion service of my ministry. The fact that there were only two of us was not unique, for there had been many such cases. But something else was unusual in this case.

We sat together and discussed our common Christian faith. I spoke to her about God's wonderful love, which was great enough to forgive all of our sins no matter how bad we have been. With tears of appreciation, she kept expressing this thought: "Isn't God wonderful? Isn't God wonderful?" It was then that I invited her to join me in the confession of our sins. As we began, her little canary started to sing and as we continued, it kept singing louder and louder, and just as the confession was completed, its voice seemed to swell into a glorious crescendo. It could have been born out of heavenly inspiration. "There is joy in heaven over one sinner that repenteth."

Each one of us has a key which will unlock the forgiving love of our heavenly Father. It is not by our good works that we gain access to this heavenly realm of grace. It is by being sincerely sorry, as a little child might be, for the wrongs which we have committed—so sorry that we resolve never to do them again. Too often we exhibit a stubborn pride—an unwillingness to confess that we have done wrong. This separates us from God and makes Him very unhappy, because He knows that with that attitude we can have no peace of mind. But "if we confess our sins, He is faithful and righteous to forgive us our sins." And when this happens, the birds of paradise sing the glorious anthem of rejoicing because the sinner has come home.

TABLE TALK: *Talk about how happy God is when each day we openly confess to Him the wrongs which we have committed, and how good we feel when we have received forgiveness.*

301

OCTOBER 28

What Are You Giving God?

Teach me to do thy will; for thou art my God: thy spirit is good; lead me into the land of uprightness. Psalm 143:10.

During the last years, more than ever before, volunteers have been called to help in various service projects. Many needs have arisen because of these hectic times in which we live. Fine people have given countless numbers of hours in helping to alleviate the sufferings of their fellow men. And it is well that we should do the same. For down through the ages the call of the Master still rings clearly: "Volunteers needed!" And the church can progress and advance only as large multitudes of its members are willing to go out and preach each day by their lives that it is worth while to be a Christian. What an inspiration it is to see people in every walk of life using even insignificant talents and dedicating them to the Lord.

Here is a man who served with the British Navy many years ago. Through the years he had grown to be an agnostic, never even bothering to seek for the truth by attending any church. But the miracle occurred. The Spirit of God captured his soul and even at a late period of life he became a flaming evangel for God. Voluntarily he surveyed the entire area in which he lived. He is now retired. Living on a small pension, he has been unable to give much financial assistance to his church, but he has given that which is worth more than money—he has given his life. Through his ministry many have found Him who is the way.

Or consider the woman who walked into the office of her pastor one day and said, "I have been so richly blessed since you persuaded me to begin having family devotions that I would like to volunteer to spend several afternoons a week, if it is agreeable with you, calling on the young mothers of the congregation and telling them of the blessings that have come to me since God has become real in our home life and encouraging them to have family prayers." That conversation was instrumental in creating a band of over one hundred voluntary parish workers in that congregation.

TABLE TALK: *What are you doing to bring others to Him? Is there anything more you can do? Discuss.*

OCTOBER 29

When There Is Power Within

And be not afraid of them which kill the body, but are not able to kill the soul: but rather fear him who is able to destroy both soul and body in hell. Matthew 10:28.

A friend of mine introduced me to a successful businessman in one of our metropolitan areas. He had previously told me much about the shrewd and honest dealings of this man in the business world. He also had made clear to me that here was a man of much faith.

I must admit I was a little surprised when I discovered that this man of business repute was a wheel-chair cripple and had been one since early childhood. Instead of losing his faith in God, he used it as a vital aid in finding his place in society.

Now he was a businessman dealing in office supplies. Materially he had grown prosperous, not because people had felt sorry for him, but rather because he was able to deliver the goods. He was capable of meeting competition, but on even terms. He had done so well that he had constructed a new and beautiful home. And there was not even a mortgage upon it.

He drives his own automobile and asks for no help to get around. In the back of his car is a bulit-in case, with doors on either side, for his collapsible wheel chair. He manages to get out of the car on his own power and, crawling on his hands and knees, opens up the case. Having assembled his wheel chair, he brings himself to his appointments by his own power. He is not only a highly respected businessman in his own community, but is known for miles around as one who is honest and fair in dealings with men. But above all, he is known as one who uses the strength and power of God to overcome a handicap and become a blessing to mankind.

Rather than blame God for physical misfortune which may come to us, let us thank God for the strength and the courage He gives us that enable us to overcome and to gain the victory.

TABLE TALK: *Have you stopped today to consider how fortunate you are? There must be many things for which you are grateful. Why not list them? Then think of others less fortunate than you. Resolve to help them.*

OCTOBER 30

As a Man Soweth

Be not deceived; God is not mocked: for whatsoever a man soweth, that shall he also reap. Galatians 6:7.

Some neighbors of Ed Jones in Topeka, Kansas, had a chuckle one day at his expense. It seemed that Ed sometime before had seeded the lawn around his home and was hoping for a nice plot of thick grass. Instead, he awakened one day to discover that right in his front yard he had a thriving crop of radishes. The seed he had planted apparently was not clover and blue grass as he had thought!

The truth of that humorous incident often becomes very real in the happenings of our everyday lives. We forget that we reap according to the seed that has been sown. We look for trust and appreciation on the part of our friends, but that cannot be expected if we speak words of slander and gossip against them. We are impatient and thoughtless, and yet we expect others to be kind and understanding. We live contrary to our professed principles and then wonder why the world will not believe that we are consecrated Christians.

A certain man constantly passed unkind remarks about his neighbor. Later he discovered that many things he had said were untrue. We admire him for being big enough to seek the forgiveness of the one he had wronged. But when he went to him he learned a lesson he could never forget. He asked him how he could ever win back his faith and trust. The man told him to gather an armful of feathers and then go from house to house in the village dropping a feather at each doorstep. When he had done this he had fulfilled his request. Then he was asked to go and pick up the feathers again and, lo, they were blown away and many of them could not be found.

TABLE TALK: *Have you ever passed on gossip or rumors about someone that may not have been true? Have you ever stopped to consider that when you make unkind remarks about someone, true or untrue, you are showing that you yourself are not the kind of person you should be, and you harm the person about whom you are speaking more than you can ever undo?*

OCTOBER 31

Living Consistently

And he said unto them, The sabbath was made for man, and not man for the sabbath. Mark 2:27.

You must often have thought of the fact that all history is today reckoned from the coming of the Master into our human life. For there are only two chief divisions of history: B. C., the years before Christ, and A. D., the years of our Lord. Truly His coming has revised our calendar.

But besides dividing history into two parts, Jesus revised it in another way. For He gave us a new interpretation of the Sabbath and its use. On the Sabbath, after attending a synagogue service, He walked with His disciples across a grain field. Some of the disciples stopped and picked some grain. They cupped it in their hands to let the chaff blow away, and then munched on the kernels much as we eat popcorn today. The Pharisees who saw them said, "Jesus, are you going to allow that? It is against the law. Our law says that you can't pick grain on the Sabbath." These ceremonialists were trying to trip Jesus at every turn.

Then Jesus told them that the Sabbath was made for man and not man for the Sabbath. By His example on many occasions He showed them that by doing good and showing love on the day of rest we keep His commandment as much as by our worship.

Besides, Jesus taught that every day is to be one of worship. Religion should not be like a Sunday suit which you put on when you go to church and take off when you go to work, as if you thought your religion did not fit into your everyday living. There is something wrong with it if it does not. Jesus said our living must be consistent with our profession.

Now this does not mean that Sunday is not a special day, set aside for divine worship. Nor does it mean that we should turn it into a day of work or in any way misuse it. It means, rather, that our manner of life shall be consistent both on Sunday and on the weekday.

TABLE TALK: *Discuss ways of making your Lord's Day what Jesus would have it be. What should you carry with you through the week?*

NOVEMBER 1

It Takes Time

Be patient therefore, brethren, until the coming of the Lord. Behold, the husbandman waiteth for the precious fruit of the earth, being patient over it, until it receive the early and latter rain. Be ye also patient. James 5:7-8.

A minister in a small country church was calling on one of his members who lived on a farm. As he and the farmer were walking through the fields he noticed that some of the soil seemed lifeless and incapable of growing good crops. He mentioned this to his friend who replied, "That's right. But now I am going to plant sweet clover in that field. The clover roots will reach deep down into the earth and draw up the valuable minerals that the other plants do not find. So next year the soil in that field will be ready for another good crop again."

That story illustrates our spiritual lives. Sometimes we drift away from God. Our lives grow shallow. We need spiritual nourishment. We need to become more deeply rooted in the soil, if the harvest is going to be plentiful. We need to spend more time reading God's Word everyday. We need added assurance to keep going no matter how difficult the way might be, and courage to battle the good fight of faith.

Sometimes we need to have a long talk with God about the things which are troubling us, concerning the problems we have to face and the task He has assigned for us to do. We should spend quiet moments with Him, just strengthening our friendship, coming to a closer understanding, and letting Him know how grateful we are for all that He has given us.

The encouragement of our spiritual life does not happen just by chance. We need to draw upon the very depths of the Master's love and mercy so that real living will result, filled with happiness and an undying faith. Whenever you find yourself drifting so far away from God that you fail to use His strength and ask for His help, then it is time for you to stop in the day's busy occupation to find and walk the narrow pathway again.

TABLE TALK: *What spiritual nourishment do you take daily? Perhaps you will discover that you need more time for daily devotions.*

NOVEMBER 2

Find That New Horizon

I form the light, and create darkness; I make peace, and create evil; I am the Lord that doeth all these things. Isaiah 45:7.

No doubt you have meditated upon the events that surrounded the death of Christ on Calvary. It seems so tragic that such a wonderful king as the Master should have to die in such an ugly and shameful way.

But as you think it through, all around the cross you can see the signs of victory quite unlike what you might expect. Jesus was not crucified in a bleak desert or upon the desolate rocks. Rather this event took place near a garden. Perhaps near the foot of the cross, which is the world's symbol of death, there were flowers growing, the symbol of life and beauty. And the wood for the ugly cross and the beautiful flowers had grown out of the very same soil.

It was God's great love for us that brought His Son to this sacrifice and it was this same love that won for us the victory. In human life there are very often possibilities at the same time for both grief and happiness to enter. He has proved that He can turn darkness into sunshine and defeat into triumph. He can do all things. In the way that He leads us, there is always a new horizon.

Your heavenly Father knows that you will have to face trouble and disappointment in life but He is also aware of the fact that He has the capacity to enable you to rise above it. There is never any temptation which you and God together cannot conquer. And you will face no problem that cannot be solved as long as you remain in partnership with Him. Remember that His great strength and power is available for the asking.

Christ has set before you an open door and no man can close it. That is the wonderful promise He has given to each one of us. That door opens into a life that is filled with all of the riches of heaven. No one but you can ever shut it: If it remains open, all of the blessings of heaven will be yours.

TABLE TALK: *Can you recall anyone who had seemingly bad luck turn into good? What lesson is there in that for all of us?*

307

NOVEMBER 3

The Captain Is on the Bridge

And, behold, God himself is with us at our head, and his priests with the trumpets of alarm to sound an alarm against you. O children of Israel, fight ye not against the Lord God of your fathers; for ye shall not prosper. 2 Chronicles 13:12.

The *Queen Mary* was crossing the Atlantic. For the first several days the waters were calm and the passengers relaxed. The farther the boat got away from the mainland, the farther those aboard seemed to be separated from their troubles and cares and worries. A jovial atmosphere was evident everywhere. There was a group participating in a ping-pong tournament, another at a swimming pool competing in races, and others just sitting in their easy chairs being warmed and tanned by the brilliant sun. Suddenly one morning the sea began to roll. The big boat tilted from side to side, sometimes almost reaching a forty-five degree angle. Ropes were stretched along the decks so that passengers could walk without falling. Dishes tumbled from the tables. All day and all night the storm persisted.

The next morning the few who came to breakfast looked like different people from those who had been there the previous day. You could see that they were concerned. Faces were drawn and anxious. Then someone entered the dining room and announced with a smile, "The captain is on the bridge. He has been there all night and will remain there until the storm subsides."

What a feeling of assurance came into the hearts of those who heard the message. Many of them had learned to know the captain. They had confidence in his ability. He had gone this way before. He had previously been victorious as he had encountered storms like this. With the captain on the bridge they were now assured that they would reach their destination.

Keeping vigil day and night is the Captain of our souls. Our God is constantly present to lead us through the storms of life to the ultimate port of our victory and the great beyond. Knowing this, our fear is replaced by our faith.

TABLE TALK: *Discuss how panic and fear become contagious. What forces of fear are loose in the world today? How can they be overcome?*

NOVEMBER 4

A Faith to Live By

Her children arise up, and call her blessed. Proverbs 31:28.

It is generally true that, if you train a child in the way that he should go, he will not depart from it. Therefore, it is of tremendous importance that we invest wisely in the lives of little children that the future might be made secure and that they might have the advantage of knowing the Christian way.

So often the destiny of an entire life is determined by what happens in the early formative years. A consciousness of the presence of God in the journey through this life and the reality of the life which is to come can even be understood by the faith of a little child.

One summer a minister conducted a camp for his young people. His own thirteen-year-old boy was with him for the entire camping period learning the gospel songs, hearing the messages from the Word, and being inspired to greater service in the Master's kingdom. The boy had often complained that his father was not home enough so that he could play ball with him and do the other things youngsters enjoy so much. But when he left camp he handed his father a letter in which he said: "Dear Dad, I want to thank you for the privilege I have had of being at camp this summer. I am going to keep all the promises I have made. I am going to read my Bible every day. I am going to stay in partnership with God and talk to Him often and I am going to try to win a person for Christ. I won't complain this year about your being gone so much as long as I know you are preaching the gospel. For though I know that we can't be together as much as I would like in this world, some day we will be together forever in the 'house of many mansions.' "

That young lad of thirteen years has a faith to live by. The investment of time in teaching him the way to go will no doubt pay rich dividends in the future as he grows up to take his place in the kingdom work of the Lord.

Invest wisely in the lives of your children and some day they will rise up and call you blessed.

TABLE TALK: *What can the parents do, beginning at birth, to prepare the child for abundant living?*

NOVEMBER 5

The Point of No Return

But Jesus said unto him, No man, having put his hand to the plow, and looking back, is fit for the kingdom of God.

Luke 9:62.

As one travels over the mighty ocean there is a place that the pilots call the "point of no return." This is a location just past the half way mark of the journey. If gas supply should run low or engine trouble should develop it would be a shorter distance for the plane to continue toward its destination. It would be a disadvantage and a great risk to turn back.

In Christian living there is also a "point of no return." That is, if you want to achieve victory in life. The Master once said, "No man, having set his hand to the plow, and looking back is fit for the kingdom of God." Once you have made the commitment of life, you can be assured of victory only if you steadfastly set your face toward your goal and, keeping your eye on the vision, continue on in spite of any outward circumstances.

When God becomes the life partner, anything is possible. In a certain small town lives a radiant soul whose husband was taken from her at an early age. She was left to raise four children, the oldest being eight years old. She was left with little material security, but with a heart that was full of the treasures of God. And these riches enabled her to find the courage to seek employment. Now she works through the whole day teaching school and comes home at night to take care of the house. And more than that, to share her own rich faith with the little ones who have been entrusted to her care.

All of the children have now grown into manhood and womanhood. She lives alone in her humble dwelling, which has been transformed into a mansion fit for the presence of the King of kings, who dwells with her and gives her the strength to keep living with a smile.

When she faced her Calvary her faith enabled her to set her hand to the plow. That was her "point of no return."

TABLE TALK: *Have you ever started a project, or a journey, at which there was no turning back? Discuss what you can learn from this.*

NOVEMBER 6

Reflect the Spirit of the Master

Blessed are the poor in spirit: for theirs is the kingdom of heaven. Matthew 5:3.

In one of our states large numbers of volunteers in various communities have in recent years made a service project for themselves by visiting the various mental institutions to bring cheer, comfort, and hope into the lives of the mentally ill.

A volunteer worker describing the condition of the hospitals tells of the improvement that has been made since the new mental program went into effect and aroused the interest of so many citizens. "Formerly," she said, "when we walked into a dark, depressing, gray room, without a touch of color anywhere, we saw women in camisoles strapped to slit benches. They screamed and raged at us and taunted us by saying, 'How would you like to be here?' The women's hair was shaved off in crew cuts and they wore similar shapeless denim dresses. It was heart-rending."

The contribution the volunteers have made has been unique in improving the program. The professional staff has been enlarged, but these volunteers bring something to the patients which the other workers are incapable of doing, and that is contact with the community. The people in the hospitals are here because they have failed to adjust to the world. When outsiders come on their own free will bringing kindness and understanding it helps give the patient courage and hope necessary to make the long journey back. The best volunteers, we are told, are the ones who genuinely enjoy themselves with the patients, who have tact and a good sense of humor.

It is thrilling to read of Christian soldiers who, like these, are helping to build houses of hope where before have stood houses of despair. Certainly something of the spirit of the Master is reflected as they go about serving a forgotten people and one that has been too frequently neglected in the years past. And they are themselves richly blest.

TABLE TALK: *What projects are there in the community in which you could take part? Think of the work of the Grey Ladies, the Red Cross Volunteers, etc.*

NOVEMBER 7

Happiness Is Within You

Happy is the man that findeth wisdom, and the man that getteth understanding. For the gaining of it is better than the gaining of silver, and the profit thereof than fine gold.

Proverbs 3:13-14.

She is supposed to have had everything: fame, adoration, wealth, luxury, and even a title. She had everything except a happy home and, lacking that, she had nothing that her heart really wanted. So she continues her long and fruitless search, which has carried her throughout the world. Time after time she had walked up the streets of luxury only to find that they do not end at the goal of happiness. What she has really wanted she has never had. Though she has had the wealth to buy the most expensive gifts found on the counters of the world's market places, she has not yet discovered that the vacuum within cannot be filled with things that money can buy. And so she remains a lonesome wanderer still searching, still traveling the highways of the world seeking for something she cannot find. She does not know that happiness must come from within.

When tragedy strikes a home, it brings sorrow. People are advised to leave for some distant point so that they can forget about it. It does not work that way. The sorrow goes with you wherever you go because it is a part of your very self. So many times when a wrong has been committed the individual involved is advised to go to another place where he can make a new start. The new start is not made at any given location. It is made within you, and conscience will not let you forget your wrong no matter how far you travel from the place of your sins.

There are so many people who, like this woman we mentioned, are traveling about on the various highways of life looking for the place called happiness. It cannot be found on any map of any country, but it can be discovered in the hearts of many people in many lands. It is something that makes no distinction, that crosses all color lines, and enters the hearts of people of all nations. Real happiness is the peace God's children know.

TABLE TALK: *Suppose you could talk to this woman. What would you say to her?*

NOVEMBER 8

More Blessed to Give

Give, and it shall be given unto you; good measure, pressed down, shaken together, running over, shall they give into your bosom. Luke 6:38.

An interesting story is told concerning a man who with his wife dropped in one night for a social call on the village doctor. Before the evening had progressed very far he was questioning the physician concerning his wife's persistent backaches and before he was through he had received a prescription from the doctor. Then settling back in his chair, he turned to his friend and said laughingly, "I want to thank you for saving us a doctor bill." "As a matter of fact," the doctor replied, "there is an old console upstairs that I thought about bringing to the shop a long time ago. Now that you are here why not take a look at it?" "Why sure," was the hesitating reply. "Let's go up and see it." The next several hours the repair man overhauled the radio under the doctor's watchful eye. Finally he put the antiquated set together and started homeward. Getting into his car he turned to his wife and bitingly declared, "Our doctor friend certainly has a lot of nerve getting me to fix his radio free. What does he think I am in business for?"

This man's reaction is very typical. He is the kind that places a value upon his own physical labor and yet does not think a thing about receiving something free from someone else.

But a constant law of life is that we will not be blessed unless we are as willing to share as we are to receive. So much of our present-day thinking centers around ourselves. Our only concern seems to be the success we can make for ourselves or the material fortunes we can accumulate. We are very willing to accept the services of others as long as it requires no obligation on our part.

The Master was always ready to give without any thought of return or reward. No less can be expected from those who follow after Him.

TABLE TALK: *Have you ever begrudged doing a favor for somebody? Discuss where you were at fault and how you can remedy your attitude.*

313

NOVEMBER 9

Reach Up!

But he said, Yea, rather, blessed are they that hear the word of God, and keep it. Luke 11:28.

A picture was printed recently of a group of mountain climbers trudging carefully along trying to reach their destination. Their pathway took them very close to a great ravine. The picture was titled "Reach Up." And the story portrayed could be told in the line found in a prize-winning poem at Oxford University written over sixty years ago, "High failure towering over low success." These words remain a constant reminder that failure that comes in attempting to reach a higher level may sometimes be a greater reward that that which comes from routine success.

In thinking about this line of poetry, various remembrances come into focus, brave men trying to scale Mount Everest, courageous men fighting in behalf of world peace, others struggling against great odds to give all people opportunity regardless of race or color. These are classic examples of those who struggle, sometimes beyond the limits of their own abilities, only to discover that when human resources run out there is a divine power that steps in, if we only "reach up." If such living is called a failure, it is a far more noble tribute to the dignity of the human race and a keener incentive to high endeavor than the laurels of a Roman triumph. The squares of Europe are full of the statues of men of war whose titles and deeds we have long forgotten. But still alive in the memory of many are heroic men and women who attempted by the grace of God more than they could carry out, but who did the best they could to serve mankind.

We are frequently tempted to do the easiest thing at hand. In such moments it is well to raise our sights, think in bigger terms, and dare to dream that even the impossible might become possible.

"Where there is life there is hope." There is still life; therefore, keep dreaming until your last heartbeat!

TABLE TALK: *Discuss some of your dreams for the future. How can God help you?*

NOVEMBER 10

There Are Times to Be Silent

But he answered her not a word. And his disciples came and besought him, saying, Send her away; for she crieth after us.
Matthew 15:23.

A former government employee criticized his country not long ago when he said that in the United States no one can say exactly what he thinks. Then he modified the remark by saying that if you agree with the majority you can say what you think, but if you are in the minority you are restrained by public opinion in the government. Then he continued, "There are many things I don't dare say. If I did I would be deprived of the right to say other things that are perhaps more important."

We are tempted to wonder if the author of this statement is as loyal to his country as he pretends to be. There certainly are times when we must remain silent, and when we have no God-given right to express our opinion. In time of war there are secrets that must be closely guarded. Were they revealed the lives of thousands of men would be in danger. There are things that must be kept in confidence. And to violate the trust makes one no less than a traitor.

There were times in the life of the Master when He thought it better to be silent than to express His opinion. We read, "He answered not a word."

Perhaps one of our difficulties is that we talk too much, especially when it comes to criticizing the actions of those about us and in speaking words of condemnation about those who have done wrong. Each of us has caused heartaches for some weary travelers along life's way by the unkind words we have spoken and the malicious gossip we have sent winging on its way.

We should never compromise with truth. We should never hesitate to speak out boldly in behalf of righteousness, regardless of the cost. Death is not too great a price to pay if that would be the cost for keeping one's faith. But we should guard our lips carefully lest the words we speak might endanger the lives of others who are also precious in the sight of God.

TABLE TALK: *When should you keep silent and when should you speak up? Discuss.*

315

NOVEMBER 11

Build That Doll House Today

Behold, now is the accepted time; behold, now is the day of salvation. 2 Corinthians 6:22.

An interesting cartoon in a daily newspaper showed a picture of a man helping to build a play trailer for a group of boys that were clustered about him eagerly watching his every move. A couple of women were standing nearby and one of them turned to the other and said, "He is the most popular father in the block. The others are too busy making money."

The cartoon reminds one of the tragic experience that came into the life of John Carmody. He was one of these busy fathers so concerned about building up material fortune that he had no time to invest in the lives of his children.

One night when he came home for dinner his little five-year-old, blond-haired, blue-eyed girl climbed into his lap and asked, "Daddy, won't you stay home tonight and build me a doll house?" "I am too busy, my darling," he answered, "I have to go back to the office and work." "But Daddy," she protested, "just a little one out of sticks and paper?" "I am sorry, my dear," he replied, "but I am too busy tonight, but I will work hard and make a lot of money and some day I will build you a doll house not out of sticks and paper, but out of precious jewels."

It was not many days later that this same father was again working busily in his office. The phone rang. An accident had occurred. His little daughter had been struck down by a truck. Hurriedly he rushed to the scene of the accident. When he arrived there, he bent over the prostrate form of his little girl. With tears streaming down his cheeks he saw her open her big blue eyes but once to say, "We didn't get that doll house built, did we, Daddy?"

Too often similar tragedy results when we neglect to take the time to do that which we ought. Today is your opportunity. Whatever the task at hand may be, live it to the fullest. Tomorrow belongs to God!

TABLE TALK: *Have you ever regretted being too late for doing something for someone? What lesson have you learned from this?*

NOVEMBER 12

Keep Becoming

Only let your manner of life be worthy of the gospel of Christ: that whether I come and see you or be absent, I may hear of your state, that ye stand fast in one spirit, with one soul striving for the faith of the gospel. Philippians 1:27.

It is important to make a good beginning, but it is much more important to keep "becoming." Good beginnings are often helpful in achieving the final victory.

In the athletic contest, the team that can carry the kickoff back to a touchdown has an advantage; the person running the hundred yard dash who gets off to a lead could be more sure of victory; a baseball team piling up a series of runs in the early innings is in a very strategic position. But none of these acts assures the ultimate victory. Staying power is more important than beginning power.

There are those who have come from behind to gain the prize after it has seemed that they were facing ultimate defeat. They were those who never gave up, but who kept on playing the game to the utmost of their ability, and who gained the reward because they gave all that they had. It is important to make a good beginning but it is more important to keep "becoming."

In the long ago it was said of the Master, "As many as received him to them gave he the power to become." You are just a fraction of what you are meant to be, and to the world. A personality expert has indicated that the average person is only ten per cent of that which he is capable of being. Think of what life holds in store for you! If you love life today, multiply it tenfold and you will see the possibilities that are before you. Many of us die with too much unexpressed music left in our souls. We have failed to give to life what God has intended us to contribute.

We are the keys, He is the organist. As we allow Him to come into our lives to play the melody which lies latent in our souls, we will realize the contribution He has intended each one of us to make toward the great harmony God wants in His world.

TABLE TALK: *What more can you do as a family and individually to make this world better, in the work for peace, in politics, in charity, and in all fields? Discuss.*

NOVEMBER 13

Meet Each Day As It Comes

But be ye doers of the word, and not hearers only, deluding your own selves. James 1:22.

Have you ever thought how fortunate it is that we do not have the capacity to look ahead to see what is going to happen? We are called upon to meet things one by one as daily they confront us. God will renew our courage when we meet the separate blows that fall upon us. There is value in not knowing about the future. Only when we try to anticipate what might happen and become concerned over the uncharted future do we lack the capacity to meet life's day victoriously.

Zane Grey gives these keys to greatness: "To bear up under loss, to fight the bitterness of defeat and the sickness of grief, to be victor over anger, to smile when tears are close, to resist evil men and base instincts, to hate hate and love love, to go on when it would seem good to die, to seek ever after the glory and the dream, to look with unquenchable faith in something ever more about to be—that is what any man can do and so be great." But this kind of greatness and courage cannot come from man alone. It comes only when the empty hand is reached heavenward to receive the bountiful gifts of the Father.

Meet each day as it comes. By constantly keeping in touch with the Eternal make sure that your resources are greater than those which you have in yourself. God will give you the capacity to make your dreams come true. Do not think about things as they might have been or philosophize about the mistakes of the past. Do the task at hand to the best of your God-given ability. God will bless you for it.

The eminent philosopher John Dewey once found his son in the bathroom, the floor flooded with water. The professor began thinking about what could have caused it. After looking for a few moments, the son turned to him and said, "Dad, this is not a time to philosophize; it is a time to mop!"

There is a time to dream, but also a time to work.

TABLE TALK: *Perhaps you know of someone who laments over the past or worries about the future. What can you say to them which might give them more security?*

NOVEMBER 14

Words with Great Meaning

And now abideth faith, hope, love, these three; and the greatest of these is love. 1 Corinthians 13:13.

There are many beautiful words in the English language. When they are spoken they recall associations that are unforgettable. For example, there is the word "courage." Whenever it is spoken there flashes through the mind the dauntless spirit of the early Christian fathers or of the pioneers who trekked across the country in caravans of primitive mode, or of valiant souls struggling heroically against insurmountable odds, or of an athlete struggling for a prize. There come into focus those who have set their vision on things beyond, those who keep looking up until they have scaled the peak.

Or take the word "service." Immediately we think of those we know who believe that life is a trust which must be administered unselfishly. They know the meaning of being their brother's keeper. They not only believe but truly live the philosophy that it is more blessed to give than to receive.

Or consider the word "memory." Have you ever thought of what a wonderful mechanism the mind really is? What a tremendous library is catalogued in even the smallest of human brains. Here is an art gallery with pictures painted by the Almighty, such as golden sunsets, gardens of multicolored flowers, great expanses of water, and snow-covered mountain peaks. There are memories of friends who have been kind and good and who have done things to give rich meaning to our lives.

But there are three greater words. The first is one that gives us the capacity to remove mountains. It is the word "faith." The second is one that gives us vision to keep dreaming in spite of anything. It is the word "hope." The third is one that prompts one to give his life. It is the word "love." "But now abideth faith, hope, love, these three; and the greatest of these is love." For "God is Love."

TABLE TALK: *Play a game of words. Make up a list of words and register your reactions to each by smiling or frowning as they are said. Discuss what each of the words, faith, hope, and love, mean to you.*

NOVEMBER 15

Keep the Channel Open

Jesus said unto him, If thou canst! All things are possible to him that believeth. Mark 9:23.

"Dear Mr. Creator: Will you please tell me what the universe was made for?" This question was asked of God by that great naturalist and scientist, Dr. George Washington Carver, an outstanding Negro of the South who made a great contribution to the welfare of all people. Dr. Carver frequently talked to God through the course of the day. At work and at play he was in constant conversation with Him, keeping his soul in tune with the will of his great Creator. This is the answer he said he received to his question about the universe: "You are asking something that is too big for your finite mind to understand. Get down to your own level and ask a question whose answer will be within your reach."

So he turned to God and asked again, "Mr. Creator, will you tell me what man was made for?" Once more the great Deity replied, "You are still asking a question out of your size." And a third time he said, "Will you tell me what the peanut was made for?" And this is Dr. Carver's testimony: "Then God right before my eyes in the presence of my mind opened up the peanut and put it back together again." History records that God revealed to George Washington Carver processes whereby the lowly peanut could be used to produce over two hundred separate products, everything from face powder to axle grease. It was all done because a single soul teamed up with Almighty God to perform a miracle, a miracle that has helped to stabilize the economy of the South.

If we keep the channel open, power from God will always flow through us. The condition is always the same, to walk and talk with Him as "good friends should and do." It is to be willing to accept His will and direction and find the task assigned for us to do, and then to launch out in faith, knowing that because He is God anything becomes possible!

TABLE TALK: *Did you talk to God today as you went about your daily affairs? How can you be silent partners with God?*

NOVEMBER 16

You Belong to God

Ye should walk worthily of God, who calleth you into his own kingdom and glory. 1 Thessalonians 2:12.

There is something more important in life than just to eat, drink, and be merry. This type of uninhibited existence has become far too prevalent in this day. There are just too many who are compromising their Christian faith, pretending to be followers of the Master while they still cling to the things of the world. There are not enough people who are going "all out" for God. They are allowing sin to tempt them. They are forgetting that if they get too close to the fire, they will surely be burned.

In a company of people who were visiting a coal mine was a woman dressed in white. Turning to the guide, she asked, "Mister, is it all right for me to go down in the mine with this dress on?" The guide's answer was, "Well, there is nothing to keep you from going down into the mine wearing a white dress, but there is plenty to keep you from coming out that way."

The Christian is always concerned about keeping himself "unspotted from the world." His white garment is not a dress to put on, but a holy faith and a pure heart. He can "walk worthily" wherever duty calls him. Power is always available to him to enable him to withstand and remain pure in spite of any temptation.

In the days of long ago, an attempt was made to discredit one of the good kings of France. They took his young son and placed him under the influence of a wicked woman who, as his governess, was to teach him to cheat, lie, swear, and steal. But every time she would try to induce him to do something wrong he would square his little shoulders in princely fashion and say, "I can't do that because, you see, I am the child of a king."

God has not promised that when we become Christians He will take us out of this world so that we will not be subject to temptation. Though we remain in the world, He assures us of power to remain firm. For we are children of the King.

TABLE TALK: *How do we compromise our Christian faith? What tempts us?*

United We Stand

But if we walk in the light, as he is in the light, we have fellowship one with another, and the blood of Jesus his Son cleanseth us from all sin. 1 John 1:7.

In one of our magazines of national circulation there was an unusual advertisement. At the top of the page was a beautiful colored painting of a covered wagon caravan fording a stream. Beneath the picture was an account of the story which had inspired it. It told of the dread in the minds of the leaders of these caravan trains at the prospect of fording the Platte River.

This was the main obstacle on the westward trek. The reason for this concern was that the current of the stream was so changeable in its mighty strength that even the most experienced of the leaders could not predict where the pockets of quicksand might be. It was tragic, of course, when one of these prairie schooners would strike such a bog and get stalled midstream. Almost without exception the wagon would overturn and the family and all their goods would be dumped into the stream.

But experience taught the travelers that there was a way of crossing that river quite safely. The caravan would halt at the edge of the river, and the men would unhitch their ox teams from their respective schooners. Then they would hitch all the oxen together to pull each of the wagons across in turn. If any team should get into difficulty, the rest would have sure footing and could forge ahead, pulling until the floundering team would get its bearings again. The wagon load itself was saved from being upset.

That experience, repeated so many times in the 1860's, holds a real parallel for our twentieth century living. In fact, it has a meaning for all time. All of us face circumstances which we cannot handle alone and still come through victoriously. We need each other; we need God. We need the church; we need "the tie that binds our hearts in Christian love."

TABLE TALK: *Discuss instances when there has been strength in unity—political issues, church projects, Christian movements, public opinion, etc.*

NOVEMBER 18

O Love That Will Not Let Me Go

And ye shall be holy unto me: for I the Lord am holy, and have severed you from other people, that ye should be mine.
Leviticus 20:26.

Somewhere I read a story that came out of the last war concerning a little nine-year-old boy in Italy. Some soldiers were driving along in a jeep one day when they noticed this young lad sitting on the porch of a bombed-out house sobbing his heart out. They stopped and talked to him, and they discovered that his name was Tony. He told them that his mother and father had both been killed when their home was bombed. Their hearts went out to the little lad. They put him in the jeep and took him back to camp. One of the soldiers became very attached to little Tony and took a special interest in him. He received permission to have a soldier's uniform cut down to the lad's size and had a little soldier's cap made for him. Often Tony would join in the maneuvers, standing as straight and erect as the rest.

One day, an order came that all refugees and waifs had to be returned to the central station. It became the duty of this particular soldier to tell Tony the sad news. This was his approach: "All good soldiers take orders, don't they, Tony?" The boy replied, "Yes, Sir." Apparently he had become reconciled to his fate. That night, when the men lined up he was not in the background, but up beside the captain standing like a good little soldier. Finally after the golden sun had sunk in the west and the last notes of the bugle had been played, Tony started to march to the waiting jeep. But half way there, Tony, the soldier, became Tony, the little boy. He stopped and burst into tears. He turned around and ran to his soldier friend throwing his arms about him as he said, "I can't go, I won't go! I belong to you!"

God never sends us away from Him. This is His reassuring promise, "Lo, I am with you always, even unto the end of the world." His is a love that will never let you go.

TABLE TALK: *Recall the story of the Prodigal Son. What was the lesson taught in that story?*

323

NOVEMBER 19

There Is Joy in Living

Freely ye received, freely give. Matthew 10:8.

A poor family once lived out in a hollow close by a certain city. About the only time they were seen was when occasionally people would bring something to them, such as a basket at Thanksgiving time. They were always receiving, but what the people did not know was that the mother of this family was implanting into her children's minds the fact that some day they must also share. Because they were so poor, that day had not yet arrived.

After the mother had gone home to heaven, the oldest girl, to whom the mother had most often talked, was out walking one day. She had picked some blue flowers, for these were the ones that her mother had most loved. She was walking back to her house when she met two ladies. They greeted her with a smile. She stopped because she was not used to having people smile at her. Then one spoke to her: "My, what beautiful flowers you have!" The little girl became stony cold inside. She did not know exactly what to do. She had been at the receiving end of life all the time. People had always given her things, but now, in one quick act, she thrust out the flowers to the ladies and said, "Here, you take them."

Then she ran home as fast as she could. Her face was radiant. She found her brother. She fairly shouted to him, "Listen, I have given somebody something!"

The entire life of this little girl was transformed by this act of kindness. A miracle took place. From then on she became the happy person that only unselfish living can make of anyone, as she learned the truth of the words from Scripture, "It is more blessed to give than to receive."

How often we complain because we do not have enough. We are so dissatisfied with our present state and are always wishing for things beyond our means. Let us remember that happiness is not so much the result of what we have but rather, the radiance that comes within when we are willing to share.

TABLE TALK: *Discuss the people you know who are happy because they are always living such unselfish lives.*

A Parable of Life

But if thine enemy hunger, feed him; if he thirst, give him to drink: for in so doing thou shalt heap coals of fire on his head.
Romans 12:20.

Good and evil are incompatible. They are constantly at odds. One must move over to make room for the other, depending upon which exercises the most force. In his letter to the Romans, Paul makes a very practical suggestion. He says that, if you have an enemy and he is hungry, feed him. That seems like strange advice. But the likelihood is that you both will be winners in the end, that is, if your enemy is not so hard of heart that he cannot appreciate the gesture of kindness.

One Thanksgiving season some young people were to deliver a basket of food to the tumble-down home of a woman. They were bringing these gifts in the name of the church. This woman had once spoken very bitterly concerning the church to some of the young people in this very group, and so they had debated among themselves whether or not they should bother about packing and delivering a basket to her house. After a few moments of hesitation, they realized that it would hardly be the Christian thing to pass her by for she was in need. Perhaps the stop at her home was the happiest of all the day's happenings, for these visitors had conquered themselves and now God was flooding their hearts with joy.

Several of the girls stayed on to visit with the old lady. They offered to put away the food, but she said, "I don't think you can find room in these shelves for any of it. They are all too full." Upon investigating they discovered the shelves loaded with empty jars and bottles. There just was not room for the food.

What a parable of life! We fill our shelves with empty bottles of misunderstanding so there is not room for the things that can feed the soul and nourish a happy life. Each day our prayer should be to enthrone Christ and let unimportant things go.

TABLE TALK: *You have heard of misers who, though living in apparent poverty, have thousands of dollars secretly stored away. Discuss what these people really have missed in life. What was their need?*

NOVEMBER 21

Spring Will Always Come

And I, if I be lifted up from the earth, will draw all men unto myself. John 12:32.

When fall departs and winter comes, it seems as though the world takes on a different spirit. This is a time when the flowers have withered and the trees have lost their leaves. And everything outside looks as if it had forgotten about beauty and had just prepared for a long, cold sleep. We like to huddle around a fireplace and feel the warmth and comfort of home. But no matter how cold it gets or how deep the snow, we can be certain that some day we will once more see the miracle of spring when the buds on the trees will begin to open and the flowers will bloom in all their glory.

Our lives are made up of seasons. Sometimes we are bright and cheerful. At other times we are sad and lonely. We live on the mountain peaks for a while and then suddenly we slip into the valley below. When moments of despair come, we should always think of the assurance we can have that there will be a springtime of new hope and happiness.

When winter descends upon us in all of its fury, and we have to battle the cold and the snow, we many times get so discouraged and depressed. One storm seems to follow after another. "Will winter never end?" we ask. Then spring and summer come and we soon forget the hardships we have endured. So in life, if we keep faith, we will never lose hope.

Spiritual living seems to be like a rose. At first it seems beautiful in its simplicity as a bud, but soon the petals begin to open and we discover an even greater richness. Every day it seems more wonderful than it was the day before. But life is different from the rose in that it never withers away, for the Master Gardener comes to touch our hearts and adds meaning to every moment that we live. Higher and higher He carries us upward to our home in heaven.

TABLE TALK: *Recall times when you have felt like you were in the Valley of Despair, other times when you felt yourself climbing, and again when you have felt the jubilation and exhilaration of life on the mountaintop.*

NOVEMBER 22

God Is Love

Like as a father pitieth his children, so the Lord pitieth them that fear him. Psalm 103:13.

Perhaps you have read Coventry Patman's "Story of Toys," written in verse form, in which he tells about a father reprimanding his child very severely and then sending him up to bed unkissed. The boy cries himself to sleep. Finally the father goes up the stairs, too, and discovers his boy sleeping with eyes still moist with tears. He goes around the room, picks up a few of his son's favorite shells, coins, and books, places them on a little stand beside the boy's bed, then leans over and kisses him goodnight leaving there some of his own tears. Then Patman goes on to say that the father stood there a moment and asked himself this question: "Could it be that God in heaven has much the same feeling toward His children as I have for my little boy?"

Yes, we can know that our God is love. In spite of the fact that God must be so busy these hectic days with all of the troubles that abound in this world, it is a glorious assurance to have the faith to believe that He still knows every little hurt of every life. As the Good Shepherd, He tenderly feeds His flock. As the Great Physician, He binds up all their wounds. He knows us all by name and had we been the only persons who needed salvation, He would have died for us.

Too many of us today really do not know what victorious living is because we carry in our consciousness the remembrance of all the things we have done wrong. The burden weighs heavily upon us and unless we can find someone to bear it for us, it will eventually break us down. The promise of the Master is not only to forgive but also to forget. There is real glory in living when you come to the knowledge that because of the love of God your past can be separated from you and that because of His grace you have a chance each day to begin again.

TABLE TALK: *Do you nurse a grudge against someone in your family or circle of acquaintances? Try today to forget your petty complaints and love that person sincerely.*

NOVEMBER 23

No Sacrifice Too Great

Through him then, let us offer up a sacrifice of praise to God continually, that is, the fruit of our lips which make confession to his name. But to do good and to communicate forget not: for with such sacrifices God is well pleased. Hebrews 13:15-16.

One day a little boy went out too far into the deep water. He began calling for help. A man rushed out in an attempt to save him. Unable to swim this man was lost under the waves. A second rescuer rushed to the scene and saved the little boy. As he wrapped the lad in warm blankets, the boy who was suffering from shock asked anxiously, "Where is he?" "You mean," he said, "the first man who tried to save your life?" The boy replied, "Yes." "I am sorry to tell you, Sonny. He lost his life. Can you give me any reason why he might have done that for you?" The boy dropped his head and replied in a soft and quivering tone, "Yes. He was my father."

Each day we are reminded that God is good and His mercy endureth forever. Let us remember the tremendous sacrifice made for us. When all of the forces of evil were lined up against Him, Jesus willingly gave His life as a sacrifice for each one of us. That is the greatest evidence of love that a man can show— the giving of his life.

Certainly such devotion should not go unrewarded. Every day we have the opportunity of showing God our gratitude for what His gift means by proving that our life has been worth saving. So many opportunities of service surround us. Christ has no hands but ours to do His work today. He cannot command us into action because He has chosen to give us a will that can determine the way that we will go. But pleadingly He invites us, hoping that His ever great love will be the compelling power to send us on errands of mercy in behalf of Him and His kingdom. No sacrifice is too great in the fulfillment of Christian service.

TABLE TALK: *Love will impel you to sacrifice for others. What sacrifices do you make for your parents, your friends?*

NOVEMBER 24

The Power of Faith

And the Lord said, If ye had faith as a grain of mustard seed, ye might say unto this sycamine tree, Be thou rooted up, and be thou planted in the sea, and it would obey you. Luke 17:6.

Less than thirty-two years ago a small group of people gathered together in a little frame house located on the outskirts of one of our metropolitan centers. The purpose of their meeting was to organize a church. There were just an insignificant number present but from the very beginning they seemed to hear the voice of one who promised that if we have faith, even though it be small, we shall have power.

The road ahead was not easy. The first meeting place was an old post office building. Boards were used for benches. An old reed organ provided the music. But as God showered His blessings, the faith in the hearts of these people continued to grow and they began to see the vision of what they could become through Him.

A new frame chapel was erected and soon that became too small for this growing congregation with a growing faith. An addition was made and then plans for a new church were drawn. A large sum of money was gathered together, but everything seemed lost when the bank failures of the early thirties wiped out practically all the assets. That is, it took from these people most of their material assets, but they still had God, and that was worth more to them than all the money in the world.

Then a second new church was built and it was not long until four indentical services had to be held each Sunday to accommodate the congregation. God's great gospel and His message of faith was spread to more and more homes.

They did not give up, but hand in hand with the Eternal they kept marching on. And God rewarded their faith. Once again money was raised and a beautiful new church constructed. Each member became a witness, and as a result more and more joined hands in God's great work. As the congregation grew, four services had to be held each Sunday morning.

TABLE TALK: *Discuss the growth of your church. Name all the elements which make a church grow.*

NOVEMBER 25

Tomorrow May Be Too Late

But God said unto him, Thou foolish one, this night is thy soul required of thee, and the things which thou hast prepared, whose shall they be? So is he that layeth up treasure for himself, and is not rich toward God. Luke 12:20-21.

Recent history has often been called the Era of Indecision. Since the world has very little idea of what the future may bring, it finds it difficult to travel a steady, designed course. As a result, the governments follow one pattern one day and another the next. There is no fixed policy and purpose.

Though these uncertain days may keep right on being a time of indecision in world affairs, they can be quite the opposite for you in your daily life. Today can be a great day of decision. Today you may choose to leave the crooked and treacherous road of hatred and selfishness and begin to walk the way of love and truth. The choice you must make is between the riches of the world and the riches of the soul. If you are not willing to follow the Master at any cost, you reject His offer of peace.

Some years ago the people of a small coal mining village gathered together for worship one Sunday evening. After an inspiring service, the minister noticed that one man remained seated at the rear of the church after all the others had left. He sat down beside the man and asked him about his troubles. The man told him how he had never been able to make the final promise to God. Then he added, "Before I leave the church tonight, I am going to settle the question of my soul's salvation." Together the man and the pastor read from the Bible and prayed. A great peace came upon him, and he returned to his home. The next day there was a tragic explosion in the near-by coal mine. This very man was among those injured. As he was brought out of the mine, his friend stooped over to moisten his lips and to offer a word of encouragement. He could only answer, "I am glad I said 'yes' last night!" Decide today to go God's way.

TABLE TALK: *Mention people whom you know who have put off the decision to go God's way, and whose lives have been suddenly required of them. Mention also people who so live that whenever the call may come, they are ready.*

NOVEMBER 26

Always Present

The Lord is with you, while ye are with him; and if ye seek him, he will be found of you; but if ye forsake him, he will forsake you. 2 Chronicles 15:2.

Each one of us has been given the privilege of choosing the way that he will go. When we come to the crossroads no one can force us to travel in any one direction. Christ is always there pleading with us to go His way so that His power and strength might be ours. But He reserves to us the right to make our own decisions. What glory there is in living if one has caught the vision to which the hand of God is pointing! How He wants us to go that way that happiness and victory might be ours!

A missionary once told of a young Chinese Christian whose name was Lo, who as he read the twenty-eighth chapter of Matthew came across the verse, "Lo, I am with you always." He was amazed to think that God was speaking to him so directly. It gave him wonderful assurance. He was right in his thinking. Jesus has made that promise to each one of us. You can substitute your name, whatever it might be, in that verse of Scripture and the promise will remain true: "Mary (or John, or Jane), I am with you always."

One of the thrilling discoveries of this adventure with God is that He is not just a part-time King. He is always alert to our needs and ready to share our joys. His care and vigilance are more perfect than the undying light of the stars. He guards our lives not only in times of prosperity but also in times of despair. He guides our footsteps whether the day's journey is over smooth and easy ground or takes us through rugged and dark places where, without Him, we would be afraid. The truest meaning and happiness is to discover His eternal love and mercy.

There is only one victory road. It is the road that leads up to Jerusalem and to Calvary. But also to the open grave and to eternal life. The Master has traveled it before you. The Master can lead you safely along this road to your eternal destination.

TABLE TALK: *Have you ever found something in the Bible which fit you particularly? What is one of your favorite verses? Make it a point to learn more verses.*

NOVEMBER 27

There Is a Time to Speak

A time to rend, and a time to sew; a time to keep silence, and a time to speak. Ecclesiastes 3:7.

The writer of that fascinating book in the Old Testament called Ecclesiastes tells us that "there is a time to keep silence, and a time to speak." There was a reminder of these words in a recent radio program. The master of ceremonies was interviewing a little boy who was very timid. It was his first time before that ominous instrument, the microphone. The friendly interviewer asked the little fellow his name and the town from which he came. Falteringly the boy replied to each question. Then the man asked him, "And, Sonny, just how old are you?" There was an extra long pause, but presently the radio listeners heard a chuckle by the master of ceremonies and a wave of laughter from the studio audience. "In reply to my question, 'How old are you?' the little man is holding up three fingers."

How often the time comes in life when we should speak and we keep silent! It is true that sometimes actions speak louder than words, but there is also very definitely a time for us to speak out boldly. In the case of the little boy, only the people in the studio were in a position to get his visual message. They could see the action and understand what he meant. But the vast radio audience had to depend altogether on sound to catch what was going on just then. Someone had to translate the boy's actions into words before the listeners could understand.

Each day we are faced with important circumstances which give us an opportunity to speak. Surely each one of us is given from time to time the opportunity to witness for Christ. If our Master means anything to us at all, we certainly will want to share the peace of heart and the security of faith which we know in Him. Let us ask God for the grace to be articulate in telling others of the faith that means so much to us. There is a time to speak!

TABLE TALK: *Discuss times when you have had an opportunity to speak to others about God, and have failed to do so. There must be times when you have taken advantage of this opportunity. Did it not bring you joy?*

NOVEMBER 28

A Spot of Creation

Ye are the light of the world. A city set on a hill cannot be hid. Matthew 5:14.

For a long period in the history of keyed instruments the thumb was never used and the little finger but rarely. It was J. S. Bach, in fact, who introduced the use of all fingers. Think of all the music which the world before that time failed to hear, just because it was not known that greater harmonies could come from the added use of two seemingly insignificant fingers.

Life is meant to be a glorious symphony and each one of us has a part to play in it. Our part might seem inconsequential and small. And yet if we fail to make our contribution there will be less harmony and beauty because of it.

One day at a great orchestra rehearsal the conductor dropped his baton and commanded, "Stop!" He pointed to the man with the piccolo and said, "Why haven't you been playing?" The man replied, "Because my instrument is so small and insignificant, I didn't think that anyone would notice the difference." God's ear is attuned to the song that is being played. As the great Director He knows when we fail to make the contribution which He expects from us according to the talents He has given us. The biggest things in life are not always the most important.

Over in England there was an artist whose studio was located in a little house on a city street that led to the busy downtown section. In front of his place he had a cobblestone walk. Every morning after the traffic had dirtied up the stones, the artist could be seen with his pail of water and scrub-brush working feverishly to clean up the walk. At night when passers-by had again soiled the walk, he would repeat the same process. One day a friend asked him, "To what avail is all of your work?" The artist replied, "I know of no better answer to an avalanche of destruction than a spot of creation!"

You may be such a spot of creation that can help save the world.

TABLE TALK: *Discuss the means you have to contribute to world unity such as voting wisely for good representatives, being informed, writing to foreign friends, sending CARE packages.*

NOVEMBER 29

When Night Becomes Day

Even so reckon ye also yourselves to be dead unto sin, but alive unto God in Christ Jesus. Romans 6:11.

A Christian life is to be lived today, not yesterday or tomorrow. It means facing squarely the tasks at hand and sharing the joys and problems of this very moment.

But even though the Christian life is lived in the present tense, it does give you an understanding of what has gone before and a hope for that which lies ahead. Some time tomorrow will become today. If Christ is by your side, that is the most glorious experience to anticipate.

A very wealthy businessman had been told that he did not have much longer to live. He had been a success at virtually everything he had ever attempted. He always had been faithful to his church and willing to share his wealth with those who needed help. The startling news concerning his own incurable illness did not lessen his faith in God. If anything, it made Him all the stronger. His last days were a witness to the deep conviction he had in his heart. When the inevitable time came, one of the friends said, "I knew he would see God. It was just like waving farewell from the deck of a ship that was starting on a new journey."

The Master has the power and the willingness to change night into day, and to turn the end of a road into just another beginning. Your life is not a room that is padlocked by time. It is a hallway into a mansion where there is an eternity of light and love. That is the kind of tomorrow you can be building today with God's help. He has promised you His mercy and forgiving grace as the stepping stones which lead to the ever open gates of heaven.

God in your life can be real in daily living. He takes away despair and unhappiness and transplants His own hope and joy into your every moment. He is not a proud dictator who lives in some far away palace but a kindly Father who is willing to answer you when you call upon Him.

TABLE TALK: *Death is only a beginning. How could you explain this to a little child who does not understand?*

NOVEMBER 30

You Are Important

Fear not therefore: ye are of more value than many sparrows.
Matthew 10:31.

One day when Jesus had His disciples together, He was speaking to them about the things of the Kingdom. He was telling them about the day that was coming when there would be a great accounting, when everyone would have to give evidence of his stewardship. It was then He spoke to them the parable about one man who received five talents, another who received two, and a third man who received one. Then the giver went away. When he returned at an unannounced time, he asked the man with the five talents what he had done. The man replied, "I took the five talents which you gave me and invested them and here I have made five more." The man with the two talents said, "I took the two that you gave me and invested them and here I have made two more." But the man with the one talent had a different story. His answer was, "I was afraid I might lose the talent you gave me so I went and buried it in the ground." This man had hidden his talent, and, as a result, it was all that he had to show.

Perhaps the man with the one talent failed to do anything with that which he had been given because he was unhappy when he noticed how little he had, compared to his friends. The world needs five-talent men and two-talent men; but remember, it needs one-talent people, too. Even the smallest of our possessions can become significant when linked with the power of Almighty God.

A small fuse hardly an inch long was found on the floor of my car one day. Because this little part of a complex mechanism was not serving as it should, it was impossible for me to use the dictating machine I have attached to my car. Your life may not seem like very much but its worth can be greater than you think.

TABLE TALK: *What talents do each of you have to use for the glory of God? Do you sing in the church choirs? Do you support the church generously? Do you work for the church in word and deed? Take inventory. What more can you do?*

335

DECEMBER 1

Our God Is Color Blind

Honor all men. Love the brotherhood. Fear God. Honor the king. 1 Peter 2:17.

If we are going God's way, then we are no respecters of persons. Then we believe that He has made of one blood all the nations of the world. Then we respect all men regardless of the color of their skin. A Christian will fight with all his might to rid the world of the prejudice which is so evident at every turn.

A challenging cartoon was printed in one of our daily newspapers. It showed a beautiful swimming pool located in a luxurious estate. The Negro caretaker was standing on the edge. In the pool was the owner. Having gone into water too deep and being unable to swim he was calling for help. The Negro was answering back in a plaintive voice, "I certainly would like to help you, my friend, but you understand I can't. You see, Negroes are not allowed in this pool." The cartoon tells a story that we might well take to heart. Not only does injustice result because of our prejudice, but our own lives may be affected thereby.

A little boy who had just started school kept telling his mother about the new friend he had found whose name was Jimmy. One day when the mother visited the school, she inquired of the teacher concerning the friend that her boy had made. Much to her surprise she was told that he was a Negro. That evening she called her son to her side and said, "It is all right for you to keep Jimmy as a friend, but don't you think you should also find some others? You know, Jimmy is a Negro." "Oh, is that so?" replied the boy, looking surprised. "I really hadn't noticed that."

Our God of love is color blind, and if we follow in His pathway we must be, too. We must fight to give everyone the God-given right to live in a community and share equally in its opportunities. When there are people who are discriminated against, we Christians must be the ones to declare our allegiance to God by helping protect the rights of His children.

TABLE TALK: *The newspapers carry stories of prejudice and persecution. What have you read about recently? What organizations are there to bring about better understanding? Discuss.*

DECEMBER 2

Your Unseen Friend

Greater joy have I none than this, to hear that my children walk in truth. 3 John 1:4.

An advertisement in one of our daily newspapers made this statement: "Whether you go by bus, or by train, or by plane, you have an 'unseen friend' in nickel." It went on to say that if you go by bus, this metal goes right along with you as your "unseen friend," not in the driver's seat, but down underneath in the strong, tough axle that "cradles" our ride, in the steering gear that directs it, and in the brake drum so essential to your safety.

Go by train and this "unseen friend," nickel, is your constant companion. The bearings you roll on, the truck frames on the car, the cylinder and pistons in the locomotive, and many other vital parts are often made from this metal.

Go by plane and this "unseen friend" takes to the sky roads with you. In one form or another it is in the engine's crank shaft, gear valves, and cylinder heads, and it is there for one main reason, to help the airlines add safety, speed, and comfort to your trip into the great blue yonder.

Then the advertisement went on to say, "Yours is the going country." One thing that helps keep it going is nickel. Your buses, your trains, and your planes all use this metal. Your "unseen friend" helps you reach your destination.

One cannot help but observe as he reads this statement that something else is very necessary, too, if life's journey is to lead him successfully to his ultimate goal. No matter how beautiful or efficient any of these physical conveyances might be, there has to be some power in the engine that will keep them going. There is the real "Unseen Friend" who is present always to give us that capacity that will enable us to have staying power so that we can reach our destination.

It takes strength beyond our own to live this day. Our resources fade out. The only security is to take the hand of the Master and say, "Lord, I will live life with You."

TABLE TALK: *Sing together the song, "What a Friend We Have in Jesus."*

DECEMBER 3

Let God Give Direction

And the Lord direct your hearts into the love of God, and into
the patience of Christ. 2 Thessalonians 3:5.

One day three young children found the keys to the family
automobile. They were thrilled at the idea of taking the car for
a drive. With the eleven-year-old lad behind the wheel, the
three youngsters got in the car and started down the road.
Of course, the young man at the wheel knew very little about
driving, but he managed to steer the car safely for about a mile
or so. Then suddenly the car went careening into a ditch. Each
of the children received bad cuts and bruises. They found out
that driving by themselves was not as simple as they thought.

Some people think living is merely putting the keys in the
ignition switch and taking off down the road. They feel quite
capable of steering their lives by themselves until suddenly
something happens which quickly brings them to the consciousness of their inadequacy.

God has not intended that we should travel alone nor that we
should direct our own living. He knows that we have neither
the knowledge nor the ability to steer our lives in the safe way.
That is why He stands ready to give us direction and guidance.

The greatest tragedy in any life is an unwillingness to claim
the great promises which God has given for more abundant living. The story is told about a man who bought a cello and played
it each evening for nine years never moving his fingers from
one certain place on the strings and keeping up precisely the
same see-saw with the bow.

One night his wife, after returning home from a concert,
interrupted the cello session. "George," she said, "I saw a man
play the cello, and he moved his fingers up and down the
strings." "He's just looking for something," said George. "I have
found what I want."

So often we make the same tragic mistake. Let God give
direction to more abundant living.

TABLE TALK: *Have you ever tried to do something without
first learning the procedure? Discuss the need for advisors.*

DECEMBER 4

God Provides Windbreaks

But thou, why dost thou judge thy brother? or thou again, why dost thou set at naught thy brother? for we shall all stand before the judgment-seat of God. Romans 14:10.

Whenever the wind would blow, especially on a stormy night, a little girl would plead with her father to go out and chop down the trees outside the house so that the wind would stop. Since she heard the noises of the rustling of the leaves, the breaking of little branches, the whistling of the wind in the trees, she thought they were the makers of the wind. She looked with unbelieving eyes at her father when he tried to explain that the trees did not make the wind. In fact, he went on to inform her that he had planted them as a windbreak to stop the force of the wind as it came to their yard.

If we are honest with ourselves, we must all confess that our thinking is sometimes just as childish as that of the little girl. Many times it is in direct opposition to the actual truth.

This kind of thinking can take on many guises. We look at another person and judge that he is proud when all the time it may really be that we are envious of his achievements. We say that a certain person gets all the breaks. Things just have a way of opening up and falling together right for him. Perhaps if we were fair in our reasoning, we would have to admit that we have not applied ourselves to the task in hand as earnestly as our neighbor has to his opportunities.

We even criticize God. We wonder how He can allow some things to come our way as they do. We must remember that it is not God that has stirred up the tempests in our lives. It is human willfulness and a refusal to go God's way. But God does raise up walls of resistance aganist these destructive forces that try to play havoc with our lives. Sin is rampant in the world. All knowing and realistic souls certainly recognize this. But let us also discover the windbreaks that God is providing to protect us.

TABLE TALK: *Discuss what is the best remedy against un-justly criticizing the achievements of others?*

DECEMBER 5

Give Your Best

Search me, O God, and know my heart: try me, and know my thoughts: and see if there be any wicked way in me, and lead me in the way everlasting. Psalm 139:23-24.

It is difficult to believe that there are people in this great country of ours who would be disloyal to it. Yet constantly there are rumors about men and women in high office in our government being in some way identified with a movement that would overthrow American democracy and lead us into some other way of life. And some there are who have been found guilty.

It is important that there be loyalty to the country we love, but even more important is the loyalty to a greater realm, the kingdom of eternal significance. There is no doubt in the mind of God as to the loyalty of His children. It is not something that can be stored in secret files, or hidden under a disguise of high-sounding words, or expressed only in outward acts. For God knoweth all things.

If you have ever walked famous Broadway in New York City, you may have seen a certain bronze statue. It is of young Nathan Hale, and bears on its base the inscription: "I regret that I have but one life to give for my country."

Each one has but one life to give for his country, and each day we should give the best we have because we shall not walk this way again. We should also remember that we have but one life to give to God. If we are honest with ourselves, we must admit that too often we have been disloyal not only in the things we have done, but also in the things we have failed to do.

The words we speak today, the things we do, and the thoughts we let pass through our minds shall be strung together as a chain, a chain that will either be of rough ugly links that some day will bind and choke us, or that will be gems which we shall wear as a sparkling necklace. We are living our one life today. There is no turning back, no chance to relive this hour.

TABLE TALK: *Discuss the qualities of good citizenship in our nation. What qualities are likewise desirable for the kingdom of God?*

DECEMBER 6

Nothing Is Insignificant

A little leaven leaveneth the whole lump. Galatians 5:9.

The feeding of vitamins to hogs seems like an insignificant issue in the business of good farming. Yet according to an animal nutritional specialist, last year there were forty million below-par pigs in the United States because farmers were feeding their hogs in horse-and-buggy-day fashion. They actually lost money because they did not pay much attention to what they termed "little things" in their business.

In living, the same tragic mistake is often made. We concentrate on what we would call the "big things," the gathering of material resources, the building of a house, the advancement of our profession, and all the time we may be losers because of our failure to concentrate on things of eternal significance. Often the making or the breaking of a life is caused by the "little things."

One little flu germ imported to America could lay low a large segment of our population within a period of forty-eight hours! Tiny raindrops descending in sufficient quantity can make rivers swell causing them to leave their banks, wrecking property, and taking lives. A small fuse sets off a big explosion. A single bomb can make a city unliveable for a period of years. A single kiss by Judas can betray the Master. One life given on the cross, the life of Jesus, brought salvation to the entire world!

In everyday life, too, little things are important. A smile, a kind word, a single act of love—these all do "big things." They may encourage one when all hope is gone, or make one feel more secure. A small gift to the church or some charitable organization has a tremendous consequence when put to work for the Lord.

Pay attention to the "little things" in life. In God's world there are no insignificant trifles. A single word spoken can have tremendous consequence. One decision can determine a destiny. Just saying "yes" can mean eternal life!

TABLE TALK: *Think of some other "little things" which actually have great importance. See how many you can name.*

341

DECEMBER 7

God's Supply Unlimited

And he hath said unto me, My grace is sufficient for thee; for my power is made perfect in weakness. Most gladly therefore will I rather glory in my infirmities, that the power of Christ may rest upon me. 2 Corinthians 12:9.

For many years Minnesota has been supplying the world with one of its most important resources, iron ore. From its great mines have come the material with which to build steel products for every corner of the globe. Through the years millions of tons of this rich iron ore have flowed to giant steel plants everywhere. Much of the wealth of the state has depended upon these mines. But some time ago the experts reported that soon all the high-grade iron ore would be gone from northern Minnesota and the world would have to look for another supplier.

Recently, however, two executives of important steel companies of our country said the prospects were not as gloomy as many people suspect. A tremendous source of iron ore still remains untouched. Great things are expected from this important industry in the future. How serious it would be if the resources were limited!

In life sometimes it seems as if all resources are going to run out. What we fail to realize is that God's supply is unlimited. He has enough strength to defeat successfully any temptation. He has enough courage to lead one into any battle. He has enough love to forgive any sin. He has enough hope to wait for even the most faraway prodigal to return home. He has enough sympathy to be understanding about the least trouble. He has enough power to assure victory no matter how tremendous the odds.

Expect great things from God. By His hand the entire world was created and we, His children, were made in His image. In His plan we share all His riches. They are sufficient for all in this life and in the life that is to come.

God's supply of hope, sympathy, power, and forgiveness is unlimited. And it is all yours for the asking!

TABLE TALK: *Discuss the important resources of strength, courage, love, hope, sympathy, and power.*

DECEMBER 8

Our House of Hope

For freedom did Christ set us free: stand fast therefore, and be not entangled again in a yoke of bondage. Galatians 5:1.

A constructive program to better conditions in the mental hospitals was initiated recently in one of our communities. The leadership of the state combined with the efforts of public-spirited citizens resulted in vast reforms as "dungeons of despair" became transformed into "houses of hope." Previously strait-jackets, camisoles, handcuffs, and the like, had been used to restrain the patients. Now more loving and humane types of therapy were administered to the patients. These have brought much better results.

Immediately upon the taking away of the old restraints, a new attitude was seen in the patients. Much to the surprise of many, very few unpleasant incidents occurred even when visitors came, for the patients seemed to know that now they were being treated not as prisoners, but rather as innocent victims for whom there was hope.

After this program had been in effect for several months, a great demonstration was arranged. All of the shackles previously used were taken outside and piled high. A program was presented in which many of the patients participated, giving evidence of talents which many never even knew they possessed. For now they were free and were able to express themselves without fear. Then at a very dramatic moment, the leader of the state stepped forward and told in inspiring terms of the program for the future and made the promise that no longer would these patients be the forgotten people but that a loving state would care for them. Then he took a match and set fire to this great pile of material restraints. A great cheer went up from those who saw them burning.

A comparable but definitely greater movement was the one on Calvary, where all the chains of sin were piled high upon the shoulders of the Son of God. No longer need any of His children fear, for He came to set us free that we might live abundantly.

TABLE TALK: *Discuss why love is more effective in dealing with any situation than force.*

343

DECEMBER 9

Stay Within Your Limits

Let not sin therefore reign in your mortal body, that ye should obey the lust thereof. Romans 6:12.

There have been instances when people have built beyond the limits of their own property so that the building has extended into the neighbor's lot. Many times lawsuits have resulted. These have sometimes involved years of wrangling and dispute and tedious search for evidence. Many times in the end the property has been legally forfeited by the original, rightful owner to the invader. It had gone on too long. It was too late to establish the claim.

In our living we would do well to clearly define our property lines. When a man or a woman has pledged his life to Christ, he belongs to God. That man does well to set up a property line to guard the title to his time, his talents, and his means, so that not one evil thing can trespass the boundary line. He must say "no" to temptation and to all the forces of the world which would press in upon him from all sides. Firmly he must declare, "Beyond this line you cannot intrude. My life and all that I have belong to God. I stay within these limits!"

Far too many people have faced the sad consequences of trying to play with sin. They allow it to come just a little way over the boundary line and it finally settles as a habit. At last it has permanent claim on that soul. If that person should awaken to what has happened, he finds great difficulty in attempting to prove the rightful owner. There is very little evidence left of a life and a heart that belong to God.

"Let not sin therefore reign in your mortal body, . . . for sin shall not have dominion over you." Christ tells us to whom we rightfully belong. "Ye are Christ's," He says. It is He who has the rightful claim upon us, and we would be wise to guard faithfully that which He has committed unto us until that day when earthly bounds shall merge into the limitless boundaries of heaven, where there shall be peace, joy, and righteousness.

TABLE TALK: *What habits or desires do you have which might make claim upon your soul? Discuss the harm of anger, jealousy, deceitfulness, etc.*

344

DECEMBER 10

How Is Your Vision?

Then again he laid his hands upon his eyes; and he looked steadfastly and was restored, and saw all things clearly.

Mark 8:25.

A blind man once came to Jesus. The Bible tells us that the Master laid His hands upon the man's eyes and his sight was restored so that he "saw all things clearly."

Let us think about that blind man for a moment. The outside world did not change when he was given the ability to see. Everything that he saw after his healing was just as it had been before his sight was restored. His friends, his family, the flowers, the trees, and the sunsets, were there all the while. But the mechanism of his own eye was faulty, and he could not experience the sight of all these things.

Many of us are missing some of the wonders and marvels of living—in fact, some of the greatest things of life—because we, too, are blind. Something is wrong within us, within our hearts. We lose our ability to see the lovely things of the spirit. We are blind. But the same Jesus who laid His hands of healing on that blind man on the streets of Bethsaida in that long ago still has the power and the great desire to touch our eyes and to give us the vision of things as they really are.

Perhaps when you have been washing windows in your home you have learned this lesson: Even though the windows are clean from the outside, if they are dirty within, the vision is not clear through them. Like those windows our lives must be clean both without and within if we are to give the clear view of the Christian way of life which we profess. We cannot be something at church which we are not at the office, or at the club, or in the social world. There must be a consistency, if our living is to ring true. Thoughts of hatred cannot be hid under the motions of pretended kindness. A witness must be consistent. The outer life and the inner life must be the same.

TABLE TALK: *Analyze your daily actions. Are you consistent? What should you do if you are not?*

DECEMBER 11

Is It Good?

And God saw everything that he had made, and, behold, it was very good. Genesis 1:31.

Reading the creation story in the Bible is like sitting down and thumbing through a snapshot album and seeing the series of pictures of God's creation as it proceeded step by step.

First God created the light. Then He stepped aside and took a view of it and declared that it was good. Then He made the sky and separated the land from the water beneath it. Once more He judged, "It is good." The next picture introduces all the vegetation which He caused to spring up and grow. The story continues with the arrangement for the seasons and the stars, the sun, the moon, the fish, the birds, and the cattle. Then finally, crowning His whole creation, He made man in His own image. After each addition to this earthly Paradise, God took off some time for reflections. And the picture which He saw pleased Him. "It is good," He said.

Each day great sermons are preached by pictures. Our actions are like candid shots to the eyes of others. We are making an impression upon someone. Every day there are cameras clicking about us, very silently and unobtrusively, perhaps, but people are seeing what we do. The impressions go into the imprint of memory for good or bad. They may influence a lifetime!

We should remember that God also keeps an album and carefully enters into it a picture of our living each day. As we face temptation, as we are challenged by the impossible, as we stand at the crossroads deciding which way to go, let us remember to make such choices that as God continues to turn the pages in the album which record our life through His loving eyes and with His forgiving heart He might be able still to say, "It is good." To attain that result we must be exposed to the healing sunlight of the forgiveness of our sins. We must seek daily to walk in His presence.

TABLE TALK: *Read or retell the Creation story as found in Genesis. How does God daily create?*

DECEMBER 12

There Is Wonder-Working Power

Having eyes, see ye not? and having ears, hear ye not? and do ye not remember? Mark 8:18.

Many of us are missing much of the glory of life because our vision is not complete. We may look but we do not see. From the psychology class room we learn that we can look at the same objects every day of our lives and still know very little about them. For instance, do you know how many steps you take when you walk down the stairway to the basement of your house? How many trees do you pass in the first block in walking from your place of residence to the store? How many houses in your block have shutters on their windows? What color is the trimming on your neighbor's house? How many panels on your back door? Most of us are amazed to discover that these things, so commonplace in life, have escaped our observation.

It really does not make very much difference whether or not we know how many steps there are or what color the window trim of our neighbor's house is. These facts are inconsequential. However, there are many things we are passing by which would help give our lives a more beautiful melody. We do not begin to fathom the possibilities of the hope that God gives; we cannot anticipate more than a fraction of what God has in store for us.

If Christ could be raised from the dead, surely there is power available for you and me to rise high above our pettiness, our critical attention to our neighbor's business, our neglect of our own duty, our self-seeking. We can have the vision to see that God gives us the power to overcome all these things.

Only as the Lord removes from our lives haziness and dullness can we see clearly the wonders of the possibilities about us. Put your life into proper focus and you will discover the opportunities for good which surround you every day.

TABLE TALK: *See if you can remember how many steps there are to your front door, how many houses in the block, how many windows in the house, etc. To what conclusion do you come?*

Roundabouts

But they hearkened not, nor inclined their ear, but walked in their own counsels and in the stubbornness of their evil heart, and went backward, and not forward. Jeremiah 7:24.

One of the curious experiences of an American traveler in the English countryside is the constant encounter with what are called "roundabouts" along the highways. Each is a circular plot of ground placed in the center of highway intersections. American tourists driving through the English countryside can become very much vexed because of the slow speed at which they move from place to place. The "roundabouts" demand almost a stop as one approaches the hublike arrangement from which the various highways branch out. Located there are signs which tell the distance to the important towns and the road to be taken. One has a choice as he makes the circle. However, if he does not know where he is headed, he will shortly land right back where he entered the "roundabout."

But the wise man has studied the map. He knows where he wants to go and he is alert to the signs. He will have little difficulty in finding the way to his goal.

For each of us there come times of slowing up. Some of these may be of our own choosing. Or God may allow us to be laid low for a while. Illiness may intervene to interrupt our plans. Even at times like this the great mercy of God can be at work. It could be that at these moments our souls are much sicker than our bodies. But many of us do not realize this until the physical breakdown comes. As we are thus stopped at the "roundabout," we are given time to consider the way that we are taking.

Whenever these moments come, let us use them rightly. There is a destination ahead. We were not meant to dream, to drift, and to wander aimlessly. Ours is a high and honored calling to the perfecting of a life that is redeemed from wrongdoing and evil thinking. The command of God is, "Go forward!"

TABLE TALK: *Have you ever had an illness which made you stop and think? How could you arrange to have a frequent stopping place for meditation?*

DECEMBER 14

Keep Looking Up

But the word of the Lord abideth forever. And this is the word of good tidings which was preached unto you. 1 Peter 1:25.

There is no doubt about the fact that we take a lot of things for granted in this life. As long as we are well and healthy, we forget about the hospital with all its sick people and the doctors and the nurses who are on the job day and night. When everything is peaceful and ordinary, we do not think about the police force standing ready to protect us at all times. We are not particularly interested in the fire department and the service it stands ready to give us until our house is burning down.

Some people think about God in pretty much the same way. As long as everything is in order and life runs smoothly they go on their way forgetting Him who is constantly present not only to be our friend when emergencies come but also to walk and talk with us as a good friend in the joyful moments of life. It is when trouble comes that many people go running to God for help. Loving God with all your heart means much more than just calling upon Him when there is disappointment or sorrow.

God is our heavenly Father whose eternal vigilance watches over us day and night, in good times just as in bad. He not only helps us when we are in trouble, but if we live with Him at all times, He steers us away from those things which would keep us from a full life. His is a love that does not know any boundary of time or space or distance.

The story is told of a father who took his young son with him when he went out to steal potatoes from his neighbor's field. They crept along the fence in the shadows of the trees and then suddenly they stopped. The father looked carefully in all directions to make certain that no one was watching and then he started to climb over the fence. At that moment his young son said, "Daddy, you forgot something. You didn't look up."

Keep looking up in good times as well as bad. Then you will know abundant living.

TABLE TALK: *Imagine how different the world would be if everyone realized that God was always watching. Discuss this modern Utopia. What would you do differently?*

DECEMBER 15

Our Symbol of Victory

For the Lord thy God is a merciful God; he will not fail thee, neither destroy thee, nor forget the covenant of thy fathers which he sware unto them. Deuteronomy 4:31.

Because our Master conquered worldliness and sin we have the opportunity of sharing a great victory—one which we could never know if we had to depend upon our own strength.

The cross is the symbol of our victory. Its meaning has preserved so many thoughts and values in life. Instead of despair, there has come hope. Instead of defeat, there is victory. Though we are not worthy in our own right to be called children of God, Christ has suffered for us our shame and humiliation. And because He is the advocate pleading our case the heavenly Father turns to us and says, "I understand, My children, and since you have proved you are sorry, I will not forget you nor forsake you. I can only freely forgive you."

The people in the time of Jesus thought if they could just get rid of Him, all of His followers would soon disappear and His teaching would die out. So they crucified Him.

John Masefield has written a book in which he imagines a conversation that might have occurred shortly after the Good Friday crucifixion and the first Eastern Morn. He sees a Roman soldier hurrying to the wife of Pontius Pilate to bring the news that the stone has been rolled away and that the tomb is empty. Excitedly and in great fear she asks the soldier: "Where do you think He is?" He replies, "Let loose in a world where no one can stop Him!"

His truth goes marching on. His is a love that can never be destroyed nor will the time come when He will refuse to offer it in all of its abundance. You may choose to accept or reject it. But if you claim it for your own, you come into possession of the richest gift you will ever know. It is the only price by which the doors of heaven will open for you.

The Cross is our symbol of victory. We need never know defeat if we trust in Him.

TABLE TALK: *Some think that they can get rid of Jesus even today. Discuss why He will always be in the world.*

DECEMBER 16

When You Never Have to Worry

Take my yoke upon you, and learn of me; for I am meek and lowly in heart; and ye shall find rest unto your souls.

Matthew 11:29.

A young lad one day happened to meet a man who was an officer in the Navy. The boy was anxious to know what all the emblems and stripes on his uniform meant. He pointed to one of the insignia and asked what it was. The officer explained that it was an anchor with a cross on it. "That means I am a chaplain, a minister in the Navy," explained the man. "Well, does that cross keep you up on the water?" asked the little boy. The chaplain smiled, thought for a moment and then replied, "Yes, that is exactly what it does. The cross keeps you above the water when the storms are raging and the waves are high. My Son, you never have to worry as long as you cling to it."

There are times in life when we are tempted to slip away from the cross. At moments like these we are in danger of losing our security unless we come to ourselves and take a tighter hold. These are days when the storms of the world rage fierce and furious. They try to sweep us away from God and His wonderful love. But as long as we hold on to the cross we do not have to be afraid, for there is no storm that can conquer it and no battle in which we cannot be victorious.

Do not forget God today. He has the power to save you from every sin and gives you the strength to resist all the temptations that the devil can put before you. His is the only power great enough to win the victory over worldliness and hatred.

It is impossible to put into words the rich blessings which come from giving your life to the Master. The whole world takes on a new vision and the things which are lasting and worth while come clearly into view. A refreshing spirit fills every moment of the day, and becomes a real part of eternity.

He stands at the door of your heart. He is food for the hungry, rest for the weary, love for the lonely. He never fails!

TABLE TALK: *A chaplain wears a cross on his uniform as a means of physical identification. Comment on how a man of God can be identified without insignia.*

DECEMBER 17

The Master Is Here Today

For it is written, As I live, saith the Lord, to me every knee shall bow, and every tongue shall confess to God." Romans 14:11.

These are names that are familiar to all of us: Bethlehem, Nazareth, Jerusalem, Emmaus, Bethany. They are the villages which Jesus visited two thousand years ago.

So often as we recall this story of long ago we forget the fact that Christ today is still walking the streets of our very own town. He visits the shops of "Main Street." He stops at every home along the way and is still the friendly confidant of anyone who will stop to listen and talk to Him. And so many people just pass Him by. His kindly words and gentle deeds go unnoticed in the midst of the hurry and the scurry of our modern-day living.

The Master is just as concerned for you and me today and can be just as real as He was to those people He met face to face long ago, as He journeyed across the ancient Holy Land. He understands our twentieth century living just as He understood the life of the faithful shepherds in the Judean hills and of the eager merchants of Bethlehem. His love has not changed. It is the same for us as it was for them.

When Jesus saw that His earthly ministry was drawing to a close He commissioned a band of His faithful followers to continue His preaching and teaching among the people of every land. Into all the world they were to go. He counted on them to carry the message of salvation into the hearts of men and women in every station of life. Upon the shoulders of His disciples He placed a very heavy load of responsibility. But by His power they were equal to the task. Tradition says that most of them died the death of martyrs. They were willing to pay that price that they might be used as instruments in the hand of God.

Because of their devotion and zeal we are privileged today to enjoy the blessings of the gospel message. Our responsibility is no less than theirs. We are to continue to go and make disciples until "every tongue shall confess that Jesus Christ is Lord."

TABLE TALK: *Your church has a foreign mission program. What is it? How can you help?*

352

DECEMBER 18

Giving by Living

Remember the words of the Lord Jesus, that he himself said,
It is more blessed to give than to receive. Acts 20:35.

Is there a song in your heart these days? Does the melody
linger on into the lives of others? Let us ever remember that
Christmas is not only a time of receiving, but more than that,
is a time for giving. It began that way. God gave His only Son
in order that whoever believes on Him might have eternal life.
His one concern was for others. Christmas will have meaning
for us only if we reflect that same loving spirit.

There is a man who works in the veteran's hospital in one of
our American communities. His object is to make living more
enjoyable to those who have been injured in war. He has engaged an organist, who entertains the patients. The music is
broadcast to the men in their wards through earphones. The
patients listen carefully to the tunes and they joke with the
organist through a microphone carried by the master of ceremonies. This is what these men say: "The music helps us pass
away an hour each week. Four walls are pretty tough to look
at all the time."

The one who is thus sharing his talent of creating music to
give these people joy receives more happiness from giving than
they get out of receiving. There is not only a song in his heart,
but the melody lingers on in the lives of others as they become
blessed by his ministry.

There is something for each one of us to do. There are so
many people who need us. Their lives have become darkened
because of anxiety, trouble, sickness, and pain. We are in this
world not only to receive the blessings of Almighty God but
also to reflect Him in our living by the giving of our talents to
the happiness of others and the glory of God.

TABLE TALK: *Mention ways in which you can reflect this
spirit of Christ as you meet and deal with people day by day.*

DECEMBER 19

Keep Climbing

So then, my beloved, as ye have always obeyed, not as in my presence, only, but now much more in my absence, work out your own salvation with fear and trembling. For it is God who worketh in you both to will and to work, for his good pleasure.
Philippians 2:12-13.

If you have ever traveled the beautiful North Shore highway along Lake Superior, you have passed a gigantic mountain of rock called "Palisade Head." It is such a beautiful sight that many travelers stop nearby and decide to climb to the top. It is a steep rock trail that winds up through the heavy timber. You are surrounded on every side by tall stately pines blocking off any view of Lake Superior in the distance.

But if you keep on climbing, you will at last reach the very summit and there you can look out over the gorgeous countryside for many miles around. Then you will see once again the clear blue lake and the pattern of green trees and waterfalls along its shore. Perhaps the climb has been long and vigorous, but at the top you know that it was worth every effort.

Sometimes it might seem that serving God is a difficult road to follow. To be true, it is not always smooth and level, but it does keep winding upward. When you have reached the mountaintop, you will be convinced that your journey has not been in vain. It is worth every step of the way.

The wisest choice you can make is to give the Master your whole life and let Him use it as He will. Whatever your talents, whatever your abilities, be they many or few, put them to work in His kingdom. Not only are you making a wise decision, but if you keep climbing God's way you might be encouraging another fellow traveler to do the same.

There is an old motto that goes something like this: "Climb though the rocks be rugged." It will be worth it in the end because the destination you will reach after the difficult journey, will be filled with glory the like of which eye hath not seen!

TABLE TALK: *Do you recall ever having to climb a steep hill or perform a similar physical feat? Was the end worth the effort?*

DECEMBER 20

Choose the Things Eternal

But the Lord answered and said unto her, Martha, Martha, thou art anxious and troubled about many things: but one thing is needful: for Mary hath chosen the good part, which shall not be taken away from her. Luke 10:41-42.

Jerusalem is located on a high hill. Bethany is a little city less than two miles away. Living in the latter town at the time of Christ was a wonderful family—two sisters by the name of Martha and Mary, and a brother who was called Lazarus. These were special friends of Jesus. Very often when He came to preach and teach in Jerusalem, He would take the three-fourths of an hour's journey to the home of these friends where He could rest awhile. We are thinking today of one of these visits.

Jesus goes into their house, sits down, and starts talking. He tells them that He has been in Jerusalem teaching the people and they mention the fact that there is a lawyer who is going to trip Him up on His theology when He gets back. "Well," we seem to hear Him say, "I have already talked to Him. In fact, just this afternoon." And then He proceeds to tell them the story about the Good Samaritan. In the middle of the story Martha gets up and rushes out into the kitchen to start preparing the meal. She is worried about the proper care of this dinner guest. Mary is a little embarrassed but she draws her chair up closer and listens as Jesus proceeds with His story. Finally Martha becomes irritated because she has had to work in the kitchen alone. She goes back into the room and says, "Master, won't you tell my sister to come out here and help me?" Whereupon Jesus gives her this mild rebuke: "Martha, Martha, thou art anxious and troubled about many things. Mary hath chosen the good part."

Everyone of us needs to take to heart His words of admonition. We need to remind ourselves of the little boy who one day went to his mother and said, "Do you suppose Daddy will ever get to heaven?" "Of course," said his mother. "Why do you ask?" "Well, I was wondering if he could ever leave the store."

TABLE TALK: *There are many everyday things which become obstructions to the "one thing needful." How do the radio, TV, work, and worry keep us from listening to the Master.*

355

DECEMBER 22

What Is Greatness?

Hath not the scripture said, that Christ cometh of the seed of
David, and from Bethlehem, the village where David was?

John 7:42.

People are so often attracted to that which is big. This is a
"super" age, and if one were to be influenced by public opinion
one would think that just bigness makes greatness. But this is
not always the case.

The big cities of the world, like Paris, London or New York,
hold a fascination for many and very frequently one hears
people speak out how they would like to travel to these places
and how life will not be complete until they have been there.
Each of these cities seems to hold visions of delight, the big
buildings, the many activities, and the glamorous people.

After one has had an opportunity to see some of these places,
and though one may have been fascinated by them, one no doubt
learns that the value of things does not lie in size. It is not the
size of a building but what is in it that matters. It is not the
number of activities but the kind which counts. It is not the
glamor nor the bright lights nor the fancy clothes which make
the person. It is the soul and character.

Let your mind go back over the centuries and think of the
individuals who have had great influence on the lives of their
fellow men. It has not been from the great cities but from the
small towns that most of them have come. Where was Abraham
Lincoln from? A small cabin in rural Kentucky. Where did
Martin Luther first see the light of day? Eisleben, Germany.
Probably neither of these places would have been known if it
had not been for the men who rose to world fame who were
born there. And Jesus? From little Bethlehem, which was so
small among the cities of Judah, He came. Out of this little
settlement came the greatest man in the history of the World—
He who was to be the Saviour of all mankind.

Circumstances or places do not make people great. It is what
they do with the help of God.

TABLE TALK: *Think of other persons of note who came from
obscure places. What qualities have brought them success?*

Only a Penny

The wolf shall dwell with the lamb, and the leopard shall lie down with the kid; and the calf and the young lion and the fatling together; and a little child shall lead them. Isaiah 11:6.

The spirit of Christmas in the heart of a child came very close to two men who were walking in a park one evening enjoying the wintry scene of new-fallen snow. Suddenly a boy came up from behind them and shyly asked, "Misters, do you suppose I could walk along between you?" The lad seemed sincere, and the men said they would be glad to have him. They had not gone very far when the boy asked another question. "Suppose, Misters, there was a boy who lived in an orphanage with a lot of children and all the others had friends who came to see them and always brought them candy and pennies. And suppose this one little boy didn't have any friends and never got any presents. Don't you suppose someone ought to give him a penny?" One of the men answered assuredly, "I certainly do, Sonny. I certainly do." Then the little lad stopped, hung his head, and stared at the white snow as he finally said, "Well, Mister, that one little boy is me."

That small lad's wish for love and kindness touches the real spirit of Christmas perhaps closer than we realize. Deep down it is not so much the presents under the tree, or the festive dinners, or the glittering decorations, but rather it is the sense of friendship and love that makes this season more than just another holiday.

The Son of God came to earth that those who are left alone might find a friend, those who are penniless might find riches, and those who are lost might find their way. No better way could be found to celebrate the Christmas season than to humbly pray, "Thank You Lord, for coming to earth to live among men and to give peace to every heart that earnestly wants it."

Today you are a child of the heavenly Father.

TABLE TALK: *Discuss plans you could make for spreading the joy of Christmas to orphans, the sick, and the poor. Have you a family project to do something for others this Christmas?*

DECEMBER 24

There's Music in the Air

The Lord is my strength and my shield; my heart hath trusted in him, and I am helped: therefore my heart greatly rejoiceth; and with my song will I praise him. Psalm 28:7.

The business of an ordinary week was broken by a very pleasant luncheon engagement at one of the downtown banks. At noonday, I walked out in the balcony of this building and received one of the greatest thrills that came to me that Christmas season. For a period of time business had stopped in this busy place. High on the stage on one end of a long central room were a group of employees, beautifully gowned, singing Christmas carols. They were singing as if the message really came from the bottom of their hearts. As I stood there in the balcony and thrilled to the music, this thought came to me: Our old world is not quite as bad as we may think. There still is hope. If only everybody who believes in Christ and in His message of love would keep singing it, not only on Sunday but in the middle of every busy working day, that message would soon incorporate itself into our actions, and then the kingdom would surely come.

That same evening a group of young people from the church gave their time to go about singing the Christmas carols to many shut-ins who did not have the opportunity of sharing in the beautiful Christmas services. Here was another event which gave me hope for the future. These young people with all of life before them, not only had the song in their own hearts, but at an early age had decided how profitable it is to let the melody of that song linger on in the lives of others. And they were willing to take the time and to give of themselves in order to share with those less fortunate than they.

We who know the Christian way of life have an obligation to the world in which we live. There are many people who are seeking to find power beyond themselves to give them strength for daily living. If we meet them day by day in the busy marts of trade, let us so live that, in seeing us, they may be attracted to the way of Christ.

TABLE TALK: *Point out ways in which you can serve Christ in everyday living.*

DECEMBER 25

God's Greatest Gift

For there is born to you this day in the city of David a Saviour, who is Christ the Lord. Luke 2:11.

We would like to stop at your home today on a very pleasant errand. We have a Christmas package to deliver to you. There is no mistake, no mispelling of the name on this package. The card attached says distinctly: "To you, whoever you are."

The address? It reads clearly: "Wherever you are."

The return address up in the corner? Well, there is only a shiny gold star pasted there. You see, this gift comes to you from heaven above. It was wrapped for us when a brilliant star shone over a manger many years ago.

Whoever you are, God has a gift for you this Christmas time. A pastor once stood beside the bed of a man whose life was ebbing away. He had come to know the wonder of God's love and His forgiving grace. But over and over again he repeated, "I tell you, it is not decent. I have wasted years. I have missed talents that God gave me. I am wicked and unworthy. It is not decent to come to God now and expect Him to forgive all that." The pastor replied, "No, it is not decent, but it is divine."

God does not give to us because we deserve. Many choose the low road that leads to death; but since God cannot bear to see His children suffer, He gives us the possibility of the high road which leads to life. "For there is born to you this day a Saviour which is Christ the Lord." "Him that cometh to me I will in no wise cast out." "Not that we loved God, but that he loved us."

God is love and, though we can never quite fathom it, that is the essence of the forgiveness of our sins. Because of Christmas we have another chance.

God's greatest gift is for you. Will you accept it?

TABLE TALK: *Let the members of the family say how grateful they are for the gifts received this day. Emphasize how we should be most grateful to God for the gift of Christ the Saviour.*

DECEMBER 26

Forgetting the Past

And the Lord said unto Moses, Whosoever hath sinned against me, him will I blot out of my book. Exodus 32:33.

One cold wintry night a little blond-haired girl was tucked snugly in bed. She asked her mother to leave the light on because the night was dark and stormy and she was afraid. A few minutes later her mother went back to the daughter's room expecting to find her sleeping soundly. Instead she heard the child sobbing to herself.

"Are you still afraid?" asked the mother. "The light is on and I am close by if you should want me." "No, Mother, I am really not afraid any more. I am only sorry." "Sorry about what?" she was asked. "Well, I treated Little Sister awfully mean today and I told her I didn't love her any more. I am sorry for what I did and I wonder if God will forgive me." "Yes, my child," assured her mother, "God will forgive you, but tomorrow you must prove that you are really sorry for what you have done. You must tell Sister that you do love her and then treat her kindly and thoughtfully. Tomorrow you can mend the mistakes which you have made today."

We are coming very close to the end of another year. During the time past, clouds of war and unrest have seemed to blot out the sunshine. And sometimes we have been dreadfully afraid. We have prayed that the lights of peace and understanding might be turned on. If we look over the past year, we see many things in our own life for which we are sorry, unwise choices we have made, harsh words we have spoken, kindnesses we have forgotten to do. But God is always willing to forgive the repentant heart and to give us another chance to begin again.

God will erase the black marks and make the new page white and unblemished. But it is not enough just to be sorry. We have to mend the mistakes of the past. Love must replace hatred. We must prove our repentance by the things we do and say.

TABLE TALK: *Consider how our own nation has shared in the wrongs that have led to wars and other evils in the world. How can we mend the mistakes of the past?*

DECEMBER 27

There's Always an Answer

Be not therefore like unto them: for your Father knoweth what things ye have need of, before ye ask him. Matthew 6:8.

There was once a little girl who wanted above everything else a violin. She had heard a great artist play on this kind of an instrument and she had been much inspired by the concert. So when Christmas came, her only request was that she might have a violin. In childlike mind, she did not comprehend that it would take years of instruction and practice before she would be able to play. She thought that by some magic she could pick up the instrument and the same song would come forth that she had heard from the artist's hand. However, her parents were wiser than she; and when Christmas came, all she received was a toy violin. They knew what was best for her.

Sometimes we complain that God does not answer our prayers. He always does, but not always in the way that we want Him to. Our faith must first be assured that the heavenly Father knows the things that are best for us. Many times, long processes must take place before the worth-while result can be attained.

Consider, for example, the making of a violin. How particular the maker is about the wood that is to be used. He especially likes the hard wood which has come from the few trees above the timberline. Why would he choose such trees? They have stood against the storms and winds which often rage over the mountaintops, and the trees have become very strong as they have withstood these storms. Wood that has been tempered in this way is used and, as a result, more perfect sounds come forth from the finished instrument.

Lives which have many sorrows, and cares, and which have stood above these trials are often the sweetest in their witness to other people. Let us pray God that we may withstand the tests which come our way. Let us remember that the easy road does not always lead to the greatest victory or cause the most music to sound forth from a life.

TABLE TALK: *Discuss how difficulties you have encountered have enabled you to become stronger in your faith; have made of your life a sweeter music.*

DECEMBER 28

What God Is Like

Behold what manner of love the Father hath bestowed upon us, that we should be called children of God; and such we are. For this cause the world knoweth us not, because it knew him not. 1 John 3:1.

The president of Kiwanis International tells a most interesting story. He was walking to work one morning when he heard the whimperings of a little lad. He stopped to find a boy standing in the entrance of a vacant building. He stopped and asked the boy what the trouble was. "Oh, nothing is the matter, Mister," said the boy. "Oh, yes there is," answered the man. "Tell me, please."

The boy then related how he had been given a dollar by his father and told to go and buy groceries, and he was crying because he had lost the dollar. "Just go home and tell your father what has happened," said the man. "He will understand." "Oh, no," replied the boy, "he is drunk and I am afraid to go home and tell him because he will beat me to pieces."

The man took pity on the boy and went with him to the store. He then purchased the groceries that were on the list, and gave the grateful boy a dime in change. After thanking the man profusely, the boy was given this parting advice, "Now you go home and don't tell your father that anything unusual happened."

The little lad walked toward the door, then turned and looked at the one who had been his helper and said, "I wish't you was my daddy!"

Each day we can live in the assurance that our God is love. Since we are children of the heavenly Father, we never have to be afraid to return home for fear that we have lost that which has been given us. Our God will understand and in His great love will receive us back again. Our God knows our human weakness. He is well acquainted with our problems. His loving arms are always waiting to receive us.

TABLE TALK: *Discuss the ways in which we feel secure because we know someone loves us and cares for us. God surrounds us always with the assurance of His love.*

A Presence to Guide You

And he said, My presence shall go with thee, and I will give thee rest. Exodus 33:14.

A terrible snowstorm descended upon a certain city, and people were having much difficulty in reaching their homes. The hills were blocked with long lines of cars and many had to be detoured on strange and different ways in order to reach their destination. One woman found herself headed down a hill at the bottom of which many cars were stuck.

A young man got out of his car and warned her not to go down the hill because cars were lined up for a block. "What shall I do?" she asked. "I can't back up. I tried it and it was useless." The young man said, "I carry some sand in my trunk just for such emergencies. I'll put some in back of your wheels."

Though successful in getting back to the top of the hill, her troubles were not yet over. "Where shall I go?" she asked. She did not have the least idea as to what direction would take her home. But the young man was still there to help her out of her dilemma. "Where do you live?" he asked. She told him her address and he gave her careful instructions as to the way she should go. Eventually, after following his advice, she found herself on a familiar street and was soon at her home. As her car slid to a stop, another pulled up beside her. It was the same young man. "I followed you to be sure you reached home safely."

In our spiritual lives, we often get lost and confused. The storms of life descend upon us and we are afraid. There is always a Presence, let us remember, that will give us the directions we need, One who will follow us to see that we get home safely.

If it had not been for the Master, we would still be lost and confused, not knowing the way home. Because of Him, we need never fear. All we need to do is turn to Him and ask for His guidance He is with us always!

TABLE TALK: *Have you ever been lost? Describe your feelings of helplessness and insecurity. How were you reassured?*

DECEMBER 30

A Christian Is Radiant

But straightway Jesus spake unto them, saying, Be of good cheer; it is I; be not afraid. Matthew 14:27.

A writer has suggested that the wonders a smile can perform are limitless. He tells how he stopped at a certain eating place in the downtown section of a city. On the outside it looked very unpretentious, but inside the proprietor's son beamed at him as he filled the water glass, and the waiters appeared happy that he had come in for dinner. The proprietor behind the cash register thanked him profusely for his visit asking him if everything had been all right. "The effect of this," he said, "is a glow of friendliness all over the place." And then he goes on to say, as though it was almost incidental, "And the food was very good, too."

All of us have opportunities in the course of a day to make others happier. We may never know how significant might be the result of our attitude to people as we meet and greet them in the course of the day. If you are a Christian you cannot help but be radiant. No matter how dark the circumstances of life may appear, there is always a song in your heart that gives evidence to others that you are trusting in a loving Father who will never let you go. And even if materially you do not prosper, you still cling to your dreams and live by them. It was a Supreme Court justice who recently said, "It is ideas and not dollars that count. We cannot remake the world in our image, but we can help those who are seeking an escape from squalor to find alternatives to communism.'

It is true that we must constantly seek to rebuild the world beginning in the community of which we are a part. Likewise it is true that we should courageously battle for social improvement that others might have better living conditions and more equal opportunities. But even beyond these ideals, we must discover the only one who can truly give us great living. Once having found Him, we can have the inward peace that makes the spirit sing regardless of outward circumstances.

TABLE TALK: *Name people who are always friendly and smiling. Discuss the effect they have on people around them.*

DECEMBER 31

Have You Gone God's Way

But from thence ye shall seek the Lord thy God, and thou shalt find him, when thou searchest after him with all thy heart and with all thy soul. Deuteronomy 4:29.

A melancholy spirit sometimes overtakes us as we come to the end of a year. It is impossible to turn the pages back to relive, except in memory, any of the moments that have passed. It is almost inventory time. Our hearts become heavy when we think of the sins we have committed. Many times we have not made the most of the opportunities that have come to us. But we feel glad when we think of the wonderful blessings that have been showered upon us not only by friends who have been with us, but above all by Him, whose Presence has never left us and who stands ready even now to assure us that because of His love the past has been forgiven and forgotten and He will remember our sins no more.

There was a schoolmaster in England who used to keep a record each day of the misdeeds of all in his class room. Then it was customary for him every New Year's Eve to gather his students around a big bonfire. Piled high were these books in which were written the record of all the mistakes the students had made. Then he would take the books and throw them into the fire. Spontaneously the students would cheer as they saw the record of their misdeeds being burned to ashes to be remembered no more. Then the wise teacher would tell his boys that God was like that. If they would be sorry and penitent for the mistakes which they made, God would forgive them and remember them no more.

No matter how bad you may have been, God's love is greater than your wickedness. Softly and tenderly He is calling you. Why not resolve to go God's way? If you do, you stand on the threshold of life's most glorious hour. And living will become increasingly more abundant as the years roll on. A song will come into your heart as you give positive answer to life's most important question: "Are you going God's way?"

TABLE TALK: *Looking at your past and learning from it, what will be your resolutions for the future?*